CAMBRIDGE LIBR

Books of enduring

Cambridge

The city of Cambridge received its royal charter in 1201, having already been home to Britons, Romans and Anglo-Saxons for many centuries. Cambridge University was founded soon afterwards and celebrates its octocentenary in 2009. This series explores the history and influence of Cambridge as a centre of science, learning, and discovery, its contributions to national and global politics and culture, and its inevitable controversies and scandals.

Treatment of Poverty in Cambridgeshire, 1597–1834

First published in 1934, this historical survey of the application of the Poor Law in Cambridgeshire covers the period from its codification under Queen Elizabeth I to the Amendment Act of 1834. Resulting from the author's extensive analysis of parish records, accounts and court proceedings, the examination of a largely agricultural county marks it out from many other such studies. Cambridgeshire is a unique area; although under a strong metropolitan influence due to its geographical proximity to London and its links to the capital via the University of Cambridge, it contains few towns or large villages. The scattered population meant efforts to group areas for the purposes of administration during the period in question were largely unsuccessful. Instead, E.M. Hampson's study reveals that local autonomy led to large variations in the application of the Poor Law.

Cambridge University Press has long been a pioneer in the reissuing of out-of-print titles from its own backlist, producing digital reprints of books that are still sought after by scholars and students but could not be reprinted economically using traditional technology. The Cambridge Library Collection extends this activity to a wider range of books which are still of importance to researchers and professionals, either for the source material they contain, or as landmarks in the history of their academic discipline.

Drawing from the world-renowned collections in the Cambridge University Library, and guided by the advice of experts in each subject area, Cambridge University Press is using state-of-the-art scanning machines in its own Printing House to capture the content of each book selected for inclusion. The files are processed to give a consistently clear, crisp image, and the books finished to the high quality standard for which the Press is recognised around the world. The latest print-on-demand technology ensures that the books will remain available indefinitely, and that orders for single or multiple copies can quickly be supplied.

The Cambridge Library Collection will bring back to life books of enduring scholarly value across a wide range of disciplines in the humanities and social sciences and in science and technology.

Treatment of Poverty in Cambridgeshire, 1597–1834

ETHEL MARY HAMPSON

CAMBRIDGE
UNIVERSITY PRESS

CAMBRIDGE UNIVERSITY PRESS

Cambridge New York Melbourne Madrid Cape Town Singapore São Paolo Delhi

Published in the United States of America by Cambridge University Press, New York

www.cambridge.org
Information on this title: www.cambridge.org/9781108002349

© in this compilation Cambridge University Press 2009

This edition first published 1934
This digitally printed version 2009

ISBN 978-1-108-00234-9

CAMBRIDGE STUDIES IN ECONOMIC HISTORY

PUBLISHED WITH THE AID OF THE ELLEN McARTHUR FUND

GENERAL EDITOR
J. H. CLAPHAM, Litt.D.
Professor of Economic History in the University of Cambridge

The Treatment of Poverty
in Cambridgeshire

LONDON
Cambridge University Press
FETTER LANE

NEW YORK · TORONTO
BOMBAY · CALCUTTA · MADRAS
Macmillan

TOKYO
Maruzen Company Ltd

HOBSON'S WORKHOUSE AND HOUSE OF CORRECTION,
CAMBRIDGE. ERECTED 1630

The Treatment of Poverty in Cambridgeshire
1597—1834

BY

E. M. HAMPSON
M.A. (Liverpool), Ph.D. (Cantab.)
Sometime Research Fellow of Newnham College Cambridge

CAMBRIDGE
AT THE UNIVERSITY PRESS
1934

"I have heard one of the greatest geniuses this age has produced...assure me, on his being obliged to search into several rolls and records, that notwithstanding such an employment was at first dry and irksome to him, he at last took an incredible pleasure in it."

ADDISON, *Spectator*, vol. VI, no. 447

PRINTED IN GREAT BRITAIN

CONTENTS

CHAPTER XII

CHAPTER XIII

CHAPTER XIV

CHAPTER XVII

APPENDIX

LIST OF ILLUSTRATIONS

PREFACE

The present volume attempts to give an historical survey of the working of the Poor Law in the county of Cambridge from the time of the final codification of the law under Elizabeth to the new era ushered in by the famous Amendment Act of 1834.

It is true that the interest attaching to the activities of an industrial or more urbanised area is lacking in the case of Cambridgeshire, yet the county presents to the student of pauper and vagrant history not only problems typical of agricultural England but also problems distinctive in character, which reward investigation by throwing upon the subject many suggestive sidelights. The existence of the important franchise of Ely within the county borders; the numerous "open" villages and the wide stretches of fen inviting the settlement of stranger and squatter; the late date at which much of the county was enclosed; the deplorable condition of the roads which, together with the paucity of towns and large villages, rendered abortive most attempts to group areas for the purpose of administration; the connection nevertheless maintained with the Metropolis by means of the great Roman Road, and the consequent dependence of Cambridgeshire upon Metropolitan vagrancy policy; the vital significance of the university town and the keen interest taken in it by the central authorities during the period of Privy Council supremacy; the presence in early times of the world-renowned Sturbridge Fair; the importance of the border town of Royston as an index of the relative extent of vagrancy at different periods—all these features give peculiar interest to a study of the county.

Repression of the vagrant and relief of the distressed are indissolubly connected in early legislation, as they are again at the conclusion of our period. From the end of the sixteenth century, however, it is profitable to concentrate upon the pauper on the one hand and upon the offender against the Vagrancy Laws on the other. The present volume is not directly concerned with Vagrancy Laws, Game Laws, Combination Laws or the Law of Conspiracy, but it is necessary to remember that it was within this "framework of repression" that the poor were relieved throughout the centuries during which the Elizabethan statute formed the basis of the administration with which the following pages deal. Some reference is made to concurrent voluntary activities, but these play a minor rôle.

The material for this study has been drawn to a very large extent from unpublished sources. The MS. records of the Gild of the Holy Trinity of Wisbech cover, with certain gaps, the years between 1379 and 1547 and are continued as the Minute and Order Books and Treasurers' Accounts of the Corporation for the years 1547 to 1834. The records of Courts General, Courts Leet and Courts Halimote held at Wisbech exist for the period 1582 to 1619.

The MS. Corporation Common Day Books of the town of Cambridge date from 1562 to 1835. The Accounts of the Treasurer and other documents relating particularly to the history of the town during the sixteenth and early seventeenth centuries form part of the Bowtell Collection of Manuscripts in Downing College Library. The Baker MSS. in the Cambridge University Library and the Cole MSS. in the British Museum also contain material germane to the subject. These sources have been searched for fuller information on various points than is recorded in the published *Annals* of Charles Cooper.

The voluminous but ill-assorted archives of the town of Royston and the vestry books and papers of some fifty parishes in the county proper, in the Isle of Ely and in the town of Cambridge have been investigated. The earliest of these vestry books relates to the end of the fifteenth century; in a few parishes documents of the later sixteenth century are preserved; from the middle of the seventeenth century onwards many more papers have survived. In most cases the parish archives are entirely unclassified and the papers often in an ill-preserved condition. (Since the documents were examined much labour has been expended in some parishes—particularly at Royston—in remedying these defects.)

The unpublished Quarter Sessions Records for Cambridgeshire cover the periods 1660 to 1672, 1689 to 1694 and 1699 to 1834, and have been fully utilised.

The Statutes of the Realm and the Domestic State Papers—more particularly the Orders from and Returns to the Privy Council during the Tudor and early Stuart periods and the Reports of various Parliamentary Committees of Enquiry between 1776 and 1834—have contributed to the statistical surveys of certain periods and have been examined in the light of the evidence afforded by local archives.

Contemporary pamphlet literature, the files of the *Cambridge Chronicle* and the reports of philanthropic societies provide much of the social and economic background.

Indebtedness to published works of a more general character, both ancient and modern, is acknowledged in footnotes as well as in the bibliography.

The work could not have been undertaken without the continuous generosity of Newnham College. Thanks are also due to the numerous custodians of county, town and parish archives for the readiness with which they have placed papers and books at the author's disposal, and in not a few instances for the hospitality they have offered in a county still suffering from the inaccessibility of many of its villages to the non-motorist.

The publication of this volume is made possible by the benefaction of the late Miss Ellen McArthur to the University. For the assistance given, both by way of encouragement and of criticism, the author offers sincere gratitude to the adjudicators of the McArthur Prize. To Professor Clapham and to Mrs Sidney Webb a peculiar measure of obligation is owing.

Finally the author desires to express appreciation of the courteous assistance offered and the meticulous care exercised by the officials of the Cambridge University Press.

E. M. H.

January, 1934.

EDITOR'S PREFACE

I have written somewhere that the Poor Law, as the statesmen of Elizabeth made it and administrators later applied it, was "not merely a part of the English constitution but...assuredly that part of it of which ordinary Englishmen in their daily lives were most continuously conscious". If this is true, exact study of the working of the Law, district by district or county by county, is a chief task for historians of administration and society. Looking back over the centuries, the main features of the landscape have long been familiar enough; but they were lit up, and many lesser features revealed, when Mr and Mrs Webb published their *Old Poor Law* in 1927. Use was made in that volume of some important Cambridgeshire material. A year earlier, Miss Dorothy Marshall, in her *English Poor Law in the Eighteenth Century*, had also drawn upon some of the Cambridgeshire—and upon other—MS. records. It is more than twenty years since Mr A. W. Ashby published his *One Hundred Years of Poor Law Administration in an Oxfordshire Village*. Recently (1932) a chapter in Mr J. D. Chambers' *Nottinghamshire in the Eighteenth Century* has provided an excellent starting-point for a close survey of another county. Something has been done for most counties in the social chapters of the *Victoria County Histories*. This does not complete the list of good work. But outside London nothing quite so thorough as Miss Hampson's study of Cambridgeshire has yet been attempted.

The term "historical research" has many uses. Sometimes it means compilation in a warm library; sometimes transcription in a well-ordered collection of muniments. You may research in person or research by deputy. Personal investigation of the vestry books and papers, for the most part ill-kept and un-classified as Miss Hampson notes, of about fifty parishes in a "marishy" county is research of an unusually strenuous kind. The catch in these dykes and fens is not always proportionate to the fisherman's labour; but it is certain that here no labour has been spared. For some considerable time, one may certainly assume, it will not be worth anyone's while to drag the nets through them again.

No claim is made that even the most exact knowledge of the application of the Law, for more than two centuries, in a single county, shifts more than a very little existing judgments as to how that Law affected "the state of the poor" in all England. It helps, however, to make the verdict to be delivered ulti-mately—some fancied historian's last judgment—better in-formed. Meanwhile it brings those "poor" before us as they stood, at what were to them some very critical points in time—Mary Newman of Meldreth who was paid to go away and did not go (p. 143); Wm. Wrosun of St Bene't's, Cambridge, whose "family was all most Stavd naked" (p. 150); or that very tiresome whore, Sarah Gear of Royston (p. 173).

As a rule those who in the Cambridge University Press have to put works of learning in a fit state to be set up in type do not, I am told, worry much about their contents. But as this book was being prepared it was found interesting: "something that we know about", someone said. The editor takes this, and the author no doubt will also take it, as a very high compliment. They both hope that the interest will not be only local, and they believe that it should not be.

J. H. CLAPHAM

Chapter I

INTRODUCTORY: POOR RELIEF IN CAMBRIDGESHIRE BEFORE 1597

It is the particular purpose of this study to examine in detail the practical working of the Poor Law in Cambridgeshire during the centuries which followed its final codification under Elizabeth, but it would seem desirable to preface this account by a preliminary survey of the methods adopted in this county for the relief or the repression of the poverty-stricken during medieval and early Tudor days. From the dawn of the Christian era the care of the sick and needy was recognised as an important duty of the Church as a body as well as of its individual members. The institutions of religion grew up, moreover, during the Middle Ages in a society of which the fundamental organisation necessitated consideration for its weaker members—the prevention of destitution, says Miss Page,[1] was the "central thread of manorial land-law" on the Cambridgeshire manors of Oakington, Cottenham and Drayton. In the towns the regulation of economic conditions, especially during the hey-day of the gilds, did much to prevent or to mitigate want. Whilst it seems to be true that a good deal of poverty did nevertheless exist, continuous economic precariousness was not characteristic of medieval England, and the network of voluntary associations, together with the charity of individuals, met the needs of the day so long as no great strain was placed upon it.

A. PAROCHIAL RELIEF

Church rates seem to have been commonly in use in England by the fourteenth century. The churchwardens' accounts for the Cambridgeshire village of Bassingbourn, covering the period

[1] F. M. Page, *Camb. Hist. Journ.* III, no. 2, p. 125.

1497 to 1538, record occasional semi-voluntary levies of this nature and exemplify the various other sources of parochial income of the day—church ales, hocktide sports, the sale and hire of parochial property (especially live stock) and the village play. Whilst it is true that the proceeds were in the main devoted to ecclesiastical claims, a good deal of casual employment as well as enjoyment resulted—conveying the "propyrtes", cleaning the church-house and its cooking utensils, turning the "spittes", baking the bread and brewing the ale, gathering stones from the churchyard and clearing the ditches. Such work was definitely paid for at Bassingbourn at the general cost of the parish. Collections round the village were also made on occasion—for example in 1515 towards the "buriall of a poor man".

The customary collection after divine service at Great St Mary's Church, Cambridge, was still in 1515 "of every Mannys goodwill", but each individual evidently gave according to a prearranged rate—"by a certyn roll"—and from these funds the poor were regularly aided.

Among the numerous forms of bequests administered by the churchwardens (or by gild officials) on behalf of the poor, none was more common in fourteenth- and fifteenth-century Cambridgeshire than the almshouse. Not infrequently these buildings were used as an ordinary poorhouse, for casual as well as permanent cases of poverty. "Pd. for a sheet to mother maninge for a poore boy that died in the Halmes house, xii d." recorded a churchwarden of Great St Mary's.[1]

B. MONASTERIES

To what extent the poor really suffered by the deprivation of monastic alms after the "Great Pillage" is a debatable question. The complaints of the period suggest that even at that date there was some considerable measure of dependence, whether for weal or for woe, upon the indiscriminate charity which the monasteries

[1] This was as late as 1596, but the inmates early in the century were often casual paupers of this type.

PLATE II

THE OLD GILDHALL AT WHITTLESFORD IN THE SIXTEENTH CENTURY

offered. Though their total revenue was not so great as in some parts of the country, the monastic communities of Cambridge-shire formed a very significant feature in the life of the county. On an average, however, certainly not more than one village in five was within daily reach of such assistance as the monastery could give.

C. GILDS

Probably of more immediate significance to the poor in a county consisting essentially of small rural parishes were the religio-social gilds, which are to be traced in almost every village. Even where no fixed provision was made for the relief of distress,[1] it was probably customary to send round the hat among members to meet emergencies as they arose. In most cases, moreover, the expenses of burial and the celebration of masses were met by the gild—no negligible assistance in days when a fitting entry into the world and a decent ushering out were of prime significance to the happiness of man. In many villages an almshouse was supported by the gild, or was the bequest of one of its members.[2]

The county affords one outstanding example of the direct evolution of town government from its origin in a simple religious and social organisation: the early history of Wisbech, from 1379 to 1547, is the history of its gild.[3] The income of the body was derived in its early years from fees, contributions and

---

[1] For most of the larger villages the gild certificates of 1388 have not survived—*i.e.* of the gilds most likely to be wealthy and to make larger provision for succouring the poor.

[2] In not a few cases, particularly in the Isle of Ely, the old almshouse or gildhall formed—as at Whittlesford and Meldreth—the village poor-house of a later age.

[3] The "Accounts of the Brotherhood of the Holy Trinity" open with the year 1379, but record only receipts and expenditure and an in-ventory of possessions. No further entries are extant until 1423, from which date they are continuous, except for a few years here and there, till 1540. The gild was not dissolved till 1547, immediately prior to the incorporation of the town. Existing town records begin in 1560, but pages are missing for certain years up to 1584. From 1584 to 1835 the records are complete.

rates levied upon the property of its members, who increased rapidly in numbers in the century following its foundation. A school and schoolmaster were maintained apparently from the beginning and the bequest of an almshouse was received in 1477. Other gifts followed—many definitely assigned to the relief of the poor; the gild became in fact the customary legatee of all kinds of benefactions. The close association of the gild with the parish and with church affairs is evident from the outset: it was the voice of the gild which was the determining factor in parochial life as it was the voice of the township later.

D. THE STATE

With respect to one type of pauper—the wandering vagabond or the "masterless man"—from the middle of the fourteenth century the State itself was called upon to intervene in the interests of law and order. An effort to regulate economic conditions, however, accompanied the legislative repression of vagrancy. The towns, moreover, were active on their own initiative in framing economic codes.

E. CAMBRIDGE TOWN IN THE MIDDLE AGES

The regulation of supplies and the limitation of prices formed subjects of constant altercation between town and university throughout the Middle Ages—as did also the control of vagabondage. Vagrancy regulations in both Cambridge and Wisbech were frequently associated with ordinances respecting plague, for as carriers of the dread pestilence wandering beggars were peculiarly suspect. The increased sense of corporate responsibility for distress which developed in the later fourteenth century was more immediately the response to the claims resulting from extensive epidemics than to any other stimulus. It was during this period that one finds the town rulers of Cambridge acting as public trustee in the case of bequests for the poor, assuming the guardianship of orphans, granting loans to needy tradesmen and devoting fines to the relief of the poor—activities which also characterised the brotherhood at Wisbech.

By the end of the fourteenth century, however, vagrancy was obviously increasing and the State was compelled to take active measures.

F. TUDOR DISORGANISATION

The disintegrating forces for long at work upon manorial organisation were brought to a head upon the conclusion of the civil wars, yet medieval conceptions still dominated the Tudor mind. The disbanding of retainers, the growth of new trades and the rapid extension of markets, with their fluctuating demands and their encouragement of capitalism, currency inflation and debasement, the dissolution of monasteries and gilds and the spread of enclosures all played their part, whether a recognised part or not, in the disorganisation of society with which Tudor statesmen were faced.

G. CAMBRIDGE DURING THE TUDOR PERIOD

With the exception of the metropolis perhaps no place in the kingdom was so constantly in communication with the Central Government as was the university town—the cradle of clerics and statesmen. Yet even here much of the experimental legislation of the Tudor period was a dead letter, or was adopted only so far as the local rulers ordained.

Though entirely failing to grasp the significance of genuine unemployment—for the able-bodied "rogue" there was nothing but repression—the State did recognise, in the enactments of the 'thirties of the sixteenth century, the inadequacy of existing provision for the "poor in very deed". Greater precision, a stronger suggestion of compulsion and a growing suspicion of unorganised charity increasingly characterised the legislation of these years.

Cambridge authorities made no attempt to follow the letter of the laws of 1531 or 1536,[1] but they did undertake the statutory registration and badging of the licensed poor in 1536. Much perturbation was aroused by the increase of vagrancy, especially

[1] Or of the Act of 1551.

during the holding of Sturbridge Fair, but the savage legislation of 1547 only served to raise doubts concerning the efficacy of mere repression. The enactment of 1555 imposed upon officers of corporate towns the duty of supervision and co-ordination of parochial relief. A bad harvest in 1556 was followed in Cambridge by devastating plague, and profiteers saw their chance. Both town and university authorities were consequently prepared to assume joint control of the perilous situation. With the approval—in fact, stimulation—of the Privy Council, attention was first directed to the purging of market offences and the "viewing" of granaries and barns. Assuming dictatorial powers, the authorities then proceeded to assess the town and impose a compulsory poor-rate. The existing parochial lists were presented to the Mayor and Vice-Chancellor, who thereupon revised the assessments on a compulsory basis, adjusting them especially with a view to levying a rate-in-aid—such as had been suggested by the Act of 1555—upon the wealthier parishes in the interest of the poorer. Collectors were ordered to be chosen by each parish and a threefold classification of the poor was made. A list of recent immigrants was ordered to be compiled by the church-wardens, with a view to dispatching those now in difficulties to their places of settlement. In each of the four wards of the town there were appointed a superintendent and a "watcher for strange beggeres" likely to be attracted hither by the new scheme of relief. A strict prohibition of begging, under pain of imprisonment, accompanied this imposition of a compulsory rate and superseded the earlier system of licensing.[1] Notwithstanding these measures, there was much unrelieved poverty. Nothing seems to have been done in the way of providing work, and men were driven to run the gauntlet of imprisonment when starvation was the alternative. Compulsory measures had been adopted,

---

[1] Miss Leonard's claim on behalf of Norwich must, therefore, be disallowed. Norwich prohibited begging in 1571 and, says Miss Leonard, "seems to have been the first English town to prohibit begging altogether". (E. M. Leonard, *English Poor Relief* (1900), p. 106.)

yet a noteworthy reluctance to press them one jot beyond the demands of dire necessity was still manifest. If the rate continued to be exacted it was clearly inadequate only a few years later, for further avenues of income were anxiously being explored, measures adopted to check the influx of people from the rural areas, and industrial regulations enforced: if the duty of the community towards the individual demanded parental care, the right of control over individual freedom was the necessary corollary.

The Act of 1572 imposed the first general compulsory rate upon the country. Four years later it was enacted that in every corporate town, or other convenient place, the magistrates should accumulate—at the expense of a rate upon the whole area— a stock of material for the employment of the genuinely workless. Whilst at the same moment ordering in every county the establishment of Houses of Correction, where work should be supplied under disciplinary conditions, the legislature had at last frankly acknowledged that the unemployed were not all birds of the same feather.

The years between 1572 and the end of the century were marked in Cambridge by a tendency to extend the sphere of compulsion to rating for other local government purposes—a compulsory sanitary rate was adopted and even an education rate was mooted. There was, however, no thought of differentiating between pauperism and mere poverty.

The main interest of the town, as opposed to the parish, during this period lay in experimental efforts to provide work, combined with careful control of the food supply during seasons of dearth and with increased rigidity of municipal settlement restrictions. An attempt to erect a "hospital for the poor" was made in 1578; a "bedell of the beggars" was appointed in 1583, and a stringent Order from the Privy Council, prohibiting the acceptance of "inmates" and the erection of new houses on the waste, was received the following year. During the dearth of 1596–7 the Council positively bombarded the justices with Orders concerning the maintenance of a food supply, yet profiteers took advantage of disputes between Town and Gown, and engrossing and forestalling were rampant. The first workhouse scheme was followed by a project which threw the onus upon private enterprise, but in the period of stress and strain it proved unsuccessful. Further efforts were already afoot when the Act of 1597 came into being.

H. WISBECH IN THE TUDOR PERIOD

In the years which followed the granting of its charter, in 1547, Wisbech authorities pursued in the main their traditional modes of assistance. The early connection between gild and church partly explains the continued direct exercise by the corporate body of functions statutorily relegated to the vestry—a peculiarity maintained through succeeding centuries. The town rulers were anxious to retain something of the religious impulse which had stimulated the voluntary and semi-voluntary philanthropy of their gild ancestors; moreover, valuable benefactions in the control of the corporation, together with a large share of the interest accruing upon the stock of well-to-do orphans left in their guardianship, enabled the town for some time not only to give assistance to the churchwardens and to pay the salaries of public servants, but also to dispense charity directly when need arose. Freedom from the constant jealousy between two rival authorities, together with the comparative insignificance of the little town, left Wisbech, moreover, much more at liberty than was Cambridge to develop—or of course to neglect—its own organisation uncontrolled by the Central Government.

The disbursements from the town funds on account of sickness were unusually heavy and the authorities finally adopted an amusingly successful expedient. Centuries before the shadow of Mr Robert Lowe darkened the dinner-table of many a struggling schoolmaster, the Ten Men hit upon the device of payment-by-results. In June 1592, for instance, Henry Edmunds was engaged by the town to cure the leg of a pauper. Edmunds was to receive " 10/- yf he doe heale the said sore leg, viz. in hand 3/4; upon the lykyng of the Healing 3/4; and upon the full Healyng 3/4; and yf it be lyked well, to give more".

It was in connection with epidemic sickness, as in the case of Cambridge, that in 1584 the first compulsory poor-rate seems to have been levied. A rate had been imposed in 1564 to discharge the expense of the Parish Clerk's wages, and it was this basis of assessment which was presently used for other purposes—in 1579 for the support of a poor Wisbech boy at St John's College, Cambridge. In 1584 plague visited the dependent hamlet of Guyhirne and in the following year spread to Wisbech. Henceforward more or less compulsory levies were resorted to on occasions of difficulty, but a marked desire to avoid pressure was still obvious—curious mutual arrangements were at times entered into whereby rate-payers discharged their obligations to the town. The organisation of the borough into four wards, the prohibition of begging and the campaigns against "inmates" and strangers are closely reminiscent of Cambridge. The regulations of 1591 ordered more methodical "serches for inmates" and inaugurated a system of "testimonials", modelled on the Act of 1572. It was hoped by the use of an authoritative document to render the return of evicted folk less easy. Evidence of the possession of £10 in money or chattels, or the finding of surety to that extent, was demanded of all intending settlers. Mere impotence and even "insufficient ability" were regarded in actual practice as sufficient grounds for ruthless ejection.

During the acute distress of 1597 the organisation of 1587 was revived, weekly lists of the needy were brought before the town Board of Governors and a reassessment followed. Hitherto loans of money or live stock were the only modes of assistance offered to the able-bodied; but in 1598, probably as a result of legislation, the corporation took steps to "sett the pore on work".

I. THE RURAL DISTRICTS IN THE TUDOR PERIOD

As an essentially agricultural county, Cambridgeshire was less immediately influenced by industrial changes than were some parts of the country. Enclosures affected only a small area of the county, but they were, in the main, undertaken by large farmers desirous of converting arable land to pasture and of increasing the size of their holdings by intakes from the waste, and this type of enclosure was at the expense of the peasant. The extensive open-field areas, moreover, suffered from incursions of poverty-stricken strangers from neighbouring counties.

Apart from the regulation of food supplies, the main concern of the county magistrates was with the vagrant rather than with the settled pauper, until after the Act of 1597. A vigorous whipping campaign was undertaken between 1569 and 1572—the reports of the justices to the Privy Council, in 1571, show very clearly the encouragement which Sturbridge Fair offered to vagrants.

The larger villages and the small market towns, however, were interested in the newer methods of relief as distinguished from repression. The vestry records of Linton date from 1577. At that time annual "Collectors for the Poor" were rendering account to the vestry. These officials continued to be elected regularly till early in the following century. Endowments provided a large proportion of the annual funds, and collections were probably semi-voluntary. An institution called the "Taske House", partly supported by a bequest, served as a workhouse for Linton and the adjoining villages. Within a few years of establishment, however, it tended to develop into a mere asylum for the impotent and a storehouse for the "stock" distributed chiefly to home-workers. Interest in parochial employment revived in 1590, following a bequest for that purpose. Part of the old gildhall was also used at Linton to shelter homeless poor.

It is probable that the activities of Linton were fairly typical of the larger rural parishes of the county—more especially of the Isle of Ely.

J. CONCLUSIONS

The history of poor relief in Cambridgeshire during the latter part of the sixteenth century thus reveals the urban communities both influencing and influenced by the Central Government, yet manifesting no rigid adherence to the letter of the growing body of law. In the case of Wisbech, governmental stimulus is mainly indirect; in the case of the university centre, the active interest of the Privy Council rapidly increases during the century, yet here, more than in most towns, owing to the strife between two local authorities, is the control of the Council often brought to nought.

The development of interest in relief measures, as distinct from mere repression, is marked in local administration as in legislation as the century proceeds. Periods of special emergency are the starting-point of comprehensive municipal organisation, as they are of governmental activity. Interference by the Privy Council is, in the main, confined during these years to the repression of vagrancy and the securing of adequate food supplies at reasonable prices, but the machinery evolved for the execution of this surveillance necessitates constant contact with the poverty-stricken classes, and the knowledge acquired by this means has, before the century closes, already wrought radical changes in public opinion on the subject of communal responsibility for the poor. It but remains to extend to wider fields the application of the machinery. Till the end of the century, however, relief schemes are essentially dependent on local initiative and only by stringent settlement regulations can the towns, without the backing of Government, hope to achieve any measure of success.

Discussions on the treatment of poverty nevertheless pervade the air. It is interesting to notice how similar are the general lines of development in towns so widely different in type as Cambridge and Wisbech: in both cases one notes the reluctant adoption of an increasing degree of compulsion, simultaneously with the opening up of new sources of voluntary charity; in both towns coercion comes at first in dire emergency; in both the organisation designed to meet the emergency is, after a period of reversion to voluntary methods, revived to form a more permanent system. The basis of assessment is naturally some rough measure of ability; only very gradually does ability tend to be estimated in terms either of land or of money. The provision of work for the idle—distinguishing those willing to work from those unwilling —is the main preoccupation of the rulers of Cambridge during the last two decades of the century: it is not, however, till the very end of the period that Wisbech authorities take up this matter seriously. Whilst in the case of Cambridge the division of the town into fourteen small parishes tends towards the delegation of certain functions to the parochial officials, a very real control is yet exercised by the town rulers: in Wisbech still more marked is the activity of its corporate rulers, for they not only control but administer relief in detail, according to parochial officers but a very minor rôle. It is not indeed till 1597 that the legislature itself transfers from the magistrate to the overseer the duties which placed in the hands of the parish the primary control of relief.

The rural parishes move more slowly than do the towns, but at least in the larger villages much the same line of development is being followed.

The codification of the Elizabethan Poor Law in the famous Statute of 1597 on the one hand fittingly summarises the preceding era of experiment, and on the other ushers in the age of a fully elaborated national system.

Chapter II

POOR RELIEF IN CAMBRIDGE DURING THE FIRST PART OF THE SEVENTEENTH CENTURY

A. THE STATUTE OF 1597

A new era in the history of poor relief opens with the seventeenth century, or to be more precise, with the closing years of the sixteenth. A comprehensive series of bills dealing with various aspects of poverty passed on to the statute book in 1597–8. Of these the most outstanding was the famous 39 Eliz., c. 3, which, re-enacted in very slightly modified form in 1601,[1] formed the basis of Poor Law administration throughout the whole of the period with which we are concerned. It seems, therefore, desirable to recall the terms of the Act.

In every parish overseers—consisting of the churchwardens together with four[2] substantial householders—were to be nominated yearly under the hand and seal of two or more local justices. Upon these unpaid overseers, or "the greater part of them", was imposed the duty of providing, with the approval of two justices, for all those "having no means to maintain them". Power, moreover, was accorded to the overseers to raise the requisite funds by a compulsory rate, leviable "weekly or otherwise" upon "every inhabitant and every occupier of lands in the said parish",[3] under pain of distraint or if need be of imprisonment.

The poor were distinguished under three heads—the able-bodied, the children, the impotent.

---

[1] 43 Eliz., c. 2.

[2] "Four, three, or two", according to 43 Eliz., c. 2.

[3] "Every inhabitant parson, vicar and other, and of every occupier of lands, houses, tithes impropriate or propriations of tythes, coal mines or saleable underwoods, in the said parish" (43 Eliz., c. 2).

For the relief of the first group there was to be accumulated in each parish the already familiar stock of "flax, hemp, wool, thread, iron, and other necessary ware and stuff", upon which to set them "on work". Any able-bodied person refusing to be so employed was, upon warrant of a justice, to be sent to the House of Correction.[1]

For the relief of children lacking parents able to maintain them work was to be found, if the children were of competent age, or they were to be bound apprentice, with the assent of two justices—boys to the age of twenty-four, girls to twenty-one.[2]

For the impotent—the aged, lame, blind, and others "not able to work", including infants—adequate provision was to be made from the rates. "And to the intent that necessary places of habitation" might be "more conveniently provided for such impotent people", the overseers were, "by the leave of the lord or lords of the manor", to erect upon the common or waste of the parish, "at the general charges of the parish, or otherwise of the hundred or the county, convenient houses of dwelling", and were "to place inmates or more families than one in one cottage or house", should they deem it desirable.

Parents,[3] "being of sufficient ability", were to be held legally liable for the support of their children, and children for the support of their parents, but the fixing of the rate of maintenance was, in case of dispute, to be settled by Quarter Sessions.

"Wandering abroad and begging", whether "by license or without",[4] was to be punished as "roguery"; though soliciting "victuals only",[5] within the confines of the parish, was to be permitted.

---

[1] By 43 Eliz., c. 2, the alternative of the common gaol was allowed—a tacit admission that Houses of Correction had not been immediately erected everywhere.

[2] Or marriage in the case of girls (43 Eliz., c. 2).

[3] Extended by 43 Eliz., c. 2, to include grandparents.

[4] Section 16 added a proviso confirming the privilege granted to licensed soldiers and sailors to ask relief en route to their places of settlement.

[5] This exception was withdrawn by 43 Eliz., c. 2.

Meetings of the churchwardens and overseers were to take place at least once every month, in the parish church, "upon the Sunday in the afternoon after divine service". Accounts were to be submitted annually for audit by two justices. Negligence on the part of overseers was to be punished by fine, and defalcation in any form by imprisonment. All forfeitures under the statute were to be devoted to the poor.

The most important functions of the justices were thus supervisory, though certain direct duties did devolve upon them. The Mayor and other head officers within corporate towns were to exercise a similar jurisdiction within their own precincts.

The earlier principle of requiring richer parishes to assist poorer ones was clearly re-asserted. Two or more justices of the hundred were empowered to levy a rate-in-aid upon any parish within this area, and by the consent of the justices in Quarter Sessions a rate of this nature might even be levied upon any parish within the bounds of the county.

A county rate,[1] distinct from the overseers' rate, was to be levied upon every parish by order of Quarter Sessions, for the relief of prisoners of the King's Bench and Marshalsea, and also for the upkeep of county "hospitals and almshouses", where such should be erected. Any "surplusage" of this county rate was to be devoted to the relief of hospitals, sufferers from fire, water or other disaster, or to "other charitable purposes for the relief of the poor", at the discretion of the assembled Bench.

Appeal against the poor-rate, or against the action of individual justices, lay to Quarter Sessions.

The Act thus codified, clarified, and made practically enforceable the statutes of the two preceding decades.

Voluntary contributions were definitely not to be exclusively relied upon, yet two other measures, passed in the self-same session, clearly show the Government still anxious to encourage and to improve the administration of voluntary charity. The

---

[1] Not less than $\frac{1}{2}d$. or more than 6d. was to be raised in any parish, and the rate—which was to produce at least 20s. annually—was not to average over 2d. per parish.

39 Eliz., c. 6, sought to prevent malversation of charitable endowments, whilst the 39 Eliz., c. 5, facilitated the private founding of "abiding and working houses". The later stigma attaching to the rate-aided pauper, as distinct from the beneficiary of voluntary philanthropy, still found no place in the final Elizabethan scheme.

B. THE ACTIVITY OF THE PRIVY COUNCIL

It was during the last quarter of the sixteenth century that the administrative hierarchy which was now to be used to ensure the practical working of the new statute had been developed. In the course of the first four decades of the seventeenth century the control of the Privy Council became more comprehensive and more continuous in its application to the whole country than at any other period.[1] This is a marked feature, as will presently appear, in the administration of the rural areas of Cambridgeshire outside the Isle of Ely. Within the Bishop's franchise there is less evidence extant to show that pressure was directly brought to bear by the Council, though in the larger parishes one does find developments following much the same course as in the county proper. Wisbech, the one urban community within the Isle,[2] had already, during the sixteenth century, given proof of its enterprising spirit, independently of governmental stimulation, but the proximity of the town to the East Anglian counties, with which the Council was in constant communication, no doubt influenced the policies pursued. The Ten Men, or Capital Burgesses,[3] of Wisbech in fact deliberately sent embassies to glean information on the organisation of neighbouring towns, and invited manufacturers and dealers from these areas to engage in industrial undertakings for the employment of the poor of Wisbech.[4] Whilst it can hardly be said that the grip of the Council on municipal and academic affairs in the university town was

[1] E. M. Leonard, *English Poor Relief* (1900), pp. 165–83.
[2] Apart from one or two small market towns.
[3] The governing body of the town.
[4] Cf. *infra*, pp. 34, 37, 61.

closer in the early seventeenth century than it had been in the sixteenth, it is noteworthy that matters concerned with the relief of poverty were more often the peculiar occasion of intervention. The developments which followed the passing of the 39 Eliz. in the town of Cambridge may be examined first.

C. THE WORKING OF THE STATUTE IN CAMBRIDGE

(1) *Parochial Response*

A circular communication was sent by the Privy Council, in 1598, to the Sheriff and to the justices of all counties and corporate towns, among which Cambridge was included, requiring them to see that the new Poor Law was put into operation. During the previous year, however, a lively correspondence had arisen between the Council and the two authorities in the town, concerning, among other subjects, the new scheme which had been formulated for the erection of a combined workhouse and bridewell.

It is probable that regular compulsory poor-rates were being levied in all the parishes of the town before the Act came into being, but compulsion did not solve every problem. It was already found impossible to raise sufficient sums in the poorer parishes, and in 1599 the Mayor and Vice-Chancellor exercised the powers vested in them by the recent Act to direct that a rate-in-aid should be levied upon the wealthier parishes of the town to assist the overburdened parishes of St Giles, St Andrew and Holy Trinity. Town and Gown were for the nonce in harmony, yet the order was not complied with till 1601.[1]

Direct commands to the overseers to give relief in certain instances were occasionally issued by the town magistrates and grants from corporation funds were also sometimes made. Such activities were not new but they do imply that the compulsory rates were kept down to the minimum.

---

[1] Chief Justice Popham, in 1601, censured the Mayor and his predecessor for its non-observance up to that date. (Cooper, *Annals of Cambridge* (1842), II, p. 594.)

"Given to Mr Cutberdes daughter, sometyme of the parish, being in great want, by yᵉ apoyntment of Mr Pottall deputy maior, 6s. 8d.", recorded a churchwarden of Great St Mary's in 1614. The entry is interesting, for it is suggestive of that spirit of narrow parochialism which was beginning to manifest itself in other directions also—in opposition, for example, to rates-in-aid. Various writers have been at pains to point out the absence in the Statutes of 39 and 43 Eliz. of any rigid limitation of settlement to the bounds of the parish. The stricter enforcement of the law during the early seventeenth century nevertheless inevitably brought more into the foreground the question of who were or were not entitled to parochial, as distinguished from municipal, relief. "Cutberdes daughter" had evidently moved out of the parish, and discussion had arisen regarding her settlement; relief was eventually granted, however, without returning her to Great St Mary's. There are other similar instances recorded during this period.[1] A dispute which arose, in 1631, respecting the exact boundary of Great St Mary's parish, and the consequent liability to provide for certain paupers,[2] betrays again the tightening of the parochial net which accompanied the strict enforcement of parish responsibility, and offers an early example of a type of dispute exceedingly common after the passing of the Settlements Act of 1662.

This attitude on the part of the parish authorities in no way lessened the earlier anxiety of municipal governors to restrict the number of newcomers. In connection with the control of vagrancy and plague, repeated injunctions had been issued by the Privy Council, during the first four decades of the seven-

---

[1] In 1619, for example, 5s. was allowed by Great St Mary's "for a child at Chesterton". Another instance occurred in 1629. (*Churchwardens' Accounts of St Mary the Great*, ed. J. E. Foster, 1905, pp. 331, 352.)

[2] Only "a parte of the Inn called the ffalcon" lay within Great St Mary's parish. Whilst any unfortunate inmate chancing to fall upon the rates was carefully housed on this side of the inn and demanded relief from Great St Mary's, inmates of ability refused to acknowledge the legitimacy of assessments laid upon them by the vestry of that parish. (*Ibid.* p. 442.)

teenth century,[1] against the taking of inmates and the erection of pauper dwellings in Cambridge. The policy was largely inspired by a desire to cut down the poor-rates.[2] The tendency to migrate to the town was in part due to the negligence of various rural authorities in Cambridgeshire to provide work for the unemployed.

The difficulties experienced in securing the smooth working of the Poor Law and in obtaining adequate supplies through the medium of the rates are evident in the reluctance of "substantial householders" to accept the office of overseer. Goaded by the justice, reviled by the rate-payer, unremunerated for his service, the lot of the overseer was hard, and it is not surprising to observe already a tendency for the office to fall into the hands of petty men who had an axe to grind. In 1613 John Crane paid his ten-shilling fine rather than serve as overseer of Great St Mary's, yet Crane— a large benefactor to the poor forty years later—was just the type of man whose services were the most valuable. In 1621 the increased difficulty experienced by the same vestry in this matter led them to raise the fine to forty shillings. Some years later it was plainly alleged that parish officers were guilty of corruption in the levying of the rates.

(2) *Municipal Action and the Able-bodied*

It was partly the unsatisfactory working of the parochial system, combined with the curiously persistent reluctance to call upon

[1] Privy Council Orders on these subjects were issued in 1619, 1623, 1631, 1632 and 1635–6. Regular supervision by the Assize Judges was decreed in 1632, and in 1636 steps were taken at the Quarter Sessions of the town to enforce the regulations. Movement even from one parish to another within the town was forbidden without written permission of the Vice-Chancellor and Mayor, or of the two nearest justices, together with a majority of the officers of the parish concerned. Infringements were to be dealt with by Quarter Sessions or even by the Privy Council itself, "according to ye qualitie of ye person and nature of ye offense". (Cooper, *op. cit.* III, pp. 126, 158, 241, 252, 272.)

[2] A desire equally manifest at Wisbech during the seventeenth century.

the rates for the relief of the able-bodied, which led the corporation to renew their own efforts to deal with this class.

The bad harvest of 1622 and the crisis in the cloth trade had evoked much activity on the part of the Council in the eastern counties. The woollen trade was a strictly local one in Cambridge, but here, too, unemployment was a serious question. In 1627 the corporation decided to lease out Jesus Green for seven years and devote the rents to "setting the poor on work" and "raising a stock for their maintenance". Institutional provision—semi-workhouse, semi-bridewell—was again the favoured plan. The following year it was agreed to apply the fines for negligence in cleansing and repairing the streets to the upkeep of the proposed House of Correction. In July 1628 Hobson, the famous carrier, took his first step towards furthering the scheme, and conveyed to twelve trustees[1]—six representing the university and six the town—the ground on which the building was being erected. £500 was raised in addition by a public "collection"[2]—whether voluntary or compulsory is not clear. The workhouse side of the establishment received attention first as meeting the more pressing need of the moment, though an adjoining House of Correction was also contemplated—the necessary complement to effective provision of public work.

(3) The Book of Orders. Plague. Unemployment. Maladministration

In 1629[3] a bad harvest again coincided with a crisis in the cloth industry. Directions from the Privy Council to the counties peculiarly hard hit were followed by a general proclamation

---

[1] To be appointed respectively by the Vice-Chancellor and Mayor.

[2] In the petition to the Privy Council, in May 1631, the Vice-Chancellor and Mayor declared that "before the visitation began they had exhausted themselves by a collection of £500, wherewith they built a workhouse for the poor, and furnished the same with some stock, intending for the better ordering of the said workhouse, to build a house of correction". (Cooper, op. cit. III, pp. 230–40.)

[3] Bad harvests recurred from 1629 to 1631.

commanding the due execution of "the Lawes made for setting the poore on worke". In June 1630 a special committee of the Privy Council was nominated—the "Commissioners for the Poore". Local commissioners and sub-committees were in their turn appointed to bring pressure to bear upon the Circuit Judges. It was early in the following year that the famous "Book of Orders", which formed the basis of Poor Law organisation till the outbreak of the Civil War, was issued by the Council. Emphasis was laid upon the duty of magistrates with respect to rates-in-aid, and the administrative measures to be adopted were laid down: monthly meetings of the justices in their respective districts for the review of the activities of constables and overseers; quarterly reports of the justices to the Circuit Judges;[1] the final reports of the Judges to the Lords Commissioners. The enquiries made by the justices concerned not only every side of Poor Law administration—the relief of the impotent, the apprenticeship of children, the employment of the able-bodied —but also the closely allied questions of the management of charitable bequests and the observance of the Statute of Artificers.[2] Orders were also issued, after the manner of the sixteenth century, with respect to the provision of corn.

In the spring and summer of 1630 a powerful stimulus to exertion was provided for the town of Cambridge by a violent outbreak of plague.[3] So catastrophic was the tragedy that it was necessary to petition for a Royal Brief. A deficient harvest, combined with the fear of entering the afflicted town professed by the farmers and corn dealers of outlying districts, threatened the town with famine. Following the precedent set during the distress of 1587 a careful enquiry was instituted: 468 quarters were consumed monthly, it was estimated.[4] Only about 2050

---

[1] Through the agency of the Sheriff.
[2] As well as the repair of the highways.
[3] Cooper, *op. cit.* III, pp. 222 *et seq.*
[4] About 1070 quarters monthly had been deemed necessary in 1587. (Cooper, *op.cit.* II, p. 435.) Of course the mortality was very heavy in 1630 and the colleges were closed. In London, 1630, about ⅛ peck of corn per

quarters were in the hands of the farmers, bakers, and brewers of the town, and available for use before the next harvest. An Order from the Privy Council was issued to meet the situation: farmers were to bring their corn to market notwithstanding the plague. Distress was on a scale hitherto unexampled, but assistance from other regions was generous.[1]

The plague passed, but it left a grievous trail of unemployment in its wake.[2] Attention was consequently again turned to the completion of the institution "in a great part erected and built",[3] and Hobson once more came to the rescue. By his will of December 1630, he left in the hands of the former trustees a further bequest which included the whole of the building site, together with sundry "farms, gardens, curtilages, courts and gardens thereto belonging with all their appurtenances, in the parish of St Andrew without Barnwell gate",[4] on condition that the establishment should be finished within four years, "as well for the setting the poor people of the said University and Town to work, as for an House of Correction for unruly and stubborn rogues, beggars, and other poor persons who should refuse to

head per week was reckoned as requisite (*vide* Leonard, *op. cit.* p. 188). In 1587 Cambridge—in consideration, perhaps, of its privileged university—had calculated on the far more liberal basis of 1 peck per head per week. Now, however, in 1630, the total amount necessary was said to be less than half the amount in 1587.

[1] It is interesting to note this reliance on the ancient device of a Brief at a moment when the Council was reminding justices that it was their duty to levy divisional or county rates in similar cases of distress. During the plague of 1665–6 the County Bench did levy rates upon the whole county in aid of stricken parishes, but there is no later evidence of such policy.

[2] It was estimated in 1630 that there were 2800 persons out of work in addition to the infected, and that the cost of maintaining the poor reached £150 a week, whilst there were not above 140 persons able to pay the rates. The following year the position was even worse. (Cooper, *op. cit.* III, pp. 223–30.)

[3] Hobson's will. (Bowtell MSS. Downing Coll. Libr., also MS. Corp. Com. Day Book, 1630.)

[4] The site of the present Police Station.

work". In "convenient time" the trustees were also to provide "a sufficient stock of wool and flax, and other materials". The buildings and stock were to be "sufficiently maintained", and a salary of £30 allowed to the Keeper from the rents and profits arising from the bequest.

If the terms of agreement made with the Keeper in 1675 were those customary at the opening of the institution—as seems probable—wool was to be provided for five combers of the town, and spinning and weaving for any unemployed weavers or other poor people of the town who desired work. Payment was to be made "at the usuall rates and prices as usually are paid by others". Whether miscreants in the bridewell department were also to receive the same full remuneration is not clear.

The dual nature of workhouse and reformatory is far more characteristic of these town establishments—especially when the foundation was of a semi-private and voluntary character—than it is of the county Houses of Correction, which tended to become more gaol-like after the Act of 1610.[1]

In May 1631[2] a petition was presented to the Council asking permission to devote the remainder of the money collected upon the Brief to the building of the House of Correction and the provision of stock for the workhouse. Leave was also sought to enclose for ten years fifty acres or so of Jesus Green and other common land, "for the yearly maintenance of the said stock and workhouse". With a view, moreover, to enforcing the Statute of Artificers, and thereby preserving the privileged trades from intrusion by the unemployed or by immigrants to the town, the petitioners further asked the Council to insist upon the observance of the seven years' apprenticeship clause.[3] The Council duly

[1] One of the directions issued with the Book of Orders, in 1631, was that the House of Correction should be erected near the gaol. (Cf. *infra*, p. 50.)

[2] Cooper, *op. cit.* III, pp. 239 *et seq.*

[3] It was necessary two months later for Thos. Buckell, who had served his apprenticeship as a chandler in Cambridge, to obtain the direct consent of the Privy Council before setting up as a draper in the town. Certain clauses of the Statute of Artificers were clearly enforced in Cambridge at

issued Orders in compliance with the requests, stipulating only that those who had "any particular interest in the said commons be fairly treated with".[1]

A report from the town concerning the steps taken to observe the Book of Orders accompanied the petition: weekly meetings, it was asserted, were held for the consideration of constables' reports; watch and ward were kept; such penalties as were legally so disposed of were devoted to the poor; the monthly poor-rates in every parish had been trebled and even quadrupled to meet the distress of the "late heavy visitacōn"; all such poor as were able, "beinge of seaven yeares of age and upwards", were set to work or bound apprentice; the monthly meetings of the overseers were also regularly held. The "Assize of bread and beare" and the punishment of "bakers, bruers, ingrosers, forestallers and the like", added the town authorities rather bitterly, "we leave to the vicechancelor and governors [of the university], accordinge to there Charter of priviledge wch they challendge".

This self-drawn picture of efficient, detailed administration suggests an easy working of the local machinery which is hardly borne out on closer investigation, though there was unquestionably a good deal of activity. An attempt on the part of the town magistrates to levy a rate-in-aid of the poorer parishes, in 1636, led the officers of Great St Mary's to lay their case before two of the Assize Judges.[2] The dispute shows quite clearly the friction with which the wheels revolved. The overseers complain of the "unequall rates" in the town. A sum of £4 monthly, they maintain, is expended by the parish in relieving its own poor —"so as none of them begg in any other parish". The further

this time. It was generally to the interest at least of the university to insist upon the fixing of prices. After a heated dispute, in 1629, between Town and Gown on the old subject of candles, the Council again upheld the privilege of price-regulation by the university.

[1] Corp. Cross Book 1631; MS. Baker, xliii, 152. (Cooper, *op. cit.* III, p. 240.) An Order again enforcing the regulations respecting inmates and cottages was issued by the Council at the same time.

[2] Great St Mary's MS. Vestry Book.

sum of £62. 18s. has been expended in the past year on "keeping of Nurse children, putting out of Apprentices, and clothing of poor children sent to the hospitall".[1] Notwithstanding these efforts the parish poor "daylie increase, in soe much as 80 ffamilies wch have to the number of 350 children and servants in them, are utterly unable to contribute to others". Vagrants also are "dayly releeved". Yet "it hath pleased the Justices, without any information in what case the state of our Parish now standeth, to look upon us as if we were able now as wee were 35 years since, and because we then yielded releefe to other parishes, when far more able, to lay an imposition of 26s. 8d. a month more upon us, to releeve other parishes who have impoverished themselves by errecting new cottages, and receiving of Inmates daily to them". The justices have rated "Clement parish at 5s. 6d.; St Edwards at 8s.; and Bennitt parish but at 4s.; every of those parishes being as able, if not better, to pay equall with us, the richest and most able men in the Towne being the most erectors of cottages and inmates". Complaint to the justices, the overseers allege, has merely resulted in a reassertion of the demand with a promise of consideration at the next Sessions. But, say the wary officers, "we have just cause to feare if we once pay, yt will still be exacted upon us". They therefore beg the Judges to appoint "three or four Justices of the Universitie, and as many of the Towne, to renew and amend the said Rates according to equitie". "We doubt but then there wilbe sufficient releife for the poore, without this new imposition",[2] they add. A strict order issued by the Town Sessions the previous January, and backed up by the Privy Council, directed against the influx of "strangers out of the country", the erection of cottages and the taking-in of lodgers, lends some colour to the justice of the above complaint, but objection to a rate-in-aid had been strong in 1599, despite the present naïve admission that the parish was then in a position to pay it! The two Assize Judges,[3] however, duly

---

[1] Apparently a children's home of some kind.
[2] Great St Mary's MS. Vestry Book, 1635–99.
[3] John Bramstone and George Croke.

appointed a committee of seven magistrates of the town and university, "to consider of and amend the said rates as they shall see cause, agreeable to justice and equitie".[1]

(4) The War Period

The outbreak of Civil War, whilst providing employment for many of the able-bodied, seriously complicated other sides of Poor Law administration. The supervision of the Privy Council ceased, and the justice of the peace became pre-eminently a justice of the war. As the headquarters of the Eastern Association after December 1642, Cambridge suffered very directly from the presence of troops, and continual sickness added to the burden of war taxation. The claims of the impotent could hardly be disregarded, but much difficulty was experienced in the gathering of the rates, and negligence and collusive action on the part of the overseers were justly complained of—the churchwardens and overseers of Great St Mary's were presented before the Town Sessions, in 1646, for "neglecting to collect the severall rates upon severall persons within the said parish".[2] Rates in relief of the poverty-stricken parishes of St Giles, Holy Trinity and St Andrew were once again ordered by the Town Bench to be levied upon the parishes of Great St Mary and St Edward, but the fiat was flatly set at nought. Even after a repeated order the rate was only collected by means of distraint upon the goods of the churchwardens and overseers. The officers of Great St Mary's were furious and promptly sought legal opinion. The magistrates do seem to have overstepped their legal authority, but in the absence of Privy Council intervention redress appeared to be unattainable. The officers of the three distressed parishes, it is pointed out, suffer their poor to beg in other parishes of the town, and when complaint is made to the magistrates, "noe punishment: noe reformation" follows. Divers persons in these parishes, "especially the abler sort", are underrated, but the

[1] Cooper, *op. cit.* III, p. 272.
[2] Great St Mary's MS. Vestry Book, 1646.

justices take no action. Even the "overplus" left after execution of the distress warrant has not been restored to the penalised officials. Counsel[1] advised that the warrant, under 43 Eliz., ought to have been issued against the individuals refusing to pay the sum assessed upon them and not against the officers, who could only legally be called upon to forfeit 20s. for negligence; that in any case the "overplus" ought to have been refunded, but to advise an action for trespass—"the taking being by Officers, and the order an act of Court, and treble damages, with costs, being given in case of miscarriage"—was too risky a procedure.

In 1649 the rate-in-aid was still being paid, and the alternative plan of equalising the poor-rate throughout the town had fallen through.

The administrative machinery certainly worked with many creaks and groans.[2] There was, on the part of some, a readiness to enlarge the parochial unit by equalising the rates over the whole town, but failing this condition there was a marked determination to limit the claims upon the parochial purse to settled parishioners.

Negligence on the part of the town rulers was manifest in other directions: the legacy of £200 left by Roger Thompson to Hobson's Workhouse, in 1642, lay idle for four years whilst Vice-Chancellor and Mayor wrangled[3] over right of precedence in the deed which made the bequest effective.

The unrelieved poverty in the town at the conclusion of the war was sufficiently obvious to draw from the university a promise to contribute £120 per annum in lieu of £48.[4] At a meeting of the town authorities, in 1652, some corporate action on behalf of the poor was contemplated, though it appears to

[1] Robert Bernard of Huntingdon.

[2] Two "collectors" were specially chosen in 1650 to assist the overseers of Great St Mary's to gather the bad debts. (Great St Mary's MS. Vestry Book.)

[3] First before the Court of Chancery and then before the House of Lords.

[4] Cooper, *op. cit.* III, p. 439.

have died at birth: it seems possible that the procuring of a private Act for the establishment of a body similar to the London "Corporation of the Poor" had formed the abortive project.[1] So much for the working of the compulsory statutes.

D. VOLUNTARY CHARITY IN THE TOWN

It was no part of the aim of Elizabethan legislators, as already stated, to discriminate between voluntary and compulsory charity, and this attitude continued to be shared by administrative authorities during the early seventeenth century. Constant emergencies—bad harvests, sickness and fire—did much to delay any tendency to distinguish between the pauper and other distressed persons.

The co-ordination of corporate and private charity was very evident at Cambridge in the plague organisation of 1630, and in the mode of foundation and maintenance of the workhouse and bridewell of the town. Private benefactions to an increasing extent took the forms suggested by statutory relief. Endowments for workhouses, for "stock" to set the poor to work, for the apprenticing of children and for erecting almshouses for the impotent were among the commonest types of charity. The ever-growing call for capital, moreover, induced many philanthropists to leave money to assist small tradesmen to set up in business, or to recover from fluctuations in trade. Such funds were in some cases administered by private trustees, but they also formed at this date an important part of the general means at the disposal of town or parochial officers.

Stephen Perse, in 1614, left habitations for six poor women, in addition to founding a free-school. Wm. Baldwyn, in 1620, left £100, to be divided among the several parishes of the town, for the apprenticing of poor children. Henry Wray, in 1628, left to Trinity parish the means whereby a hospital, or almshouse, for eight poor widows and widowers might be established. Elizabeth Knight, in 1647, bequeathed £440 to build almshouses for six poor women, to be selected by the corporation; a yearly

[1] MS. Corp. Com. Day Book, 1652.

allowance of £3 was to be made to each inmate.[1] Mrs Knight also left £20 to be loaned, on security, to young tradesmen "of godly life and conversation". John Sherwood, in 1642, similarly left £200 to be loaned to ten tradesmen. Alderman Foxton, in 1649, left £25 for the same purpose—the money was not made use of till 1656 and in less than twenty years the fate so usual with loans had befallen this benefaction. Taking special precautions to avoid loss, John Crane, in 1652, left £62 yearly to be loaned out by the town authorities of Cambridge, Wisbech, Lynn and Ipswich in rotation.[2]

The churchwardens' funds continued to be drawn upon for the relief of the poor simultaneously with the poor-rate proper.[3] At Great St Mary's, for example, even freer use than formerly was thus made of the church-rate. The almshouses in this parish still sheltered rate-aided paupers as well as other poor. Together with benefactions the communion collections taken at the church festivals provided the major part of the charity administered by the churchwardens, but the church-rate was also at times frankly used for the same purpose. In 1635, for example, "a halfe Easter Booke ffor and Towards the orderinge and clothinge of poore childrene and ffor other disbursements" was "agreed vppon". Three years' communion money, amounting to £4. 7s. 5d., was expended in 1600 on making "ix gounse of ffrese for our Almes fokes,[4] viz. vij gownes for wemen and two gownes for men". The details of the churchwardens' expenditure on the poor in this parish were usually entered separately in "the Booke which is kept for their vse", but occasionally an officer recorded the items along with his charges connected with the church. One thus learns that the types of folk relieved by the churchwardens, in their capacity as such, were much the same as those aided by

[1] Not an ungenerous allowance. "Old Hall", the sexton of Great St Mary's, earned only £4 a year about this period.
[2] *House of Commons' Reports on Charitable Endowments*, 1786–8, pp. 102–4. (See also Cooper, *op. cit.* under respective years.)
[3] J. E. Foster, *op. cit.* pp. 273, 309, 328, 340, 353, 369, 370, 409, 475.
[4] The designation "Almes fokes" was used here for parishioners in receipt of any form of regular relief.

the overseers. In 1619 there were thirty-one individuals—some of whom were almshouse inmates—relieved by the churchwardens. Many of these must also have been on the overseers' books. The sums given ranged from 5*d*. to "Nurse Corbit" to 9*s*. 4*d*. to old "goodman warren". The list included six widows, ten other women, four children severally boarded out, two children living with their father, and seven old men. "An old man for a losse by fire" received 18*d*. and "a poore travalinge woman and her child", 3*s*. To the Tolbooth prisoners 3*s*. 4*d*. was allotted and 8*s*. was spent on "Coles to the poore". Burial expenses were also occasionally paid by the churchwardens. In 1627 the following entry occurs: "Item ffor burieing of one John Harrison, a poore man, £00. 2. 00". Magistrates' orders for relief, too, were sometimes paid from the same source, and in 1621 even the statutory contribution to disabled soldiers was drawn from church funds— "Layd out for mayne souldiers, to Moses Horne ye Constable, xv^s". The Report of 1631, sent to the Privy Council, stated that the apprenticeship clauses of the statute were carefully observed by the overseers. Children were also bound out, however, by the churchwardens—mainly by aid of bequests left for the purpose. Thus, in 1613, the churchwardens of Great St Mary's paid £3 "for puttinge forth a child of wilsons". "Henry ffrancke", an orphan, was placed out in 1609 with a Mr Burwell, who agreed "to brynge hym vp in learninge yerby to make hym fytt for his trade", in consideration of a premium of "ffyfty shillinges" annually for three years. The insistence upon careful instruction and the precaution taken to pay in instalments were not always so marked, but a reasonable amount of care does seem to have been generally exercised in the town parishes at this time: no apprentice was indentured without discussion before the assembled vestry.

In 1633 two parishioners were appointed by Great St Mary's vestry to hold a careful enquiry into the management of the charitable endowments of the parish.[1] Local administrators in Cambridge very clearly adopted the attitude of the legislature respecting the relation between public and private charity.

[1] J. E. Foster, *op. cit.* p. 457.

Chapter III

POOR RELIEF IN WISBECH DURING THE FIRST PART OF THE SEVENTEENTH CENTURY[1]

A. EMPLOYMENT SCHEMES FOR THE ABLE-BODIED

Compulsory rating was well established in Wisbech for more than a decade before the enactment of 1598, though all sides of relief continued to be administered much more immediately by corporate, as distinguished from parochial, authorities than was contemplated by the sponsors of the new Act.

By far the most interesting of corporate activities were the endeavours to provide work for the unemployed. It was possibly the influence, direct or indirect, of governmental measures that determined the Ten Men of Wisbech, faced with the serious economic difficulties of 1598, to follow the precedent of Cambridge and of the still nearer East Anglian towns, and in July of that year to "purchase an howse of Mr Styrman to sett the pore on work". The moment was propitious, for a recent bequest of £100 relieved the rulers here, as at Cambridge, of the necessity of further raising the rates, and rates for the relief of unemployment were still eyed with deep suspicion notwithstanding legislation. The first plan seems to have met with little success, for a new scheme was adopted eighteen months later. The corporation entered into an agreement with certain local manufacturers who were to employ, "in bunchinge of hempe, pashelinge, hicklinge, and spynnynge of candleweek", all poor—vagrant or settled—sent to them by the town officials. The corporation purchased the hemp and tares wholesale and sold them at cheap rates to the employers, who themselves paid the poor for the work according to a fixed scale—"for the bunchinge

[1] MS. Corp. Minute and Order Book, Wisbech.

of each stone of hempe three pence, and for pashelinge one halfe penny, and for each stone of teare hicklinge fyve pence, and for each pounde of Candeleweeke spynninge one penny". The employers also undertook the marketing of the products and in return for their services claimed the profits accruing. The hemp trade was good[1], and as certain of the manufacturing processes did not require a high degree of skill the enterprise appears to have been run successfully for the ensuing twelve months—the three employers, Mr Wilks, Thomas Pite and Wm. Thompson, continued at any rate to purchase the raw material from the corporation.[2] Soon, however, the town became so attractive to folk in search of work that the labour market was glutted; the Ten Men were obliged to return to their former practice of ejecting strangers, and the undertaking petered out.

The authorities then turned to the expedient of granting monetary loans to enable folk to purchase hemp for themselves, leaving them to make their own bargains for the sale of the work. Items such as the following occur in the town records:

> 1608: To James Pemberton. Lent him to buy hempe to sett himself one work, by consent of the Companye, 10s.
>
> 1609: To Henry Coward. Lent him to sett him to work, 5s.

In 1614 attention was directed to the employment of children: it was easier to exact continuous labour at low wages from unresisting infants, and a glowing conscience rewarded such devotion to the duty of disciplining youth. Part of the town bridewell[3] was transformed into a School of Industry, and some

---

[1] There was a considerable demand for sailcloth and ropes for the shipping of Wisbech and the ports with which Wisbech communicated.

[2] January 29th, 1600–1: "The same day was paide in by Mr Wilks 29s. 7d. for certeine hemp—viz. 9 stone. Wch. some of 29s. 7d. was paide into the hands of James Gaylebanke the same tyme, to be expended about the poore. Itm̄ there is oweing by To. pite for 9 sto. hempe, 29s. 9d. Itm̄ due by Willm̄ Thompson for 2 sto: hempe, 6s. 2d." (MS. Corp. Minute and Order Book, Wisbech.)

[3] In 1613 the Court of Quarter Sessions for the Isle issued some order concerning the Wisbech House of Correction. The details are not re-

fourteen to twenty children were set to work there under a certain James Pite. They were apparently neither lodged nor fed on the premises—though they may have had meals in an adjoining room, for the Town Bailiff was ordered to allow "for their maintenance of diett at the house of Mathias Tailer, or els where, at 2*d.* the day a peice": Taylor was the Treasurer of the Bridewell and as Constable of the Castle[1] occupied adjacent premises.

A vigorous policy of extrusion of undesirable strangers was in vogue at this time, as it was at intervals during the greater part of the century, for further efforts were to be made to deal with the unemployed, whose ranks needed no recruitment by outsiders.[2] The bridewell at Wisbech did duty for the whole of the northern part of the Isle, and a good deal of reparation or extension of the building was taking place,[3] for it was determined to treat with no gentle hand the vagrant or deliberate idler. A new Town Hall, or Market House, was also in course of con-

corded, but in view of the legislation of 1610 (7 Jas. I), one would surmise that steps were being taken to emphasise the penal aspect of the bridewell. (MS. Corp. Minute and Order Book, Wisbech.)

[1] He was a Capital Burgess and was also Chief Constable of the Hundred. (*Ibid.* 1613.)

[2] Bonds of security were demanded of persons permitted to settle in the town in four separate instances in 1614. (Cf. *infra*, p. 128, note 2.) In 1674 Benjamin Wright was paid 10 shillings per quarter for "tacking care to give notis to the Justeses of pease, Constabl and Colektors, for the better keeping oute poore strangers that shall come to setell heare to be a charge to oure Towne". Similar appointments continued to be made for some years. The salary was doubled in 1676—again in connection with schemes of work for the unemployed. In 1676 the Court of Quarter Sessions issued an order for the pulling down of various cottages. In 1693 the Bishop, as Lord of the Manor, was desired to give consent to the demolition of certain cottages, "to ye intent y^t theire may be no more erections upon ye said Waist without ye Consent of ye Capital Burgesses". In 1697 the policy of payment by results was resorted to: John Walpoole was to have "for every family he turns out of Towne as Inmates 18*d.* a family, and for every single pson one shilling". (MS. Corp. Minute and Order Book, Wisbech.)

[3] 2000 bricks at 15*s.* 8*d.* per 1000 were delivered there.

struction on the adjoining site; the building was required, among other purposes, as a storehouse for hemp or other stock used in setting the poor to work. It was proposed to carry on the municipal purchase of raw material more extensively, with a view to retailing it cheaply to the unemployed, crediting poor folk, if need be, with certain quantities until they had effected a sale. In 1616, for example, the Town Bailiff allowed "unto old Blessing towards his relief, for the buying of one stone of hempe, that he may labor for his lyving, 4s."

The House of Correction up to this point had been merely a deterrent institution,[1] so far as adults were concerned. By 1620 it had become clear that neither employment on the outwork system, nor harsh institutional discipline, met the situation with complete satisfaction, and a deputation was sent to Swaffham, in Norfolk, to "vewe" the bridewell there. After consideration of the report it was decided to convert the new Town Hall of Wisbech into a House of Correction and make some attempt to deal with certain types of the able-bodied by providing them with work on the premises, carried out under supervision. The Keeper of the House of Correction was receiving, in 1622, a salary of £12[2] for supervising and instructing, and was thus not dependent for his own maintenance upon wringing a profit out of the inmates, who were paid by the corporation at fixed rates for their work and appear to have been occupied mainly in weaving. Side by side with this institutional work there was a good deal of hemp given out to home-workers to be spun, prepared for spinning, or manufactured into tow, and a certain amount even of weaving seems to have been done domestically. Thomas Parke—a Capital Burgess—and Thomas Love were appointed to "oversee" the home-workers, to sell them hemp, to pay them for the yarn, tow or cloth, and to pass on some at least of the yarn to be woven in the bridewell. The cloth and

---

[1] Officially under the control of the magistrates of the north part of the Isle.

[2] In part the benefaction of Mrs Styrman, or Sturmyn. Half the salary was contributed by the justices' rate for the north part of the Isle.

other products were stored in the Town Hall and, as occasion offered, sold by the Town Bailiff to dealers.[1] The real onus of the enterprise—buying, selling, paying wages and accepting the ultimate profit or loss—fell therefore upon the corporation.

The next year 65 stone of "femble" hemp[2] were bought "as

[1] There were three buyers of cloth and one of tow in 1622.

[2] "Femble" hemp was the term applied to the fibre as prepared for use. (*Vide Oxf. Dict.*)

The following quantities were bought in November and December, 1623:

Nov.	9 stone of femble bought					for 31s.	6d.
,,	15 ,,	,,	,,	at 3/5	per st.	,, 52s.	10d.
Dec.	7 ,,	,,	,,	3/7	,,	,, 25s.	1d.
,,	4 ,,	,,	,,	3/8	,,	,, 14s.	8d.
,,	1 ,,	,,	,,	3/8	,,	,, 3s.	8d.
,,	2 ,,	,,	,,	3/6	,,	,, 7s.	
,,	5 ,,	,,	,,	3/7	,,	,, 17s.	11d.
,,	12 ,,	,,	,,	3/6	,,	,, 42s.	
,,	10 ,,	,,	,,	3/10	,,	,, 38s.	4d.

The following selected items illustrate *the payment of work, the storing of the cloth*, etc.:

"Item: The baylife appointed to pay to Mr Parke for money that he hath disbursed for hemp and making it into cloth, £9. 6. 3.

"There was delivēd by Thomas Love, wᶜʰ is left in the towne hall, vi boults of cloth, conteyning in toto 9 score and 3 yards and also 46 pounds of towe. Wᶜʰ cloth doth cost the towne in hempe, wᵗʰ the bunching, hickling, spinyng, and weaving £8. 2. 4, whereof there was formerly paid to Thomas Love by the baylife £5. And the bailife is now appointed to paie to the said Thomas Love, £3. 2. 4.

"Itm the bayliffe to pay into the handes of Thomas Parke Esq. to be bestowed by his appointment to sett the poore on worke, £10."

Payment to Master of House of Correction for wages to workers:

"Itm. Bailiff to pay to Wilcocke to be by him pd. to weavers and woork-folk about cloth, £4."

Sale of cloth to dealers:

"Item. the ballif hath received of

Mr Buckworth for cloth,		38s.	3d.
Mr ffisher	,, ,,	23s.	3d.
Mr Pigg	,, ,,	15s.	9d.

"The Bayliffe recᵈ of Mr Stanford for 46 pounds of Towe 3s. 10d."

(MS. Corp. Minute and Order Book, Wisbech.)

occasion served", and the scheme continued in full working order. The entries are somewhat ambiguous, but the corporation appear to have suffered a considerable loss on the undertaking—£11. 10s. 7d.—in the course of the year 1622–3, exclusive of £6, the half of the Keeper's salary paid by the town.[1] As recorded in rather scattered items, the outlay on hemp and labour amounted to £33. 19s. 10d.; the receipts for the sale of cloth to £3. 17s. 3d.; and the value of unsold cloth and tow to £18. 12s.

The adverse balance at the end of the next year was apparently reduced to about £2—or £8 if the Keeper's salary be added. The following items are recorded:

Payments:

		£	s.	d.
October 1623, 55 stone of femble laid upp in store:[2]		4	17	1
Nov. and Dec. 1623, 65 stone of femble bought		11	13	0
Feb. 1624, Pd to spynners, bunchers and hicklers		4	10	0
„ further to „ „		10	0	0
„ for wheele for Henry Den			3	4
June 1624, „ for bunching, hickling and making of cloth		6	4	2
October 1624, Pd to Keeper, year's salary		7	1	8
		£44	9	3

Receipts:

		£	s.	d.
June 1624, Cloth and towe sold for the yeare paste		36	8	0
Adverse balance	£8	1	3

In 1626, and for some years afterwards, a proportion of the rough hempen cloth woven by the unemployed was used in making clothing for the poor. Wool, in addition to hemp, was definitely requisitioned as raw material for the House of Correction in 1628, and possibly flax was added in 1629, for both woollen and linen cloth were then being used for clothing the poor. Though it is doubtful whether the material continued to

---

[1] £22 was expended this year in aiding the poor other than able-bodied.

[2] "Layd up in a Chamber over the House of Correction."

be manufactured by folk employed by the town, the sums spent on clothing the poor certainly increased year by year. From £4. 9s. 4d. in 1626 the amount rose to £40 in 1640, falling thenceforward to an average of £20 yearly by 1660. After 1624 there are no detailed accounts for work and during the war it was almost certainly abandoned—in spite of the continuous demand for cloth which the needs of the poor themselves would seem to have created.

In 1657 a new project was started. It was rather characteristic of the period that greater reliance should be placed upon private enterprise. The rent of a building[1] was guaranteed by the town, a sum of £250 paid down, and an additional £10 allowed to two manufacturers, Batch and Plow-wright, to "bring their materialls"—apparently they were not townsmen.[2] For the rest the two men were to undertake all responsibility concerning the poor sent to them at the discretion of the municipal rulers. This system continued to work for some years, for the rent was still being paid in 1660. Simultaneous entries such as the following, however, show that the scheme was no complete remedy for unemployment: "Two stone of hemp to be given to W. Scotred for his relief this winter".

The provision of work was the most important of the means taken in the early seventeenth century to relieve able-bodied distress, but occasionally monetary assistance was given on the grounds of a large family—the grounds so seriously criticised in the nineteenth century. In 1614, for example, the church-wardens and overseers were ordered to relieve Wm. Man for this reason. Loans also were available in certain cases, but—in contrast to Cambridge—Wisbech seems to have been more reluctant to make use of such assistance than formerly, despite increased bequests to the town for this purpose.[3] Interest at the

---

[1] £6 per annum.
[2] They probably hailed from Norfolk.
[3] In addition to Crane's bequest (cf. *supra*, p. 29), Wm. Holmes, in 1656, left £300 for loans to poor tradesmen. (*House of Commons' Reports on Charitable Donations*, 1796–8, p. 105.)

current rate of 20*d.* in the £ was demanded of Thomas Cole, to whom the sum of £5 was lent in 1623. Repayment of a loan, in 1627, took the form of supplying 60 bushels of coal for winter distribution to the poor. So far as the able-bodied poor of Wisbech were concerned, therefore, the parochial officers played no more part during the seventeenth century than they had done before the Act of 1597.

B. THE IMPOTENT

It is probable that overseers were promptly appointed as a result of the enactment of 39 Eliz.,[1] but their activities even in connection with the impotent and the children were largely dependent upon the extent to which the parish rates were supplemented by grants from the municipal chest. With respect to regular pensioners—those "on the weekly collection"—the overseers gradually came to exercise considerable discretionary powers, though at first they were closely supervised and directed as to their procedure. In 1618 the sum of £10. 15*s.* was allowed to the overseers out of corporate funds, towards easing the rates for relief of the regular poor and for the clothing of children and others. A similar grant was thenceforward made annually. In 1628 the sum of £10 was paid towards the "distribution", and cloth was given to the value of £4. 9*s.* 4*d.*;[2] in 1636 the "distribution" grant was £3 together with the "King's dole"[3] of £4; in 1640 the grant was again £10 in addition to no less than £40 for clothing. Coals for the poor were sometimes supplied by the town and distributed through the overseers—the sum of £7. 4*s.* was devoted to this purpose in 1657.

Assistance was now and again given towards the payment of house rent—in 1607, for example, 2*s.* was so allowed—but it was not a common practice. More often aged or disabled paupers

---

[1] Reference is first made to them in 1614, but in a casual manner which implies that they were then customary administrative officers.

[2] Cf. *supra*, p. 37.

[3] The sum refunded by the Court of Augmentations when the gild was dissolved.

were boarded with other poor townsfolk or were placed in one of the almshouses for which private endowments, as at Cambridge, continued to be made. Mrs Sturmyn bequeathed four almshouses to the corporation in 1616, and Hawkins left £300 for a like purpose in 1631.

C. THE SICK AND CASUAL POOR

With most cases of sickness or of temporary distress the Ten Men continued to deal directly as of yore. Allowances such as the following were made at one period or another throughout the century:

1607: Charity Russel to be allowed 5s. for curing Pierson's head, 2s. 6d. down and 2s. 6d. more "when safe and whole".

1608: To Wm Harrison to relieve him in his sicknes, 5s.

1610: 5 persons allowed 1s. each, and 1 person 6d.

1610: Widow Arnold to be allowed a nurse.

1617: Widow with children allowed 10s.

1620: The initial expenses paid for a poor woman "to travel to the bath for the cure of her infirmities".

1621: "To the wife of Wm Skerrett to help to releeive her," 10s.

1629: 20s. for a cure—10s. down and 10s. more if successful.

1631: "To Clarkes wife for reliefe of her husband being poore and sick, 3s."

1631: "Henry Coldwell, gent., to be relieved in his necessity," 15s.

1648: 20s. to "a poore sick widow, but she not to be releeved of the overseers".[1]

D. THE CHILDREN

In addition to experimenting with a School of Industry, the Ten Men maintained their earlier interest in the apprenticing and boarding-out of children. The selection of the children—two or three were apprenticed annually on an average—gradually devolved to a greater extent upon the overseers, but the formal

---

[1] In 1669 the widow of the schoolmaster was pensioned at £4 per annum.

consent of the Ten was required, for apprenticeship funds in particular were largely derived from benefactions under corporate control. The premiums paid, the conditions of service required, and the allowances made on behalf of children boarded-out were much the same as they had been in the latter part of the previous century.[1] The payment of 20*s*. to John Gogney, in 1617, "for the keeping of John Parkers Child so long as hee liveth", does not suggest much care for the well-being of the boy, but other entries do show the precautions of earlier years to be maintained: "The Baylif", it was recorded in 1625, "hath paid to John Rachel wth his Apprentice Rich. Cobbe the sōme of 33*s*. 4*d*. And he is to have so much more at the end of one yeare, if the said Apprentice live so long and is well used". Where the sums given were more than 40*s*., either for apprenticeship or board, the master was usually required to enter into a bond for the faithful performance of his undertaking. During the third decade of the century the overseer assumed the primary responsibility of arranging the contracts for children, but his expenses were regularly refunded by the Town Bailiff—a sum of £15 was thus repaid in 1629.

At Wisbech, therefore, compulsory rates merely supplemented other sources of relief, and supplemented them to a less significant extent than was the case at Cambridge. For the assistance of the unemployed of Wisbech the rates were practically not drawn upon at all; nor were they for the care, training or employment of the children; nor indeed in most cases of

---

[1] The premiums varied from 10*s*. to 66*s*. 8*d*. Clothing was frequently, though not always, given in addition. It cost about £1. 14*s*. 8*d*. per annum to board a pauper child at this time.

Most apprentices were bound out to townsfolk, though one boy, in 1629, was apprenticed as far away as London for the small premium of £1.

Contracts often, but not always, mentioned the termination age limits of twenty-one and twenty-four, for girls and boys respectively.

Babies were allowed for at the rate of 6*d*. or 8*d*. per week, dropping to 20*s*. per annum when the child was old enough to be of some service. Illegitimate children were customarily paid for at the rate of 1*s*. per week, refunded by the parent.

sickness or casual distress. Even for the relief of old age and permanent disablement voluntary endowments provided some part of the means. The primary duties of the town authorities were certainly not confined to the supervisory functions envisaged by the Act of 1597. There is little evidence of direct influence being exerted by the Privy Council upon the town, yet its rulers continued to control social and economic life as vigorously as in the preceding century.

Chapter IV

POOR LAW ADMINISTRATION IN THE RURAL AREAS DURING THE FIRST PART OF THE SEVENTEENTH CENTURY

A. LOCAL RECORDS OF THE RURAL VESTRIES

It is probable that in those country parishes where distress was marked the new Poor Law was at least to some extent put into operation for the time being, in compliance with the Privy Council Order of 1598. Such early seventeenth-century rural vestry records as now exist, however, give no indication of any sudden or widespread change of policy. In many small parishes benefactions still met the normal claims of poverty, and were supplemented by a special collection, or by an occasional compulsory rate.[1] The customary "collektors" certainly did not universally give place at once to legally appointed overseers, though it is probable that the change occurred in some of the larger villages, and spread during the second decade of the century.

At Linton[2] the more important principles of the Act of 1597 had been adopted earlier, but had fallen into abeyance before 1590. The benefaction of that year, designed for the relief of the unemployed, remained legally in the hands of the widow until her death. In 1618, however, sensible of the needs of the parish, she voluntarily passed on the bequest to the overseers, who were by that date regularly elected. The stock of flax and hemp seems, as in former days, to have been distributed among home-workers, as well perhaps as supplied to the residents in the old "task house" and gildhall, which continued to be let out cheaply or freely as lodgings.[3]

---

[1] This custom did not end even with the seventeenth century. Cf. *infra*, chap. xiii.   [2] Cf. *supra*, chap. i, p. 10.

[3] There was no attempt to make a profit out of the rent of the rooms, though expenses were usually narrowly cleared.

PLATE III

THE OLD GILDHALL AT WHITTLESFORD
after conversion into a workhouse

At Whittlesford very similar conditions prevailed: the gild-hall began to be used for housing the poor soon after the dissolution of the gild in the sixteenth century, and probably spinning was introduced about the same time. The ground floor of many of these gildhalls was in one entire room, well suited to use as a storeroom or workroom; the upper story—at least in the seventeenth century—was usually partitioned off. Thomas Watson[1] was appointed as Superintendent of the workhouse at Whittlesford about the year 1635. Such of the inmates—mainly aged folk and widows—as were capable of work were employed in spinning, but Watson was also responsible for the distribution of wool to domestic workers and for the collection and disposal of the yarn. Most of the larger villages of Cambridgeshire had earlier possessed a gildhall,[2] and the uses to which the building was put at Linton and Whittlesford were probably charac-teristic of many rural parishes during the early seventeenth century. By 1654 all reference to work at Whittlesford had ceased.[3]

In some parishes there is no trace of any communal building, either for employing on the premises or for housing the poor, though domestic work seems to have been going on. At Little-port, for example, such entries as the following, for the year 1624,[4] appear to indicate that home-spinning was encouraged by the overseers:

Laid out for papere for to set the pore a worke, 1d.[5]
Paid for Spindeles and wharles,[6] 2s.
Paid unto Nucklas Sare for spinners, 18d.

As the seventeenth century proceeded, the proportion which

[1] The building was still used as a workhouse in 1805, when the Keeper was still a member of the Watson family. (Notes by Maynard, Saffron Walden MSS.)

[2] Cf. *supra*, p. 3.

[3] The disbursements of 1654—sums varying from 1s. 6d. to 5s. per week—were given exclusively to women and children.

[4] MS. Overseers' Accounts, Littleport.

[5] Apparently for the purpose of recording their work.   [6] Wheels.

benefactions bore to the whole outlay on relief in normal years perceptibly, but by no means sharply, diminished. Whereas, for example, at the end of the sixteenth century more than half of the funds at Linton consisted of endowments, by 1652 out of about £50 expenditure[1] £32 were derived from the rates. There was, however, no distinction in these rural parishes, any more than in the towns, between the uses to which the respective funds were put. During the earlier part of the seventeenth century the annual outlay on the poor, in the villages of Cambridgeshire, averaged only about £20 or £30 per parish, hence benefactions might easily cover expenses in fortunate parishes during favourable years. At Ickleton, for instance, even as late as 1658 the whole needs of the parish poor were normally thus met—seventeen cottages were in the hands of the overseer, as well as lands, rent charges, and gifts for poor widows, more than equal to the value of the cottages.

The vestry records of Sawston and Littleport may be taken as characteristic examples of the type of information most commonly to be gleaned from the local archives of the early seventeenth century. The former parish lies within the county proper, the latter within the Isle of Ely.

"The statute enioyneth a booke of record to be kept, that the names, numbers, and necessities of the poore may be seene", explained a writer of 1601,[2] but the injunction was by no means always observed at this date.

The earliest overseers' book at Sawston refers to the year 1617; it was in this year that overseers were probably first appointed.

The doale at Easter, vi li.
Item layd out at the doale at Christmas—
Item given to poore people at Severall times as appeareth in his bill
of Accompts—
      The whole summe of this Accomptants
      Layings forth for this last yeare, £30. 19s.

---

[1] This included the maintenance of an illegitimate child, whose father refunded the parish.

[2] *An Ease for Overseers of the Poore* (Anon. 1601), p. 2.

Thus did the vicar of Sawston, in 1617, incompletely summarise and enter on record the accounts kept by an illiterate overseer on loose scraps of paper which were then apparently destroyed. The record for 1621 is somewhat more informative:

For the 2 doles at Easter and Christmas,	£15.	19s.	6d.
Given to the poore at divers times in the year as need required,	£8	17	2
	£24	16	8

The two doles, at Easter and Christmas, evidently constituted two-thirds of the year's entire disbursements to the Sawston poor. Only £25 were required annually, and to meet this need £27 were available from the rents of 61 acres of arable land, an orchard and pasture, and there was in addition a balance of £3 from "the last accomptant". Hence there was no need at the moment to resort to a rate at all. Regular compulsory rates were not in fact demanded at Sawston till 1658.[1]

In 1635 Elizabeth Wakelin left lands, part of the profits of which were to go "towards a stock for poor labourers". The accounts for this period do not record details, but by 1659, when particulars are given, nominally at least there was no relief offered to the able-bodied. Apart from the occasional placing-out of a child, the only folk registered as receiving assistance are those indicated in the entry of that year: "Given to poore not able to worke, £41. 5s."

At Littleport a few stray overseers' bills for the year 1624 are extant. One of these records the weekly list of recipients of out-relief, another the miscellaneous casual payments. The more or less regular pensioners cost the parish about £9. 12s. per annum, and the "bye" expenses amounted to about £25 at this period.[2] The moneys seem to have been raised by a rate at Littleport.

---

[1] In 1694 the rents from the parish lands amounted to £36. 6s. 11d.; the rates to £16. 11s. 8½d.

[2] This distribution of expenses as between regular pensioners and casual payments was exceptional at this date.

The lists vary a little from week to week, suggesting frequent revision. For the first week in June the list was as follows:

To the Wid.	Hargrave,	3*d*.	
„	„ Boner	3*d*.	
„	„ Lumbe	3*d*.	
„	„ Hodlinton	3*d*.	
„	„ Spencer	4*d*.	
„	„ Mendham	6*d*.	lay sick
To Briget Cattlyn		—	
„ father Poter		3*d*.	
„ father Barkum		4*d*.	
„ Robert Meadows		3*d*.	
„ Robert Lumbe		12*d*.	
		3*s*. 8*d*.	

Briget Cattlyn, Robert Meadows and Widow Mendham received nothing for certain weeks—presumably they occasionally obtained sufficient employment. Widows, it is to be noted, figure prominently. The smallness of the sums allowed seems to imply that the recipients were not entirely destitute of other means of livelihood. Allowances in aid of wages must in fact often have been given in certain cases long before the practice became systematised and applied regularly to the able-bodied at the end of the eighteenth century. The encouragement given to home-spinning has already been mentioned. Various paupers were boarded out with other parishioners but, except in case of "suckenesse" or entire decrepitude, the payments—a penny or twopence per week—could not possibly have included at this date more than the barest shelter; part of the expense of even a room may in fact have been paid by the poor themselves. The overseer, for example, "paid unto Henry Baly for lodging the widow Spenser for 6 weeks, 7*d*." and for "harboring of Thomas [?] one monthe, 8*d*."[1]

---

[1] It cost 6*d*. to 8*d*. a week to board a child fully at Wisbech in the early seventeenth century. (Cf. *supra*, p. 40, note.)

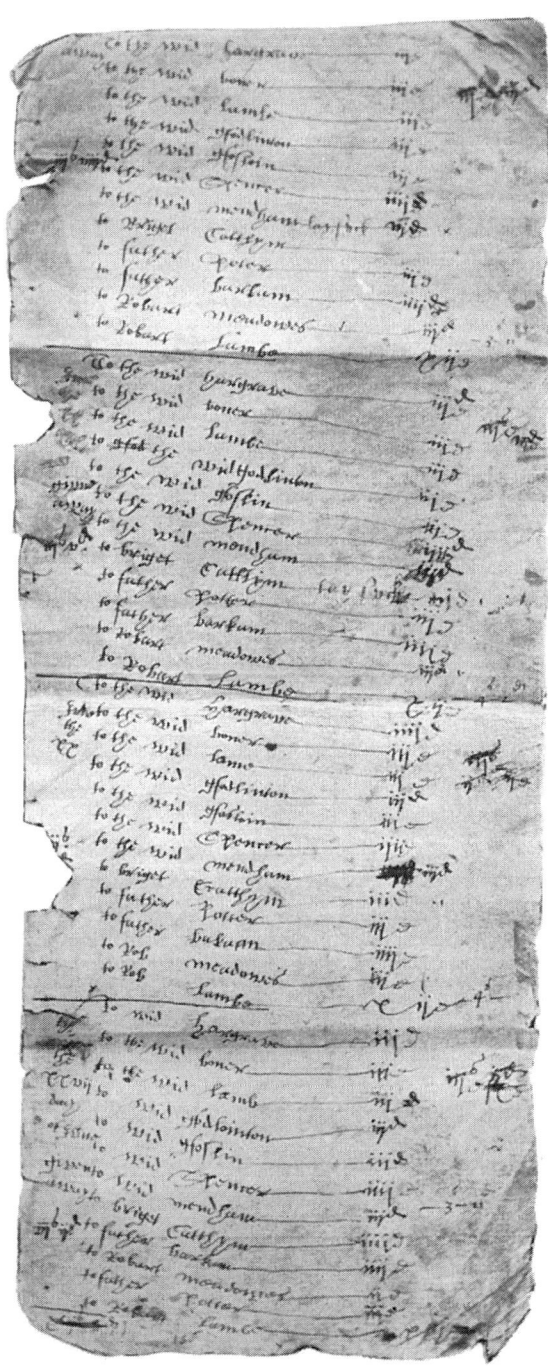

PLATE IV

OVERSEER'S ACCOUNTS, LITTLEPORT, 1624

In addition to the dozen or so more or less regular pensions there were many allowances for temporary sickness:

Paid unto Gorg Lendal the 13 day of March when he lay sucke, 4*d.*
Paid for Lendal the 20 day of March when he lay suck, 11*d.*
Paid unto John Baxter when he lay suck, 6*d.*

The services of a doctor were not directly paid for by the rural parishes at this date. The overseers of Littleport did, however, deal with the tailor or dressmaker directly. There were numerous payments for the making of clothing—an expensive item, for even the clothes and needles of a vagrant pedlar who died on the hands of the parish fetched 3*s.*

The ease with which overseers could defalcate is most obvious. The accounts at Littleport are not signed or examined at this period; they are not entered up by the vicar as they are at Sawston; marginal corrections are numerous, and even the totals at the foot show inaccurate addition, which is not amended. Judging by the handwriting, each overseer took service in turn for one month at a time—a method unlikely to secure either accuracy or continuity of treatment.[1]

It is possible to supplement such fragmentary evidence as is derived from existing parish records by reference to the reports of the justices compiled in obedience to Privy Council Orders.

B. REPORTS OF THE RURAL PARISHES TO THE PRIVY COUNCIL

(1) *The Statute of Artificers and the Supply of Corn*

Following the bad harvests of 1629 and 1630, and the consequent rise in prices, there was much complaint that the rating of wages, enjoined by the Act of 1563, was not being practised. In September 1630 the Privy Council therefore proceeded to arouse the justices of Cambridgeshire:[2] "These hard and necessitous

---

[1] Overseers more usually worked simultaneously at this date than they did at the end of the eighteenth century.

[2] And also those of Norfolk, Suffolk, Essex and Norwich. (Leonard, *op. cit.* pp. 162, 163.)

tymes", wrote the Council, "doe require some better care to be had in that behalfe....The Statutes of 5 Eliz. and 1 Jas. having so carefully provided against these inconveniences,...this Board cannot but be exceeding sensible of any neglect or omission". The implication seems to be that assessments had been made at an earlier date, but that magistrates had grown negligent. The towns of Bury St Edmunds and Norwich, which had received similar communications from the Council, definitely did draw up new assessments as a consequence. The neighbouring county of Hertford did so a year later. No Quarter Sessions' Records for this period are extant for Cambridgeshire, but it is clear from the replies of the justices who met at Longstanton, in 1632, for the hundreds of Chesterton, Papworth and North Stowe, that the Order was not complied with at least in some areas of Cambridgeshire. "For the statute of labours, retayneinge of servants and ordering of wages", they admit, "we have taken it into our consideracōn, but have perfected nothinge, the care of the poore and puttinge forth of apprentices hath imployed soe much of our tyme."[1]

(2) *The Carrying-out of the Poor Law*

The observance of the directions issued in the Book of Orders, concerning the carrying-out of the Poor Law, certainly did receive respectful attention fairly generally at the hands of the Cambridgeshire magistracy.

In April 1631[2] it was reported from Whittlesford, Chilford and Radford hundreds, that the impotent were "releeved", the able poor "provyded for or sett to worke", and that between six and seven score children had been apprenticed—a number which suggests considerable negligence in the preceding years.

---

[1] *State Papers Domestic* (henceforward quoted as *S.P.D.*), Chas. I, vol. 216, no. 45. (Leonard, *op. cit.* pp. 359, 360.)
[2] *Ibid.* vol. 189, no. 75; also Leonard, *op. cit.* p. 253.

In July 1638[1] the impotent were still said to be relieved and the "other poore provided of worke".

Chesterton, Papworth and North Stowe hundreds reported, in 1632,[2] that regular monthly meetings of the divisions had been held and the High Constables, together with the petty constables and overseers of every parish, summoned to render "a strict accompt" of their doings, "accordinge to the instruccons sent vnto us". The impotent poor were "sufficiently relieved". The "Towne stockes" for the unemployed had been found less satisfactory and directions had been given to most parishes that they be "increased and duly imployed". The subsequent improvement had been so marked within a short time that the justices had deemed it wise to be "sloe in punishinge", seeking rather "by gentle means to incourrage them, where we find the law to give us that liberty". Over 150 apprentices had been put forth at the several divisional meetings: within three of the hundreds this matter had, in fact, occupied much attention, for obligations had frequently been evaded by masters who had "putt away", on frivolous pretences, the apprentices bound to them. The necessary pressure had now, however, been exerted in order to "settle them againe".

The apprenticeship clauses of the final Elizabethan Poor Law had indeed from the outset encountered opposition. The extreme youth and sometimes weakly constitution of the children did not recommend them to enterprising masters. It was seemly, in the view of the earliest interpreters of the law, that pauper children should be put forth "very timely"[3]—at the age of seven—but practical difficulties led even the most energetic justices to enquire only concerning children above the age of ten. Unwilling masters, "by some devise or hard intreatie", frequently provoked their apprentices "unlawfully to depart"; other masters accepted the child and made of him a household slave, frustrating

---

[1] *S.P.D.* Chas. I, vol. 395, no. 114; also Leonard, *op. cit.* p. 253.

[2] *Ibid.* vol. 216, no. 45; also Leonard, *op. cit.* pp. 359, 360.

[3] *An Ease for Overseers*, p. 7. This was the opinion expressed also by Michael Dalton, *The Country Justice* (ed. 1630), p. 105.

thereby the intention of the legislature to give him "experience of his trade",[1] and ultimately turning him adrift to seek employment in the over-supplied market of unskilled labour.

The county House of Correction lay within the hundred of Chesterton. "We have yett had noe tyme or means to alter it," write the justices of this division, in 1632, "but we shall carefully and speedyly obey commandemt."[2] The institution already complied with the Council's directions in so far as it adjoined the gaol. The Legislature in 1610, and the Council in 1630, were stressing the punitive aspects of the county bridewells. For the whole of the rural county, however, outside the Isle of Ely, there was but the one House of Correction: hence no parish authorities at any distance would be likely to dispatch thither any but the recalcitrant poor or the criminal misdemeanant. It may indeed be that the provision of work in the bridewell had fallen into entire neglect and that the Council's Order was one requiring amendment in this respect. Later in the century, though the county House of Correction was certainly not designed to house the genuine seeker for work, it was nevertheless an institution distinct from the county gaol and it did provide remunerative labour for its prisoners. Through the difficulties of communication the bridewells of the county, as distinguished from those of the towns, early became merely disciplinary in character.

---

[1] It is clear that the statute was officially interpreted as requiring that children should actually be taught a trade—whatever happened in practice—and that the evils of blind-alley occupations were evident even as early as 1601. (Contrast Dunlop, *Apprenticeship and Child Labour*, p. 251. Cf. also *infra*, p. 156.)

Miss Dunlop's reading of Dalton seems hardly justifiable. Dalton insists upon the necessity of the child being properly instructed: "Lest the apprentice consume his time without learning anything: for the word apprentice...sheweth that they are to be bound to, and brought up in, taught, and instructed by the master in some art, mysterie, or trade". (M. Dalton, *The Country Justice*, ed. 1619, p. 104.)

[2] *S.P.D.* Chas. I, vol. 216, no. 45; also Leonard, *op. cit.* p. 358.

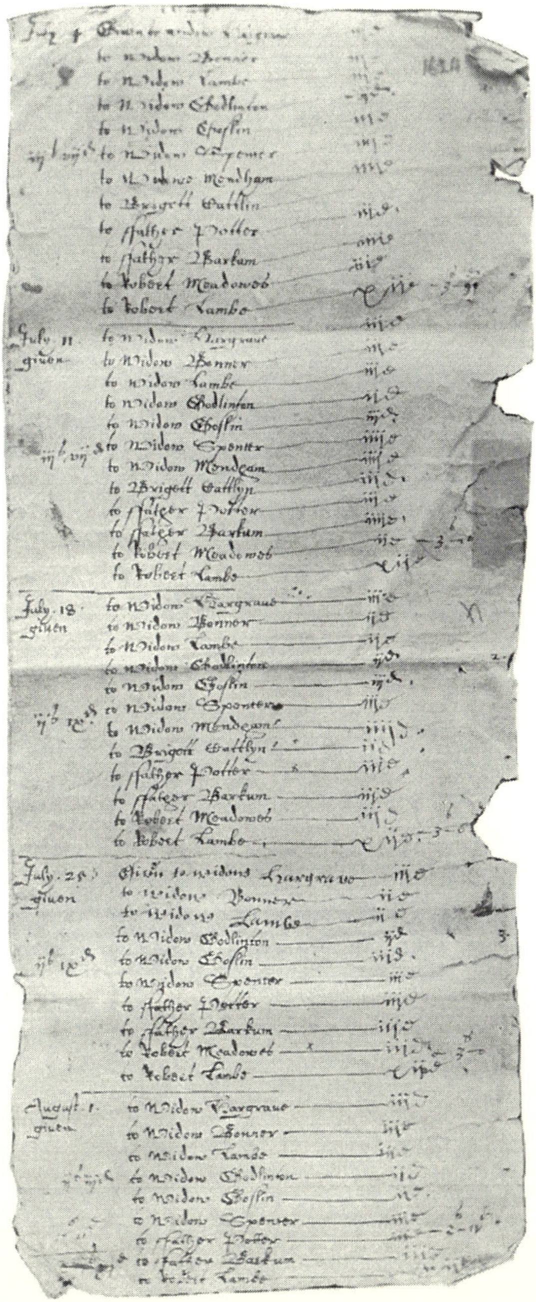

PLATE V

OVERSEER'S ACCOUNTS, LITTLEPORT, 1624

Chapter V

WAGE PROBLEMS. THE PROFITABLE EMPLOYMENT OF THE POOR. FIRST PHASE OF THE MOVEMENT

A. THE DOCTRINE OF PROFITABLE EMPLOYMENT

The social and economic dislocation ensuing upon the war naturally manifested itself in certain areas in the form of unemployment. Legislative steps were presently taken to facilitate the reabsorption into industry of men whose war service had interrupted their term of apprenticeship, but the old industrial system was itself breaking down in face of the demands made by rapidly expanding trade: the beginnings of a *laissez faire* attitude were already evident both in the newer doctrines of certain contemporary pamphleteers[1] and in the practical breaches of restrictive commercial and industrial regulations, everywhere apparent notwithstanding the attempts of municipalities, gilds and companies to reassert control. The fear of Dutch rivalry, moreover, pervaded economic life no less than political, and the resulting demand for cheap home production favoured low wages and stimulated the desire to employ pauper labour profitably to the nation.[2] "The general leprosie of our piping, potting, feasting fashions, and mis-spending of our time in idleness and pleasure", had been deplored by such writers as Thomas Mun in the 'thirties of the century. "The poverty and misery of this Kingdome" were due, in the opinion of a converted highwayman[3] of the 'forties, to "Sodom's sin of Idleness", for which the creation of workhouses "in all cities, market-towns

[1] T. E. Gregory, "Economics of Unemployment, 1660–1713" (*Economica*, 1921).

[2] Some argued that the Poor Law should be abolished in order to force the poor to work sufficiently hard to provide for their own old age.

[3] *Stanley's Remedy* (1646), title-page.

and able parishes" was the prescribed remedy. By the time Mun's words appeared in print, in 1664, a Restoration public applied them to the labouring classes only.

Even in the most active years of the Privy Council régime difficulty had been experienced in enforcing that part of the Elizabethan Poor Law which concerned the unemployed: upon the cessation of warfare unemployment faced a Government bereft of its most effective machinery for the control of local administration. It was the "want of a due provision of the regulations of relief and employment" in many areas which, according to the legislators of 1662,[1] led folk to leave their own parishes in search of work under more enterprising authorities.

B. THE ECONOMIC POSITION OF THE RURAL LABOURER IN CAMBRIDGESHIRE

Whilst the transitional stage through which the country was passing inevitably involved social strain in commercial and industrial districts, in purely agricultural areas, not affected by enclosure movements, the position of the labourer was on the whole peculiarly strong. There was here an actual scarcity of hands, whilst at the same time the marked rise in the price of manufactured goods, during the latter half of the seventeenth century, was not accompanied by a corresponding rise in the price of food products—a matter of prime significance in the rural labourer's cost of living.[2]

Unemployment arising from local circumstances did of course occur in rural parishes, and overseers were as frequently neglectful of their duties, as well as flatly dishonest, here as in the towns. An overseer of Coton was sued before the Bench, in 1664, for retaining in his own hands the money (£3. 10s.) put aside "for setting the poore on worke". At the same sessions the overseers of Cottenham were fined 33s. 4d. each for failing to make provision for the poor: the brazen officials responded

[1] Preamble to Settlement Law of 13 and 14 Chas. II.
[2] Cf. J. E. Thorold Rogers, *Hist. of Agric. and Prices* (1866), v, pp. 672 *et seq.*

by calmly paying the fine out of the poor-rate! In 1670 the overseer of Stetchworth was fined 40s. for negligence.

The Poor Law was but one aspect of the comprehensive social legislation promulgated by Tudor statesmen: the prevention of poverty was to them even more significant than its cure. The famous Statute of Artificers was framed largely from this point of view. The breakdown of State regulation on the industrial side, after the Privy Council ceased to intervene, is of less moment in agricultural Cambridgeshire than the effort to enforce certain clauses of the statute[1] in the teeth of opposing forces.

By the terms of the Act magistrates were empowered to compel—subject to a minimum property qualification—males between twelve and sixty years of age and unmarried females between twelve and forty, not being otherwise legally retained, to enter regular service in husbandry, or to assist with the "inning of the crops" during harvest. In order, moreover, to discourage unsettled modes of life, as well as to minimise fluctuations in the supply of labour, with their inevitable tendency to undermine the stabilisation of wages, the statute sought to restrict mobility by requiring "testimonials" to be obtained by folk desirous of removing themselves from the town or parish in which they were last employed. Perhaps, however, the most significant clause of the statute was that which required the justices, yearly at their Easter Sessions, "calling unto them such discreet and grave persons...as they shall think meet", to "rate and appoint the wages" of labourers, servants and artificers, taking into consideration "the plenty and scarcity of the time", to circulate throughout the county the assessments so drawn up, and to penalise by fine and imprisonment any breach of the law.

The statute itself cannot fairly be regarded as a piece of deliberate class legislation, but from the very outset—except as regards the textile industries—according to traditional policy the fixing of wages was interpreted by the justices as the regulation of maximum and not of minimum rates. This was a duty which rural magistrates, as landed gentry, were unlikely to evade

[1] 5 Eliz., c. 4.

even when Privy Council supervision was a thing of the past.[1]

The severe scarcity of agricultural labour in various parts of Cambridgeshire is evinced in the activity of the County Bench during the Restoration period.[2] The subject of rating[3] still came up at this time for annual discussion. At the Easter Sessions of 1661 the "rates and proporcōns for wages" were "sett forth and appointed" by the County Bench—in a schedule which, unhappily, was not copied into the Order Book. Whether the old scale was revised, after due consideration of prevailing prices, or merely re-issued is not clear. The approved assessment was, however, circulated to the Chief Constables of each hundred, who were required to seé that it was "openly published and proclaymed" in every parish. It was particularly enjoined that no person "for the year ensuinge presume to give, take, or directlie or indirectlie, agree or contract for any greater wages then in the said Rates are expressed and sett downe, upon payne of sufferinge and undergoinge the penaltyes of the Statute". The wording of the order is most suggestive: clearly the whole motive force was directed to keeping wages down. It is, moreover, evident that Cambridgeshire farmers were prepared to attract the all-important supply of labour by circumvention of the statute even when not by direct disregard.[4] The Law of Supply and Demand eventually proved irresistible, but the County

[1] The fact that the number of small landowners in seventeenth-century Cambs. was large also worked in favour of the enforcement of agricultural regulations of this type.

[2] The MS. Quarter Sessions Records extant for the county begin in the year 1660. (Henceforward referred to as MS. Q.S.R.)

[3] The search for examples of wages assessments has been a favourite sport of economic historians: a hunt through the Cambs. records comes excitingly near running the quarry to earth, but actual copies of assessments seem, most unfortunately, to have perished.

[4] The higher courts had indeed decided before 1635 that "masters may reward a well-deserving servant, over and above his wages...so it be not by way of promise or agreement upon his retainer". (Cf. Brown, Bland and Tawney, *Select Documents*, pp. 315 *et seq.*)

Bench did not give in without a prolonged struggle. In October 1661 divers single persons, able of body, belonging to the parishes of Chesterton and Horningsea, presumed to refuse full-time work under the conditions laid down: they were peremptorily bidden to "place themselves in service" within a week. The orders of the Bench were no mere formality; the House of Correction was more fully utilised for the reformation of the idle at this period than at any other till the nineteenth century.[1] Nicholas Blunt, for example, was dispatched there by the Court, in 1662, for "living out of service". Nevertheless the plaint of non-observance continued to be "great and generall", and the Court proceeded to commit a whole batch of offenders to the bridewell. Five young women of Soham, for instance, were ordered, in 1667, to choose between going to service or to prison —possibly a "great ryott" at Soham the same year, necessitating assistance from the Sheriff, was connected with the attempt to enforce economic regulations.

A sessions' entry of 1670 makes it clear that even the prescribed rates had been subject to revision—concessions to the demands of the labour market had proved inevitable. Elizabeth Gooch of Caxton, openly engaged at the Hiring Sessions in 1670, contracted to work for 50s. a year—an advance of no less than 25 per cent. upon the recognised rate of only three years before, and prices had not risen to anything like the same extent. The woman had, nevertheless, broken her agreement in favour of more advantageous service elsewhere. Failing satisfactory explanation, she was ordered to be committed to the House of Correction.[2] At the same sessions the Bench made a further determined effort to enforce the statutory wages. Many persons, it was averred, did give greater wages than appointed by the magistrates, and naturally frequently failed to "regyster" such contracts at the High Constables' Sessions, held in the respective hundreds. As a result, it was stated, "many servants depart from

[1] MS. Q.S.R. Cambs.
[2] Notwithstanding the wording both of the statute and of the justices' orders not a single entry records the penalising of a master.

their services before their times [are] expired, and are retained into other services without sheweing any testimoniall, as by the statute made 5 Eliz. they are required to doe". For the effective working of the law much depended upon the publicity of contracts made between masters and employees. Agreements were therefore ordered to be made in the presence of the Chief Constable at the Statute Sessions or Hiring Fairs. As a means of remedying the laxity so much deplored, all Chief Constables were directed to enforce the regular holding of annual Statute Sessions and to present before the next assembly of the Bench the names of masters who had, after a certain date, failed to record their contracts.[1] The form of testimonial prescribed by the 5 Eliz., together with the schedule of current official wages, was circulated round the county, in order that no excuse should exist for the prevalent negligence in the use of licences.[2]

Quarter Sessions Records for the county are missing for the years between 1672 and 1689; by the end of the seventeenth century the formal entry of the payment of £5 to the Clerk of the Peace, "for his trouble and pains in procuring the printing the Rates for Servants Wages, and prices for the Carriage of Goods, and for distributing them in every town in the said county of Cambridge", is the only reference made to a wages assessment. The colourless entry continues at regular intervals till the middle of the eighteenth century. The tempting conclusion that the payment had become by that date a mere perquisite of the Clerk must be modified by the fact that parish account books—for example at Meldreth and Histon—do occasionally bear witness to the receipt of the circular schedule, as late as 1740, though no actual table of rates seems to have survived.

In the course of the eighteenth century disputes between master and servant now and again occasioned the subject of wages to appear in the pages of Sessions' minutes, and in several

[1] The records of Constables' Sessions would prove a mine of wealth to the economic historian: a careful search for any trace of them in Cambs., among the documents preserved in the chief parishes of each hundred, as well as among Q.S. papers, has thus far, however, yielded no treasure.

[2] *Vide* Appendix I.

instances it is noteworthy that, although prices had fallen somewhat in the early years of the eighteenth century, wages had
fallen still more heavily in Cambridgeshire—in contradistinc-
tion, for example, to conditions in Warwickshire.[1] Women
servants who could obtain 50s. a year in 1670 could get but 30s.
in the earlier part of the next century, at any rate in some areas
of Cambridgeshire, for what appears to be the same grade of
employment. There were only two commitments to the county
bridewell between 1714 and 1740 for "refusing to work for the
customary wage". Probably by this date a *laissez faire* attitude
towards wages had triumphed. It is not till the troublous close
of the eighteenth century that the problem of agricultural wages
looms once again into prominence in this county.

So much for the general position of the rural labourer.[2]

C. THE TOWNS

(1) *The Charity School Movement*

In the towns unemployment was a more serious problem, and
the later years of the seventeenth century witnessed a variety of
efforts, in different parts of England, to set the poor to work in
profitable undertakings—some were the result of individual
enterprise, some of municipal action and some of private bill
legislation. Jealousy of Dutch competition played a large part
initially in fostering the conviction that pauper labour could
be made a financial asset to the nation, but other causes revived
the belief many times in the course of the eighteenth century.
Before 1700, however, there were those among the more
enlightened who had realised some of the difficulties but yet supported manufacturing projects on disciplinary grounds—"we
had better lose something by the labour of the poor, than lose
all by letting them live in sloth and idleness", argued Thomas
Firmin.

[1] Warwickshire Q.S.R. Cf. also A. W. Ashby, *One Hundred Years of
Poor Law Administration in a Warwickshire Village* (Vinogradoff, *Oxford
Studies*, vol. III, 1912), pp. 170–5.

[2] Cf. E. M. Hampson, *Cambridge County Records. Camb. Antiq. Soc.,
Communications* (1931), XXXI, pp. 134 *et seq.*

The disastrous effect on the independent labourer entailed by many of the schemes for public employment was rarely grasped by seventeenth-century advocates. Disappointing results did, however, tend to concentrate attention upon the employment of children—both on disciplinary and on financial grounds. Practical experience in the latter part of the seventeenth century was proving that in certain transitional stages of industry the labour of quite young children could be utilised. The frequent failure of apprenticeship to provide, in the changed conditions of the time, an adequate training either morally or industrially was, moreover, widely admitted. Reaction, too, against the laxity of Restoration life led religious reformers to turn an anxious eye upon the upbringing of youth. The sooner a child became an actual wage-earner, the sooner would he become "settled into good habits and the principles of virtue and wisdom".[1] "Men who are to remain and end their days in a laborious, tiresome and painful station of life, the sooner they are put upon it at first, the more patiently will they submit to it for ever after", argued Mandeville.[2]

This interest in the child resulted in two streams of activity—the Industrial School movement on the one hand, the Charity School on the other. Even the advocates of Industrial Schools would have the children taught to read and to learn their catechism, but beyond this essentially religious instruction book learning, it was contended, merely engendered a spirit of idleness and reluctance to take later to manual labour. To the supporters of the Charity Schools the practical advantage of ability to read, and even to write and figure, in a developing commercial world seemed obvious. The main aim of the Charity Schools was a religious one, but the utilitarian purpose was not entirely overlooked and the addition of manual labour to the curriculum was very generally advocated—largely as a result of Mandeville's caustic criticism—in the third decade of the eighteenth century.

[1] J. Locke, *Some Thoughts concerning Education* (1693), ed. Quick, p. 75.
[2] B. Mandeville, *Essay on Charity and Charity Schools* (1723), p. 329.

PLATE VI

I. EFFIGIES OF CHARITY CHILDREN, BOROUGH GREEN SCHOOL, CAMBRIDGESHIRE, c. 1714

II. CHARITY SCHOOL, BOTTISHAM, CAMBRIDGESHIRE, c. 1729

In Cambridgeshire signs of interest in the elementary education of the poor had begun to manifest themselves even before the birth of the Charity Schools[1]—some twenty elementary schools founded in the latter half of the seventeenth century are traceable in various records.

Industrial Schools, however, evoked little support either in the town of Cambridge or in the rural areas of a county so essentially agricultural. The real enthusiasm of the time flowed into the Charity Schools, which were established for both boys and girls of the town of Cambridge in 1704, and spread during the next two decades to some twenty or thirty of the villages. The first Charity Schools were opened at Wisbech in 1707 for boys, and in 1711 for girls. The industrial character of Wisbech rendered authorities there more alive to the possibilities of child labour and more ready to pay heed to the critics of the Charity Schools.[2] From the outset spinning and other manual work formed part of the curriculum at Wisbech.

There was behind the Charity School movement, however, no thought of increasing directly the nation's financial balance: it is in other spheres that the influence of the doctrine of profitable pauper employment, whether of adult or of child, must be traced.

(2) *Administrative Reforms and Employment Proposals*

(*a*) CAMBRIDGE

The enterprising attempt of John Cary, in 1696, to establish—by virtue of a Local Act—a common workhouse for the whole city of Bristol is a well-known story. Paupers of all ages and conditions were to be housed there, and such as were able employed in remunerative occupations. The supersession of the parochial organisation by the new "Corporation of the Poor"

[1] The S.P.C.K. was founded in 1698. An earlier educational movement in some parts of the country was in part due to efforts to circumvent the law which forbade Dissenters to teach in Grammar Schools.

[2] The schools were criticised mainly on the ground that a literary education encouraged labouring children to aspire to ranks higher than that to which Providence had assigned them.

—popularly elected, well organised, working through a permanent executive with salaried officials—and the equalisation of the poor-rates throughout the nineteen parishes of the city, were practical acknowledgments of the unsuitability of the parish as a unit and of overseers as administrative officers. The initial success of the Bristol experiment was widely advertised, and within the next fifteen years thirteen other towns had obtained Local Acts enabling them to appoint "Guardians of the Poor", working through organisations similar to that of Bristol.[1]

Caustic altercations on the subject of unequal rating had many times agitated the fourteen little parishes of Cambridge, but the opposition to municipal action evident in 1652 was still too strong to allow of the town following the example of Bristol.

The difficulties experienced elsewhere in maintaining the old economic system were nevertheless manifesting themselves in the university town—the right to exact rigid observance of the ancient terms of apprenticeship was insisted upon in 1664, when the charter was renewed.

The great violence with which the Plague raged in 1665–6 reduced the town to the straits of 1630, and in fact necessitated the levying, by order of Quarter Sessions, of a rate-in-aid upon the whole county. Unemployment added to the general distress, but no expansion of activity is noticeable in connection with Hobson's Workhouse—the "Spinning-House" as it was then called.[2]

---

[1] Cf. S. and B. Webb, *English Local Government. English Poor Law History*, Pt. I (1926), p. 120.

[2] A new Governor, John Tomasin, a worsted-weaver, was appointed in 1675, but the terms of agreement seem to be those of the original foundation. He was still, nominally at least, to provide work for five combers, and spinning and weaving for all townsfolk who should desire employment, "at the usuall rates and prices paid by others". His salary was £30. (Cooper, *op. cit.* III, p. 570.)

George Griffiths (Master of the Perse School) left £100 to Hobson's Workhouse in 1686; Dr James, President of Queens', left £50 in the early eighteenth century, and John Bowtell £500 to the Trustees, for the apprenticing of poor boys, in 1813. (*Ibid.* IV, p. 506; J. M. Gray, *History of the Perse School*, p. 69.)

(*b*)   WISBECH

King's Lynn, in 1700, and Norwich twelve years later, adopted the Bristol plan and replaced parochial administration by specially elected guardians. Wisbech did not follow these neighbouring examples so far as to obtain a Local Act. The Ten Men of the town had at no period perturbed themselves on the subject of their exact legal relation to the parochial officers. So large a share of the administration of relief already devolved in practice upon the corporate body directly that the question of obtaining legislative sanction was never mooted.

The notion that pauper labour might be made to yield an income over and above the maintenance of the worker himself did not present itself as a novelty to Wisbech authorities: as has been seen, there had been undertakings based on this assumption at the beginning of the seventeenth century. Nearly seventy years, moreover, before the Legislature sanctioned the practice of contracting-out the poor, the Ten Men, in 1657, had put up to auction the employment of the able-bodied and had paid over the lump sum agreed upon to the highest bidder, on the condition that he should take all poor folk sent to him, making his own terms with the workers and deriving what advantage he could. The undefined and fluctuating number of employees, their frequent lack of training and initiative, and the complaints that they were sweated, proved the scheme unsatisfactory, and might well have made the Ten Men chary of lending support to the prevailing doctrines of the late seventeenth century.

In 1674, however, a bid was again made to secure a three-year contract with some private dealer. Tenders were submitted by two wool manufacturers of Norfolk—Thomas Grout of "Nordrepp"[1] and John Pinchins of Cley. The Town Bailiff and one of the Ten were deputed to interview the applicants, to draw up a tentative agreement and to report to the next meeting of the Capital Burgesses. In due course the Bailiff reported that Grout had been selected "to sett the poore on workes" upon the

[1] Northrepps.

following terms: £30 was to be allowed to Grout "for the wast of wooll for the first thre yeers"; £2 was to be granted for the removal to Wisbech of his belongings; £50 was to be lent him for three years free of interest and a further £50 at the current rate; an allowance of £6 per annum towards a suitable "dweling house" was also promised, Grout finding the remainder of the rent.

In connection with the scheme it was arranged that an Industrial School should be opened, in which the children should receive a month's instruction in the art of spinning—apparently in expectation that they would then begin to earn. Four months later the Bailiff was directed to "reimburse the Overseers of the Poore such moneys as they have disbursed in providing spindles, reeles, and other materialls for the Manufacture, and in paying yᵉ women yᵗ teach"; hence it seems to have been recognised that more or less continuous instruction was called for to meet the needs of younger children gradually passing into the school as soon as they were old enough.

Certain adult weavers appear to have been employed on the contractor's premises, but there were, as in earlier days, many domestic spinners who were supplied with work by Grout. Spinning-wheels and reels were frequently distributed by the overseers during the next few years, the expense being refunded by the town.[1]

With respect to the able-bodied the overseers functioned merely as executive officers and were not required ultimately to finance any part of the undertaking. For the first few years all applicants in distress through lack of work were given assistance only through the medium of Grout.

The weekly distribution to the regular pensioners was, it is true, financed to a considerable extent by the overseers, but large supplementary sums were still derived from the Town Chest, and the levying of the poor-rate was only undertaken by the parish officers upon detailed instruction from the Ten. In 1674, for example, it was "desired that the churchwardens gather onely the single rate, and that the Towne Bayliffe pay and make up the

[1] In 1678 spinning-wheels to the value of £3. 10s. were so distributed.

rest to them soe that itt exceed not half a rate ". In the year following the establishment of Grout's "manufactory", the Ten Men ordered a reassessment of the whole town to be made. A permanent assistant overseer was appointed at the same time at an annual salary of £5. So ineffective were the parish officers that even the discretionary power which they had enjoyed with respect to the weekly doles was withdrawn in 1677, upon complaint that the townsfolk found "the charges like to bee swelling upon them" and conceived that "through care the same might in some measure be pvented and yᵉ Towne kept from some abuse". Two of the Ten Men, by rote, were in consequence required to attend regularly—under pain of fine—"to assist yᵉ Collecters and Overseers in theire weekly distribucōns".

For the first three years Grout held his own and at the end of that time consented to continue the work for only £20 per annum. The town was in the fortunate possession of valuable bequests for clothing the poor,[1] and was therefore able to expend £40 or £50 yearly in buying and making up the cloth. It was agreed, in 1677, that Grout should be allowed 2s. 4d. per yard for cloth used for this purpose. Somewhat lavish clothing of the poor followed. In January 1678 it was necessary to limit expenditure under this head to £50, but an additional sum of £10 was conceded now and again, under pressure perhaps from Grout. In 1681 the limit was fixed at £60, but in 1682 a further sum of £15 was again rather easily granted. The town rulers certainly stretched their patronage of the manufacturer to the utmost—Jas. Peddar, the Sexton, was given an extra "morneing coate of Grouts cloath", in 1682, and apprentices were rigged out more liberally than heretofore. Nevertheless, it became obvious that Grout was driving down wages in order to maintain his profit. In 1683 the Ten Men remonstrated and only guaranteed to continue purchasing cloth at the raised price of 2s. 6d. per yard if the poor were employed "at reasonable rates". Conditions did not prove satisfactory and, in 1684,

---

[1] *E.g.* Crane's charity. Coals and "meslin" were also stored by aid of this and other bequests and were sold at reduced prices—or given freely—to the poor during the winter.

the town refused to spend more than £40 on clothing, reducing the amount to £35 in the following year.

"If a right course be taken", said Sir Josiah Child in 1669, authorities need "invent no stratagems" to keep folk out of the parish, but rather will seek to bring them in. "The subtle Dutch receive and relieve, or employ, all that come to them, not inquiring what nation, much less what parish they are of."[1] Wisbech rulers did not find themselves able to dispense with such "stratagems": the most strenuous efforts were made to keep out poor immigrants at this period, but it was still necessary to grant sums of money to an ever larger number of individuals to enable them to purchase wool on their own account—"Widow Russell to be given 10s. to buy wool to employ herself about"; "a stone of wool to be given to Widow Elmar"; "lent to Samuel Secker to buy hoopes to keepe himself in worke", are typical entries. Grout's undertaking had collapsed before 1691.

With the poor who were unemployable Grout had no concern. The Ten Men themselves continued, as of yore, to administer relief directly from corporate funds in case of sickness or special emergency:

Agreed that Mr William Clarke shall have £3 for the cuting of yᵉ Legg of old Bennitt, and in Case hee make a pfict Cure of it then to have it made up Five Pounds.[2]

Thomas Freeman to have £10 towards his Charges to Bath and Wells.[3]

Dr Daves to have three pounds for cureing Winterton of his ffits, out of wᶜʰ yᵉ said Mʳ Daves is to pay for all Medicines. Mr Daves to be paid 3 months after yᵉ Cure be pfected; if he make no Cure to have nothing either for judgment or Medicines.[4]

Ordered that the present towne balife by a viallend[5] for the blynd boy.

[1] Sir Josiah Child, *New Discourse of Trade* (circa 1669), quoted by F. M. Eden, *State of the Poor* (ed. Rogers, 1928), p. 31.
[2] In 1678.
[3] In 1686.
[4] In 1697.
[5] In 1675 (a violin).

In 1691 it was decided to set up an establishment for children only: should the enterprise prove financially unremunerative, it was not to be continued merely on educational grounds. A certain Mr Henry Place was offered a salary of £20 and given £5 towards "a room for yᵉ children to work in". The arrangement was only made for one year and it was evidently doubted whether it would survive even for that period—"If yᵉ Spinning work continue not for one year, yᵉ said Mr Place is to deliver yᵉ sd Chamber up for yᵉ use of yᵉ town". The plan did not succeed and some years later the burgesses gave their support to the alternative scheme of a Charity School, "for teaching Poor Children to Spin, Read and Write"—curiously enough it was to be financed mainly out of the overseers' rate.[1]

Repeated failure did not finally destroy the belief in the profitable employment of pauper labour, but the next phase of experiment belongs to the era of workhouse propaganda and development associated with the Statute of 1723.

[1] The schools persisted through various vicissitudes for a century, when they were absorbed by the National Schools, after a period of dalliance with the rival Lancasterian Society.

Chapter VI

HOUSING PROBLEMS AND PAUPER LABOUR IN CAMBRIDGESHIRE IN THE EARLY EIGHTEENTH CENTURY. THE ISLE OF ELY AND THE STATUTE OF 1723

A. THE ORIGIN OF THE WORKHOUSE

"The parish poorhouse and the Union House of Industry[1]...were distinct in origin and purpose, but it is from the pair of them that has sprung the ubiquitous modern workhouse", says an eminent authority. "The parish poorhouse, as it existed from the sixteenth to the nineteenth century, was at the outset nothing that could be termed an institution. It consisted usually of a cottage, or several cottages, used indiscriminately as free lodgings for some of the parish pensioners, as an occasional receptacle for the disabled and sick, and as a temporary shelter for tramps and for paupers awaiting removal to other parishes. We are told that 'no regular provision for the diet is made, and little order or discipline is maintained in them. Some of the paupers who are placed there work for private employers and maintain themselves; others receive pay from the parish and also provide their own food'."[2]

The poorhouse, thus differentiated from the workhouse, was the type of building most commonly to be found in the parishes of Cambridgeshire before 1723, and in the parishes outside the franchise of Ely for more than a century after that date. There were, however, institutions intermediate in character. The old gildhall at Whittlesford, under the direction of a resident master, served both as workhouse and poorhouse during the early seventeenth century. Similar institutions existed about the same time at Dullingham and Swavesey, in the Isle of Ely, as they

[1] The House of Industry established at Bristol, in 1696, was the forerunner of similar institutions elsewhere. Cf. *supra*, p. 59.
[2] Webb, *op. cit.* (quoting Poor Law Comm. Report of 1834), p. 212.

probably did in other of the larger villages. It seems to be true that in most cases the provision of work on the premises had ceased before the Restoration era, but the "ubiquitous modern workhouse" has not always the two quite distinct sources which the above quotation assumes: the parish poorhouse was, in some instances, partly an institutional workhouse even in the sixteenth century.[1]

B. LEGISLATION AND HOUSING

The mere problem of housing the poor was always a serious one financially, apart from the provision of work. The relevant legislation may be recalled. The Act of 1601 directed that the parish rates should be drawn upon for setting the poor to work, but did not stipulate where the work should be carried on. Under this Act the overseers were further responsible for the provision of "convenient houses of dwelling for the impotent". The public support of "such hospitals and almshouses as shall be in the said county", by means of a county rate, was also authorised by the same statute.[2] An enactment of 1597[3] facilitated the building of "hospitals or abiding and working houses" by private endowment, whilst under the Vagrancy Act of the same year[4] Houses of Correction were to be established at the expense of the county.

With respect to the housing of the impotent the duty of the overseers was therefore clear, but in such parishes as were inadequately aided by bequests for this purpose the pressure of Quarter Sessions was often required before officers would apply the rates to this perfectly legal end. The Cambridgeshire justices clearly considered the overseers responsible even for the lodging of homeless poor who were not actually impotent.[5] In 1664, for

---

[1] The late sixteenth-century municipal workhouses of Cambridge, as well as Hobson's Workhouse, erected in 1630, were of a composite character.　　　　　　　　　　　　[2] Repeating 39 Eliz., c. 3, s. 13.

[3] 39 Eliz., c. 5. Made perpetual by 21 Jas. I, c. 1.

[4] 39 Eliz., c. 4.

[5] Dalton, quoting the resolution of the justices, appears to consider that the duty of providing shelter related to all poor "lawfully setled" in the parish. (Dalton, *op. cit.* ed. 1630, p. 104.)

example, John Browne, "for divers yeares last past an inhabitant of Woodditton", complained that his landlord had "put him out of his house" and that he was now "destitute of an habitation". The Court ordered the overseers of Woodditton to "finde and provide a house" for the man. In 1672 the parish officers of Hinxton were directed by the Court to levy a rate for the repair of the "Towne House". John Day, "a lame and very aged man, having but one hand", was refused relief by the overseers of Caldecot in 1700. Upon complaint being made to Sir Henry Pickering, a local magistrate, the overseers were ordered to allow him 2*s*. a week, and to provide him with a house, but the concerted action of the Bench was required before the overseers could be induced to obey the order.

After 1662 the Settlement Law was beginning to have effect in stimulating parish officers to curtail still more strictly the erection of houses of the poorer sort. By an Act of 1589[1] the building of rural cottages, not having four acres of land attached, was forbidden, but exception was deliberately made in favour of houses erected at the public expense on behalf of the poor. The Court, in 1666, nevertheless upheld the desire of the parishioners of Landbeach to demolish a cottage recently built for the benefit of "W͟ᵐ Smith, a poore, lame, aged and impotent pson", on condition that it was allowed to stand during the old man's lifetime. A similar line was taken about the same time with respect to seven other cottages. This attitude of the Bench had become more marked in Cambridgeshire by the early eighteenth century.

The most common method of providing shelter, where individuals rather than families were concerned, was naturally to place them in lodgings with humble parishioners at the expense of the rates.

---

[1] 31 Eliz., c. 7.

C. PARISH WORKHOUSES AND POORHOUSES OF THE SEVENTEENTH CENTURY

In very many Cambridgeshire parishes, urban as well as rural, almshouses and gildhouses, or cottages given by bequest, were used by the parish as poorhouses of the type described by the Royal Commissioners of 1834. The emphasis laid upon employment of the poor at the close of the seventeenth century led to attempts here and there to introduce work into these humble establishments. Doubt was raised by some as to the statutory power of the parish to erect workhouses out of the rates. Where communal poorhouses already existed, it was certainly legal to aid the impotent inmates by parish doles and the able-bodied by work, and the step from these activities to the erection of workhouses as such was a very easy one. The difficulty really lay in the heavy expenditure entailed in building or transforming houses and in employing regular supervisors, if work were to be a business enterprise: to meet such charges no statutory power to raise loans had been granted to the overseers.

It has already been seen that the town rulers of both Cambridge and Wisbech fought shy of drawing upon the poor-rate for the financing of municipal schemes on behalf of the able-bodied, and fortunately other funds were available.[1] So far as the provision of buildings was concerned, rural parish authorities also depended in the main upon endowments, but in various instances the cost of supplying the raw material—wool, hemp, iron, etc.—with which the village "task-house" should be stocked, was met by the poor-rate.

The successive failures in which the municipal projects ended have already been discussed. Attempts to reap a profit from the employment of pauper labour were doomed to even more certain disaster in the case of small country parishes. Repeatedly one finds the able-bodied drifting out of the houses, which soon

[1] The Children's Industrial School, founded at Wisbech in 1691, was financed by the overseers, and it is possible that the "subscription", in 1630, in aid of Hobson's Workhouse at Cambridge may have been compulsory.

become the residences only of orphan children, widows or impotent derelicts—a phenomenon observable at later periods also. The "Towne House" at Cottenham was an abode only of the aged and impotent in 1667. Susan Sunbury, "a young person able to maintain herself by labour", was ejected from the house in 1667 by order of the Court and her place taken by Richard Bell and his wife, "being poore, aged and impotent".

There was little in the nature of an organised workhouse at Meldreth in 1707, but wheels, reels and cards were supplied by the overseer to certain of the occupants lodged in the Town House. Other inmates found employment for themselves, and still others subsisted on doles from the parish. The house played a very minor rôle in the life of the village poor. In 1717 a new building was opened at Meldreth but it differed little in character from the earlier one.

At Linton the "Towne House" had fallen into private hands in 1646 and had so remained till 1662, when the inhabitants, intending to adopt some workhouse scheme, sought the aid of the Court in dispossessing the tenant. The revived workhouse, however, soon lapsed into the condition of a mere poorhouse. Certain of the rooms were let out at low rentals—Robert Hockley was paying 12s. yearly "for his part in the Almshouse" in 1697. The housing problem was pressing and in December 1697 an extension of the buildings was contemplated. Five months later all charity money out on loan was recalled and "a house in Symonds Lane" purchased "for the benefitt of the poor".

D. HOUSES OF CORRECTION AND THE DETERRENT POLICY

In certain counties the number of bridewells founded was considerable—in Essex, for example, there were twenty-two.[1] In such cases the distinction between workhouse and House of

[1] Justices' Orders for Relief of Poor in Essex, 1598, Harleian MSS. 7020, art. 33, p. 267. R. H. Tawney and E. Power, *Tudor Econ. Docums.* (1924), II, pp. 263–364.

Correction was fine, and the county institutions really did offer an alternative to parochial provision of organised labour. For the rural areas of Cambridgeshire proper, however, there was but the one House of Correction adjoining the Castle Gaol at Cambridge, and this, it has been pointed out, never developed as a mere workhouse for non-criminal paupers.[1]

Linton had long toyed with the pleasing notion of constituting itself the centre of a larger unit. The market town was the seat of magisterial activity in the area: monthly divisional meetings were held here and parish officers were frequently faced with the necessity of conveying convicted misdemeanants as far as Cambridge. "It is a regulation of the poor that is wanted in England, not a setting them to work", said Defoe in 1704, in the famous pamphlet[2] which opened devastating fire upon the numerous enthusiastic projects for erecting pauper manufactories. The doctrine of profitable employment of the poor had already proved delusive at Linton; in 1700 the overseers sought, and obtained, the permission of Quarter Sessions to erect a House of Correction "to employ the poor of that parish and of neighbouring parishes there to worke, and in such manner to deal with all offenders thereto committed as any other House or Houses of Correction in the same county do"—Linton was in favour of trying a stricter "regulation". Probably it was thought desirable to obtain the sanction of the Court both because the interests of neighbouring parishes were involved and because it was hoped that county funds might be available, or at least that a rate-in-aid might be levied upon the hundred. The Bench, however, gave permission only on condition that Linton bore the whole expense—the difficulty experienced but fourteen years earlier in collecting the county-rate on behalf of plague-ridden Cambridge was still fresh in memory.

Probably the scheme was somewhat modified, but in April 1700, at a well-attended vestry, it was decided to collect the "overplus" of Thorogood's charity and with the balance from

[1] *Supra*, chap. iii.
[2] D. Defoe, *Giving Alms no Charity* (1704), p. 9.

other endowments to make up a sum of £30, "for repairing the Almshouse towards makeing it a workhouse", under the direction of two of the local justices. Should £30 prove inadequate, the "Towne Stock"—which included the balance from the rates—was to be drawn upon. This institution was certainly intended to be disciplinary in character. Three years later it had become obvious that existing institutions did not meet the needs of homeless poor, for whom a strict regimen was clearly unwarrantable. The vestry therefore decided to erect, by the aid of "towne money", further "Dwelling Houses" within the "Almous grownds", for the "relefe of the Poor, in order to ease the Rents now burthinson".[1] In 1710 still further extensions of the same nature were carried out at a cost of about £36.

The note of deterrence evinced by the parish in 1700 is characteristic of the period which followed Defoe's outburst against such employment of paupers as involved taking "the bread out of the mouths of diligent and industrious families", to feed those "who ought much rather to be compelled, by legal methods, to seek that work which, it is plain, is to be had".[2] The bill which would have enabled every parish to set up a public workhouse was defeated in 1705.

E. THE STATUTE OF 1723. WISBECH AND THE ISLE OF ELY

Notwithstanding preliminary discouragement by the State, in the years which followed Matthew Marryott's experiment[3] in workhouse organisation, in 1714, amid much contention, and with variety of aims, one vestry after another began to take up Marryott's plan. It was apparently the initial success of these undertakings which led to the passing of the General Workhouse Act of 1723,[4] whereby parish officers, with the approval of a majority of the parishioners, were empowered

---

[1] Burdensome.   [2] Defoe, *op. cit.* p. 12.
[3] At Olney, Bucks.   [4] 9 G. I, c. 7.

"to purchase or hire any house or houses in the same parish", and to "contract with any person or persons for the lodging, keeping, maintaining and employing" any or all such parish poor as sought relief. Any person refusing relief in the workhouse, where such house had been established, was to be "put out of the book"—to forfeit all claim to assistance.[1] Should any parish find itself "too small to purchase or hire" a workhouse, two or more parishes, with the consent of a majority of the inhabitants, and with the approval of a local justice, were authorised to unite for the purpose of erecting a common workhouse and to come to some agreement concerning the terms on which paupers should be admitted.[2] There is here a definite acknowledgment that the parish was not always a large enough unit, but there is no suggestion of a common rating for the united area. It was partly this omission which kept alive discussion as to the possibility of adopting a larger unit for the whole administration of relief, and partly also the desire to supersede the control of petty parochial overseers.

Probably under the influence of Marryott, but before the passing of the above statute, Wisbech adopted the idea of a workhouse and in 1720 began the erection of a costly building, covering an area of 110 ft. square in the old Horse Fair. The following year the Town Bailiff was authorised to borrow

[1] Mr Fay has argued that this step was taken merely to ensure that the workhouse, if built, should be filled. It does seem, however, in view of the public attitude of the time, that the workhouse was intended to act as a "test" of destitution (Fay, *Life and Labour*, 1920, p. 89). It is, nevertheless, true that the Act in no way penalised officials for granting relief outside the house, and in actual practice certain types of applicants were from the outset frequently so relieved.

[2] Other clauses of the Act dealt with settlement questions. No settlement was to be acquired by reason of a person dwelling in the workhouse of another parish, as a result of union under the Act. By s. 4 it was required that a sum of £30 should be *bona fide* paid in order to gain a settlement by the purchase of an estate. During inhabitancy, however, no person was to be actually removable from his own estate, whatever the value. By the payment of the scavenger's rate or the highway rate settlement was not to be acquired.

£1000 under the Town Seal; a further loan of £1000 was raised, in 1722, towards the final completion of the building. A glowing account of the organisation of the workhouse appeared in 1725.[1] Up to this point it was regarded as a great success. "It is the pattern for all the rest of the Isle of Ely", wrote the eulogistic chronicler. "The method there used for maintaining the poor, is, as I take it, the best method that can be devised for that purpose; and what all their neighbours, as near as they can, endeavour to imitate."

The eighty inmates of this workhouse seem to have been chiefly, but not exclusively, elderly people and children; those incapable of work—the sick, the aged and the very young— were definitely excluded. Infants were admitted when "big enough to learn to read". At this age they were taught also to write and spin. "The children", it is explained, "spin all in one large room, under the inspection of a master; they make yarn for Norwich, as good as any is made. The whole number lie in the workhouse; the boys in a chamber by themselves, three in a bed; and the girls in another chamber, three in a bed. After the same manner likewise are the elderly people disposed of; of these only two in a bed."

The diet was remarkably varied for the time—"good beef, broth, dumplins, pease-porridge, milk-porridge, bread and cheese". The quantity was "according to every one's stomach at noon; at morning and night not so much—given out by the Mistress of the Kitchen".

The raw wool was bought directly from the "grazier", by two "managers", chosen by the town on account of their expert mercantile knowledge. This side of the undertaking seems to have been conducted most efficiently.

The women knitted the stockings and prepared the yarn for the making of all the clothing of the inmates. The baking and brewing, too, were done on the premises.

---

[1] The Wisbech experiment was described by Marryott in the *Account of Several Workhouses*, published by the S.P.C.K. in 1725 and republished in 1733.

The Master and Mistress were paid a fixed salary. The dangers inherent in the contract system on the one hand, and in the delegation of complete authority to the overseer on the other, were mitigated by the appointment of a board of managers—"four or more of the most prudent persons of the parish" being selected to direct the whole concern. The duties of the Master and Mistress were thus only supervisory: they were not dependent on the profits of the establishment; they were not allowed to draw up the diet sheet, nor to provide clothing at their own discretion. Negligence and extravagance were guarded against by detailed managerial inspection. The idle and disorderly were punishable only by order of a magistrate.

By the time the house was in full working order, the rates, it was stated, had been reduced from 3s. 6d. in the £ to 2s.; the poor were better fed and clothed than formerly; the profits of the business paid the interest on the initial debt of £2000 and left only about 1s. 6d. per head per week to be made up out of the rates.

The plan appears to have been less open to abuse than the organisation suggested by the Act of 1723. The "workhouse test" was certainly not applied to the impotent, and therefore one source of failure associated with the "general mixed workhouse" was avoided. The regulations even for the more or less able-bodied do not suggest an attitude particularly harsh, though of course the enthusiasm of the time concealed the effect of laborious hours and monotonous régime, and it is significant that within a few years the inmates tended to be limited to children or those much below par in the labour market—"what great gains could be hoped" from these? For the economical conduct of the house, moreover, much depended upon the continuous supervision of unpaid managers. Gradually the institution came to rely to an ever greater extent upon the rates.

It is to be noted that the town authorities did not hesitate to raise a loan without awaiting parliamentary approval, nor did they hesitate to continue their former custom of assuming complete control over Poor Law matters, treating the overseers as mere underlings.

For the first few years the new workhouse was regarded as the shining beacon of the Isle. Chatteris had built a workhouse modelled on that at Wisbech by 1725, and one at Ely was in course of construction.

Chapter VII

THE WORKHOUSE MOVEMENT IN THE TOWNS OF CAMBRIDGE AND ROYSTON, 1723–1785

A. CAMBRIDGE

(1) *Failure of the General Workhouse Scheme of* 1727

Matters were complicated at Cambridge by the existence of fourteen small parishes, with populations varying, in 1728, from 181 in Little St Andrew's to 720 in Great St Mary's.

In most of these parishes there were either almshouses or cottages serving much the same purpose as the poorhouses of the rural parishes. St Clement's, Great St Mary's, St Edward's, St Bene't's and Holy Trinity all had buildings of this type during the seventeenth and early eighteenth centuries.[1]

The harsher attitude adopted towards poverty, and the popular discussion of the subject of workhouses, gradually led to the practice of reserving almshouses for the shelter of those who had met with "unmerited" misfortune. It was clear, moreover, that these little buildings were unsuited to the conduct of any organised industry. The inequality of parochial rates within the town was still a bone of contention. The mere adoption of the Act of 1723 would not meet this situation, nor would it necessarily counteract the inefficient administration of certain overseers. Efforts were consequently directed to obtaining a special Local Act.

In November 1727 the Mayor and aldermen got so far as to arrange a series of meetings to consider "about obtaining an Act of Parliament for the Erecting and Establishing a publick Workhouse in this Town, and about the Corporacōn revenues to be

---

[1] The MS. Corp. Com. Day Book refers to leases of lands and houses for the purpose during this period.

collected in a better method".[1] The latter subject was too thorny ground to invite much raking over: the closeness of the connection between municipal reform and social progress was not yet fully appreciated, but the rate-payers of Cambridge had sound excuse for distrusting corporate enterprise. Moreover, the richer parishes were still undesirous of aiding the poorer, and the discussions came to nought.

(2) *Parochial Workhouse Developments*

During the next five or six years interest centred mainly in the parochial workhouses and the possibility of acquiring premises permitting of the introduction of some simple form of employment.

In 1733 St Edward's parish adopted the Act of 1723, so far as to come to an agreement with Little St Mary's to share a cottage workhouse, "for imploying their poor so as that their charge for the maintenance of the poor of each parish may in due time be lesned and made more easy to both parishes".[2]

It was found impossible to apply really deterrent principles even at the beginning of the workhouse movement in the town in the early 'thirties. Though out-relief to those able to work, and sometimes to others, was at first refused, the most numerous class of inmates soon came to consist of orphan children above the age of infancy.

In 1734 Great St Mary's appointed a committee "to enquire into the charge of making Mr Lambourn's house in Sparrow Lane into a workhouse", but the committee reporting in favour of certain cottages in Slaughterhouse Lane, these were duly acquired.

Thus far the system of contracting-out the paupers was not favoured in the town. There is no evidence even of the appointment of Masters or Mistresses. The overseers apparently en-

---

[1] MS. Corp. Com. Day Book, 1727.
[2] St Edward's MS. Vestry Book.

gineered the whole business, though the administration of these officials was subject to much criticism.[1]

In 1735 St Botolph's took steps to establish a workhouse. The overseer recorded the following expenses:

> Given to veiw the Workhouse, 2s.
> Gave Earnest for the Workhouse, 1s.
> Spent at giving warning for the poorhouse, 2s. 6d.

The indiscriminate use of the terms "workhouse" and "poorhouse" expresses the indeterminate character which these little parochial institutions assumed. The workhouse accounts for St Botolph's parish are preserved for many successive years during the eighteenth century; they afford typical illustration of the activities which can be traced—often less consecutively—in the manuscript papers of numerous small Cambridgeshire parishes, rural as well as urban.

An inventory of the workhouse was made at intervals. Two of these inventories still exist: that for the year 1739[2] conjures up a graphic picture of the small poorhouse, situate in a corner of St Botolph's churchyard. In the "Officers Room or Parlor" there stood "one large ovall table", around which were placed the "six neatt rush bottom chairs" upon which in solemn counsel sat "churchwarden stern or kingly overseer". "One firegrate" ministered to the comfort of authority. In the "Back Low Room", which served as kitchen, bathroom and workroom, "one large Copper" hung suspended above a "large Range and Grid Iron". "One Coldron, one Fryeng pan and two saws pans", six wooden dishes, eight trenchers and spoons, together with a limited supply of crockery, provided the culinary outfit. Two pails and a couple of wash-troughs sufficed for ablutionary purposes, human and other. Four spinning-wheels and two reels, a hemp block and beetle, constituted the equipment for

[1] Cf. infra, chap. xiv.
[2] The second is for the year 1747. It is quoted in the Appendix to H. P. Stokes, *Cambridge Parish Workhouses* (1911).

indoor work, whilst an iron spade may have served some pauper given the job of assisting the sexton. A "Middle Low Rome" without fireplace, on the same floor, three bedrooms on the first floor, and above these two garrets, completed the accommodation of the workhouse.

The parish had been heavily burdened by the payment of rents—there were rarely less than eight or nine persons assisted in this way between 1717 and 1735. Most of these individuals had also received weekly doles, varying from about 1s. to 2s. 6d., as did several others for whom no rents were paid. In order particularly to cut down rent charges, the "offer of the house" seems to have been made at first practically to all who sought relief—except to such children as were apprenticed. Within a year or two, however, the overseers' accounts for "extras"—or what in other parishes were termed "by-expenses"—began to include relief to various individuals who were not sent to the workhouse: Bird's wife, for example, received 1s. 6d. "on account of sickness"; White was allowed 1s. 6d. per week regularly for the maintenance of her bastard child; Bridiman, a poor man "overburdened with children", was allowed sums varying from 2d. to 5s., according to the amount he was able to earn otherwise. As early as 1746 the parish was thus occasionally making up wages from the rates on the grounds of a large family and of underemployment. By 1746, of the fourteen individuals relieved by the parish, six were not in the house. The only regular inmates were four or five children and a few aged folk. Work had entirely disappeared from the programme. It was consequently decided that the "worckhouse should be disanul'd". Doles were given and lodging found elsewhere for the occupants. Jane Newby, for example, took charge of "Dyers boy and girl", and Widow Harwood willingly augmented her meagre income by lodging "two boys of Ann wrights". £8 per annum had still, however, to be paid for the rent of the workhouse, so a few weeks later the building was again requisitioned for casual cases of distress—the former inmates remaining on out-relief. It was as a casual poorhouse and tramp-ward that the building was used till the end of 1749. At intervals of perhaps four, five or six weeks the house stood empty for a fortnight or so and the overseer recorded "no workhouse". Then the doors would again open to admit perchance some wanderer and his family returned to the parish by a removal order. They might be supplied with a spinning-wheel and allowed to retain what they could earn, but of organised labour there was no trace. Clothing,[1] fuel and provisions were bought by the overseer and distributed to the inmates, who cooked for themselves, an extra allowance being given to one or other of them to keep an eye on the children. Far more economy might of course have been achieved had the numbers been large enough to allow of the appointment of a salaried Master. Judging by the bills, the food was not supplied on the principle of "less eligibility"—butter was scarce, but cheese, meat, bread, oatmeal and roots or greens were regularly dispensed when the workhouse was open. A typical week's outlay on the inmates, in 1746, cost £1. 1s. 11½d., whilst for about the same number relieved in their own homes the expense was only 5s. 2d. The workhouse account for the week was as follows:

	s.	d.
⅙ lb. butter,		3¼
Oatemeal and Roots,		11¼
2 bus. Coal and pōr,[2]	1	5
A cheese—12 lb.,	3	0
30 lbs. Beef,	5	0
A Shin of Beef,	1	6
Bakers Bill,	6	8
Chandlers Bill,	1	5
Chippins,[3]	1	9
£1	1	11½

Rents, varying from 16s. to 30s. yearly, were again being paid

[1] 3s. was paid in 1747 for four pairs of clogs for the women at the workhouse.

[2] Porterage.   [3] Broken bread.

regularly for at least five people—all women—in 1748, and rising rates were a subject of loudly expressed dissatisfaction.[1]

At the end of the year it was decided that more commodious premises must be secured and a new policy adopted with regard to the workhouse. "One shilling as Arnest for his House for a Woork House" was paid to a Mr Lord, and arrangements were made to take possession at "St Michlemus next". In September 1749 alterations and repairs were going ahead in the new house— a bill for £7. 5s. 10d. being incurred. The building was not occupied till April 1750, when eleven persons were admitted. The cost of maintenance was now met by a contract, the flat rate of 1s. 8d. per head, per week, being allowed to Mrs Morgan, the woman contractor. The agreement seems to have included little beyond feeding the paupers and attending to the household management. There is no evidence of any new work scheme. Certain types of cases still received out-relief; for these the contractor was not responsible. There were, in 1750, eight persons assisted at home at rates varying from 6d. to 1s. per week. All additional expenses—"Extronardy Disbursements"—were paid by the overseer. Such expenses included, for example, legal advice and other charges incurred over removals, clothing bills, payment of premiums, medical attendance, drugs and nursing. In the case of inmates medicines were provided by the overseer, Mrs Morgan receiving an extra allowance for nursing. Mary Harwood and Anne Bird, for instance, contracted small-pox whilst in the house; they may have been put into a room by themselves, but Mrs Morgan continued, whilst nursing them, to mix freely with the other residents. During the middle years

[1] Micklebourgh, Vicar of Great St Andrew's, referred in his Chevin Sermon to a procession which took place in 1740—"the formidable parade of an overseer, a constable and a cart, stalking about with a slow and solemn pace, and stopping at almost every other house, to demand, to seize upon and to convey away the goods and effects of those who either could not, or would not, lay down the sums assessed upon them." (J. Micklebourgh, *The Great Duty of Labour and Work, and the Necessity there is at present for agreeing and fixing upon some Plan for a General Work-house for the Poor of this Place*, 1751.)

of the century the numbers in the house varied from five to nine.

It is unnecessary to trace in equal detail the workhouse history of the other town parishes.

The earliest extant vestry-book reference to a workhouse in the parish of St Bene't is in 1721. This building may have been merely the almshouse which had been occupied during the seventeenth century by heterogeneous types of poor. Before 1747 there was a workhouse, rented at £10 per annum, distinct from the almshouse. It was not under a contract at this time. At no period after 1747 was parochial assistance here confined to indoor relief. A workhouse inventory of 1758 shows an institution then in existence very similar to that of St Botolph's, though work occupied a sufficiently important part of the communal life to be allotted a separate "spinning-room". By this date it was evidently customary to loan out part of the workhouse furniture to paupers who were not forced to enter the house— John Haslop, for instance, was lent a bed, cupboard, table and wheel belonging to the workhouse, upon promise to return them on demand.

St Edward's parish, in 1746, relieved twelve paupers in their own homes and an equal number in the workhouse shared with Little St Mary's parish.

The first existing memorandum concerning a workhouse in the parish of St Andrew the Great relates to the year 1756, but it is very probable that an earlier institution had existed here as in most of the parishes of the town.

The main characteristics of these small parish workhouses changed little before the nineteenth century, though ever and anon the futility, the promiscuity and the squalor of the life lived within their dreary walls served as the text for some reformer anxious to supersede parochial organisation and to establish some larger institution where classification could be carried out, where regularity of life at least might be secured, and where—it was still often hoped—profitable employment might be undertaken.

In the mid-years of the century there was a vigorous revival both of proposals to this end and also of practical undertakings. The "Hundred Unions" of East Anglia, created by Local Acts from 1756 onwards, were of particular interest to Cambridge-shire.

(3) *Mid-Eighteenth Century General Workhouse Proposals*

The wide circulation of pamphlet literature on the subject of Union Workhouses had evoked much discussion. A writer in the *Cambridge Chronicle*, in 1762, entered the lists against those parish authorities who disparaged workhouse proposals—"from some interested motive, or from a desire to save themselves the trouble of inspecting them". The allegation that "there is no vent for those branches of manufacture which they are capable of employing themselves upon" and that the inmates "cannot earn by their industry so much as will pay for their maintenance", cannot, he urged, be true, when in the neighbouring city of Norwich "5000 children under ten years of age gain a livelihood by their labour". The twine and yarn at present imported from Holland might well be manufactured in our workhouses, were large, well-managed institutions set up.

Letters from one writer after another continued to appear in the columns of the county newspaper during the 'sixties, contrasting the district workhouses of East Anglia with the petty parochial houses of Cambridgeshire and the Isle, where "the allowance in many cases is not sufficient to support life", because the contractor must make a profit in order to maintain himself.

The question of a "General Workhouse" had been mooted by the corporation in 1750 and a scheme drawn up by the Vice-Chancellor agreed to, pending approval by the several parishes of Cambridge. Records of the vestry meetings held to consider the proposals are preserved among the manuscript papers of both Great St Mary's and St Edward's. In December 1750 the vestry of the former parish passed a resolution deferring final judgment until a "Coppy of the Bill intended to be brought in Parliament for the purpose of a General Workhouse be laid before this Vestry, to see how farr the same will be for the advantage of the Town". Mr Mayor was "desired to communicate the same to the Churchwardens of this parish", who "for the present do absolutely disapprove of the Governors proposed by the annexed proposal, conceiving them to be very improper". St Edward's vestry, early in the new year, preferred a similar request to the Mayor, revealing a like spirit of particularism and a dread of deputing too much authority either to the corrupt corporate body or to the university.

The Rev. John Micklebourgh, Vicar of Great St Andrew's, on January 27th, 1751, took the opportunity afforded by the annual Chevin Sermon, at which the Mayor and corporation were present, to pour forth an eloquent appeal in support of "the Great Duty of Labour and Work, and the Necessity there is at present for agreeing and fixing upon some Plan for a General Work-house for the Poor of this Place", and incidentally he revealed the condition of the existing poorhouses of the town.

"This we commanded you, that if any would not work, neither should he eat"—here was a text which lent itself admirably to the spirit of the age. Brotherly love? Charity Schools? Hospitals?—excellent; but there comes a time when a spur to industry is more needful than charity, which "for want of some restraint" is apt to become "not only useless and unprofitable, but mischievous and detrimental". There are, of course, among the poverty-stricken those who are "willing but not able to work", admits the preacher, but of infinitely greater moment are those "unwilling but able".

> Yet let us own that Trade has much of Chance,
> Not all the Careful by their Care advance;
> With the same Parts and Prospects, one a Seat
> Builds for himself; one finds it in the "Fleet".

Of the class which the poet thus recognises Micklebourgh has nothing to say: it is the second group which absorbs his attention—the profligate and lazy, "whose vitious cravings and desires are like the Grave which cannot be satisfied; whose hand refuseth to labour, whose misery is deserved, and whose acts of deceit and wickedness are often encouraged by our kindness".

How are these obvious evils to be remedied? The answer is clearly in a Workhouse Act which shall compel the poor to work: "Of all schemes a General Work-House for the poor is undoubtedly the best...where work and virtue, where religion and industry may meet together and kiss each other". Experience has proved this true "in most of the great Towns of this Kingdom". In such houses "the younger poor especially may hereafter be brought up in such a manner as to be more useful and less burthensome to the publick; where children yet unborn may learn righteousness and business so well as to be able in some measure to support the place which supported them or their parents".

This plain solution to the weighty problem is not applied because the parishes of this town are ruled by "prejudices, passions and prepossessions", by jealousies, suspicions and fears of one another. "They cannot as yet fix upon any one plan for this purpose", nevertheless a united workhouse "is as much desired as it is wanted". Glance but for one moment at the deplorable spectacle of the "little trifling houses belonging to our respective parishes" and hesitation must cease. "They are so far from refreshing the weary soul that is unable to refresh itself, that they are rather to be looked upon as nurseries of laziness, nastiness and vice, as Houses of Play and Debauchery and not as Houses of Work." This is so not merely "because the persons fed in them do little or no work, for want of proper and constant Inspectors over them", but also—and here the reverend gentleman does not hesitate to lash out against the conspicuous malpractices of others beside the poor—"because the advantages accruing from their accommodation are usually played into the hands of a few dexterous managers".

The subject continued under discussion for the next month or two. The university was the moving power, and a plan elaborated by the Vice-Chancellor was again brought before the town authorities in March, and agreed upon for submission to the respective parishes.[1] St Edward's vestry expressed itself in favour of the final proposal, "if the four persons to be deputed by each parish have an equal power to hold courts and to transact buisness in common with the Governors and other Guardians appointed".[2] Details from the other parishes are not forthcoming, but eventually the scheme fell through[3] and the attention of the university, and especially of the local clergy, was turned disconsolately to the declining Charity Schools, for even in the workhouse plan the main stress had been laid rather upon disciplinary influence than upon industrial profit.

(4) *Parliamentary Returns of* 1776 *and* 1785

The system of farming-out the poor spread in the town during the 'sixties. In 1761 Great St Mary's farmed the workhouse poor at only 1*s.* 8*d.* per head. Eight years later a certain William Endersley agreed "to find the poor with everything necessary, except physic and four chaldrons of coals yearly, on being paid 3*s.* per head per week for all the poor within the sd house".

In 1776, of the thirteen parishes of the town which sent in a return to the parliamentary enquiry, nine had a workhouse, the number of inmates varying from eight in St Peter's to twenty-four in Holy Trinity. In the whole town about 140 paupers were workhouse residents.

Nine years later the seven parishes which professed—according to the parliamentary returns—to be "setting the poor to work", expended between them only 16*s.* 5*d.* per annum.

B. ROYSTON

A particularly interesting illustration of urban workhouse history is afforded by the border town of Royston—partly at

---

[1] Cooper, *op. cit.* IV, p. 283.   [2] St Edward's MS. Vestry Book.

[3] In September 1751 a further university proposal was agreed to by the corporation and ordered to be circulated to the several parishes, but it evidently came to nothing. (MS. Corp. Com. Day Book, IV, Sept. 26th, 1751.)

this date in Cambridgeshire, though mainly within the Hertfordshire boundary.

"The Booke of Accounts for the use of the Towne" records, in 1735, the expenditure of £70 "for yᵉ bilding of yᵉ Workhous". The overseers' disbursements in the year before the workhouse opened amounted to £123; in 1737 they had fallen to £89, a slight rise was noticeable in 1739, and in this year the vestry decreed that for the future "no person should be relieved by haveing there rent paid, but they that want reliefe shall be putt into the Workhouse".

Most of the labour in the house was performed by children: in 1753 an entry records the sum of £88. 4s. 8½d. as being the proceeds of "two rates and childrens work". An entry for 1755 shows the income derived from work to be only £4. 3s. 5d. In 1766 "the boys work" brought in £5. 10s. 1d. during the year, whilst the overseers' total outlay was nearly £256.

For the first thirty years the resident Master acted only as a servant of the parish, but in 1766 the inmates were farmed to a Mr Williams for the lump sum of £160. The administration of outdoor-relief, which amounted to some £21 per annum, was retained in the overseers' hands.

Contracts of this nature were not common in Cambridgeshire. "If the contract be for a certain annual stipend for the whole number of paupers which the parish contracting can furnish," said Scott,[1] in 1773, "the hazard of unexpected contingencies must be run by the contractor." No one will undertake such risks "without a prospect of ample repayment. The gains of oppression are within his reach and he must not refuse them". The abuses to which the arrangement led were quickly apparent at Royston, and in 1774 the parish reverted to the payment of a weekly salary of 6s. to the Master for the service of superintendence only.

In January 1774 there were twenty-six paupers in the house: their personnel is interesting. Six were men. Of these three were

[1] John Scott, *Observations on the Present State of the Parochial and Vagrant Poor* (1773), pp. 40, 41.

over sixty years of age and one of them died the next June; three were young but "infirm", one of whom died in June; one—a member of a family of seven in the house—was discharged to go to service, only to return shortly afterwards "very bad": he, too, died in September. The third young man "ran away without consent". Six of the residents were women: two were very aged; one was infirm; two were widows—each with five children in the house; one was a young single woman. The remaining fourteen inmates were children, ranging in age from one year to fifteen. The fifteen-year-old boy was sent out to service a few months later. Two little brothers, named Hinkin, were allowed to go to their widowed mother, but by September she was again unable to support them and they were back in the house.

The numbers in the workhouse fluctuated more in this border town, constantly invaded by vagrants, than in either Cambridge or Wisbech. The problem of the "ins and outs" already troubled Royston. During the last fortnight of January there were added to the inmates enumerated above fourteen newcomers. Among these were an elderly woman and her three grown-up sons and daughters: the young folk seized the first opportunity to decamp, "against the gents consent", leaving their aged parent in the workhouse. A young woman, admitted about the same time, lodged her two little girls in the house and then "ran away", whilst a third woman shortly after admission also "departed without consent".

A certain Thomas Ward, who occasionally received a few pence as outdoor relief from the parish, was allowèd to find shelter in the workhouse, in 1774, but was charged 3s. a week for his board. In May 1776, 4s. a week was paid by Joseph Finch for the lodging of a boy in the workhouse—probably in this case an illegitimate child, though the practice was not confined to such children.[1]

In May 1775 there were thirty-four residents, of whom twenty-one were children—one an "ideot", one "broken" and one lame.

---

[1] Cf. *infra*, p. 94, note.

With such material as hands, it is not surprising to find the income derived from work very small. Spindles, wheels and worsted figure fairly often in the accounts, but inmates were frequently sent out to work during the day for local farmers. Two youths—Lucas and Law—thus earned sometimes 3*s.*, sometimes 7*s.* per week each, which money was paid over to the workhouse master and by him to the overseer. The earnings for one week during 1774 were as under:

Lucas, from Mr Philips, farmer	7*s.*
Law ,, ,, Fison ,,	7*s.*
2 women field-work	3*s.* 6*d.*
Spinning, bought by Mr Woodham	9*s.* 3*d.*
,, ,, ,, Spalding	4*s.* 9*d.*
	£1. 11*s.* 6*d.*

The workhouse expenses for the same week came to £4. 5*s.* 3¼*d.* Seven shillings a week was the full current wage for the period. The two youths continued to be profitable inmates for some months and, their relatives being in the house, the youths were encouraged to remain there. By April, however, Law was only obtaining three days' work per week at 6*d.* per day. Mr Britt, the overseer, himself a farmer, did not scruple to secure cheap labour at the cost of the parish, and at the cost of independent workers, by employing six of the parish lads at 4*d.* each per week. Young Joe Gailor earned 8*d.* per week with another farmer for driving hogs; his sister was sent out as a mother's help at 4*d.* per day, and even Elizabeth Smith, an "ideot" girl of thirteen, earned 4*d.* occasionally for doing a day's household drudgery. During May and June 1777 women and children were let out for housework, weeding, or spreading manure at 6*d.* per day—about the usual rate for independent labour of this type. Joseph Hay, a neighbouring farmer, employed a varying number of paupers throughout the year. Odd jobs in the churchyard were also sometimes given to workhouse people. After about 1776 there was little spinning done in the house; some of the inmates were occupied in making matches, but a very meagre income was derived from indoor work. There had never indeed been any pretence of conducting the establishment at a profit.

The diet was varied but limited in quantity. In addition to such usual items as flour, bread, beef, mutton and beer, the accounts included turnips, greens, onions, peas, beans, beef suet, lard, cheese, oatmeal, apples, "cumbers", vinegar, yeast, alspice, carraway seed, "plumbs", malagas, very occasionally eggs, and milk only on Sunday mornings. For Ralph, a chronic invalid, special "nurishment", in the form of sheeps' feet and wine, was provided. Ann Ward was considerately treated during her confinement, and in due course even the minister's fee of 1s. for her churching was paid by the parish.

Certainly the paupers seem to have lived an easier life in the absence of any contract, but the expense to the parish was heavy, and in 1781 the important step was taken of unifying the two parishes of the town, under the Act of 1723, and of reorganising the whole administration.

Chapter VIII

THE WORKHOUSE MOVEMENT IN RURAL CAMBRIDGESHIRE, 1723–1785

A. CAMBRIDGESHIRE v. THE ISLE OF ELY

The necessity for grouping parishes into larger areas was even more urgent in the case of sparsely populated country districts than of towns. In Cambridgeshire peculiar geographical difficulties were unfortunately added to those common to the rest of the country, and militated against all attempts to amalgamate, whether for Poor Law, for education,[1] or for any other purpose of local government. The fenland character of much of the county was mainly responsible for the execrable condition of the roads and for the paucity of towns or major villages suitably situated as centres for united districts. Small villages lay scattered over the shire rather than clustered together in groups. No Hundred Houses were in consequence ever established in Cambridgeshire.[2] Linton, one of the few market towns of the county, was exceptionally well placed as "the emporium of local trade",[3] yet even here endeavours to unite the surrounding parishes, with Linton as a centre, repeatedly

---

[1] With regard to education the difficulty was particularly obvious in the nineteenth century, when Central Schools were established elsewhere. It is curious to find the county in the twentieth century pioneering an educational movement based on the idea of grouping villages around a common centre—e.g. the experiment at Sawston.

[2] Gooch, *Agric. of Cambs.* (1813), p. 293. Also *P.L.C. Rept.* 1834, App. A, Pt. 1, pp. 263, 676. (All references to this Report are to the *Report from H.M. Commissioners for inquiring into the Administration and Practical Operation of the Poor Laws*, 1834, 2nd octavo edition.)

[3] *Ibid.* p. 247. Cf. also *infra*, p. 234, note 1. Two fairs were held here also.

Croxton built a House of Correction for itself and the surrounding district in 1804.

failed, and, as will be seen, later schemes within the county proved abortive till the final compulsory formation of unions in 1834.

Though it was mainly in the Isle of Ely that the workhouse movement spread, here and there in the larger villages of the county proper workhouses were established in the period between 1735 and 1745. Of twenty-five rural parishes for which the surviving records for this period are fairly complete, four erected a workhouse and fourteen others built or extended their poorhouses.

It was the poorhouse rather than the workhouse which was typical of rural Cambridgeshire proper. In many instances—as for example at Sawston—no real parochial workhouses ever existed. In other cases attempts were made at various periods to convert either the existing poorhouse, or more often some more suitable building, into a regular institution in which work could be carried on. Such institutions inevitably tended to degenerate into mere poorhouses, though the services of a resident Master or Mistress might be retained. Sometimes a deserving pauper was promoted to the post.

Within the franchise of Ely the workhouse movement was far more vigorous. In the county the standard seems to have been set by the non-industrial university centre; in the Isle the industrial township of Wisbech influenced the thought and practice of the rural parishes, and the impetus given by Wisbech in the 'twenties never completely died away.

The poorhouse or workhouse annals of several typical rural, or semi-rural parishes may be traced during the first part of the eighteenth century, before examining statistics showing the extent to which the movement had spread by 1785.

(1) *Linton*

"At a General Town's Meeting of the Parishioners" of Linton, in December 1737, it was agreed to take advantage of the Act of 1723, in order to borrow £100 for the erection of a workhouse "for yᵉ Imployment and Necessary Relief of yᵉ Poor of yᵉ said

Parish". A committee of six was then nominated to make the necessary arrangements. A Master and Dame were appointed, at a fixed salary, to conduct the activities of the house under the direction of the overseers.

The Master kept careful records of all expenditure and income and presented these to the overseer every month. In May 1739, for example, Wm. Gibbs, the overseer, received through the hands of the Master £2. 18s. 11d. for "worke" and 5s. for "ye girls board"—children here, too, were occasionally lodged in the workhouse at the expense of their parents,[1] though more often of their putative parents. All the charges of the house were paid directly by the overseer. His account for May 1739 was as follows:

To yᵉ Masters Bill for additional things					12	10¾
"	"	"	"	Wages	15	0
"	Dames	"	"	"	7	8½
"	Flower	"			10	0
"	Butchers	"			13	3
"	Shop	"			5	4
" John Webb for 20 Gall. of Beer					2	6
					£3 6	8¼

There was a considerable amount of spinning done in the house and apparently the yarn found a ready market. The Master was responsible for arranging purchases and sales, but took no

[1] The parish of Littleport submitted the following bill to a bargee whose children were accommodated in the workhouse, in 1817:
"John Crabb, Waterman,
To Littleport Parish,

	£	s.	d.
To 52 Weeks pay for Daughter in the Poor House, from Oct. 24th, 1815 to Oct. 24th, 1816, at 3s.	7	16	0
Do. from 24th Oct. 1816 to 31st Jany, 1817, 14 weeks at 4s.	2	16	0
13 weeks for other Daughter up to 31st Jany, 1817 at 4s.	2	12	0
4 Weeks for son, up to 31st Jan, 1817, at 4s.		16	0
	£14	0	0"

share in either profit or loss. There were but few cases of home-relief in the parish at this date. In 1746 the overseer made an interesting comparison between the current weekly cost of maintaining the whole of the parish poor and the cost "before the workhouse began": it had remained almost stationary.

The practice of contracting-out the poor was not common in rural Cambridgeshire before the 'sixties and seems rarely to have been adopted till after a period of trial of direct management by the parish officers. In June 1752 an arrangement was made with the workhouse Master at Linton to provide for the seventeen inmates at the weekly rate of 1s. 9d. per head—a figure which worked out at almost exactly the same total cost as that incurred on behalf of inmates by the overseer in 1746. By 1752 a number of individuals were relieved in their own homes: for these the contractor accepted no responsibility. In 1758 the parish was advertising in the *Ipswich Journal* for "a fit Person to take care of the Workhouse". A larger proportion of the poor were now relieved as inmates, under the contract system—in 1776 there were twenty-three—but the total cost to the parish was apparently reduced.[1] The sum of 1s. 9d. per head could not have supplied more than the barest necessities in 1752. Two shillings was a common rate in 1760, and Scott, the contemporary writer, considered this sum "a mere pittance", implying "unsatisfied hunger to all, and oppressive labour to many". Since, however, the contractor in this parish gained nothing from the output of the workers, he was not tempted to "turn the unable into the streets", as not infrequently happened.[2]

(2) *Sawston*

At Sawston a Town House had been in the possession of the parish from time immemorial, and had served the customary

---

[1] The totals fluctuated so greatly according to litigation expenses or the amount of sickness prevalent that comparisons in relative costs are risky—a small-pox epidemic in 1778 raised the expenses by one-third.

[2] Cf. Scott, *op. cit.* p. 44.

purposes. A building termed a "workhouse" was in use during the 'seventies—in 1779 the overseer paid half-a-crown for "removing Edward Barker and his daughter and goods to the workhouse". There were eight persons in residence in 1782, but apparently no Master or Mistress was in control. The inmates supported themselves on weekly pensions of 2s. from the parish. There were at the same date seven regular recipients of out-relief and four or five casual cases. Clothing and "weels" were bought for inmates on occasion, and bed-ticks, frying-pans and other odds and ends were supplied by the parish. During hard winters coals were provided freely. In 1791 the occupants consisted of eight widows, one other woman, three old men and a child. There was no significant change in the character of this so-called workhouse till after 1834. It was essentially a poorhouse throughout its history, as were many of the village "work-houses" of Cambridgeshire.

(3) *Bottisham*

The accounts of the overseer of Bottisham show with unusual clarity the stages of development through which the workhouse passed. Up to 1786, however, the parish possessed only a poor-house very similar to that of Sawston.

(4) *Burwell*

The parish of Burwell went to the extent of repairing and refurnishing the Town House and of supplying it with wheels, reels, and cards in 1736, but it was not until the 'seventies that a Master was placed in charge. There were twenty inmates in 1776, but no contract system was in vogue.

(5) *Soham*

At Soham the largest workhouse in the county[1] was fully organised in the 'sixties. In 1776 there were sixty residents there. The Master was paid a quarterly salary of £5,[2] the expenses of

---

[1] As distinguished from the Isle.

[2] Dropped to £3. 10s. in 1781. A contract on a *per capita* basis was arranged in 1808.

maintaining the house being met directly by the overseer. Paupers entirely incapable of work were not sent to the house, where spinning was the chief industry. The sums received for work varied from £4 to £7 per month and were paid in full to the overseer. The income from this source at its highest amounted to but one-quarter the cost of the workhouse upkeep, despite the rigorous discipline under which labour was exacted.

James Chambers,[1] "the poor poetaster", born at Soham in 1748, describes his personal recollection of life in the local "mansions of industry":

> By day I must dwell where there's many a wheel,
> And a female employed to sit down and reel;
> A post with two ringles is fixed in the wall,
> Where orphans, when lashed, loud for mercy do call,
> Deprived of fresh air, I must there commence spinner,
> If I fail of my task I lose a hot dinner;
> Perhaps at the whipping post then shall be flogged,
> And lest I escape my leg must be clogged.[2]
> While tyrants oppress I must still be their slave,
> And cruelly used, tho' well I behave:
> Midst swearing and brawling my days I must spend,
> In sorrow and anguish my days I must end.

(6) *Littleport*

There does not seem to have been any workhouse at Littleport, in the Isle of Ely, till 1768,[3] at which date a building was hired and the vestry drew up elaborate rules for the conduct of the new workhouse.

Wm. Cunington, "a wooll-stapler" of Ely, and his wife were appointed Master and Mistress for a year and, contrary to

---

[1] He was the son of a leather dealer and tried his hand at peddling, net-making and herbal doctoring in the intervals of verse-writing and begging. (T. Woolmer, *A Beggar Poet*, 1887.)

[2] Compulsory removal to a workhouse and chaining or manacling of inmates were forbidden by an Act of 1816. (56 G. III, c. 129.)

[3] Missing records would possibly reveal an earlier workhouse.

Cambridgeshire precedent, a contract at the rate of 3s. 6d. per head weekly was arranged without any preliminary period of parish management. One guinea annually was to be allowed in addition to provide a distinctive coat for the Master, who was also to be refunded the cost of maintenance of himself and family —an arrangement suspiciously suggestive of recognised abuses.

A formal indented agreement was drawn up defining the exact terms of service. The Master undertook to provide "Cloathing, Firing and Washing" for all parochial poor sent to him by the overseers, and all "other things necessary", with the exception of "bedding, physic and medical assistance", for which he might claim reimbursement, but he was to be responsible for the decent burial of any pauper dying in the house. He promised "to use his utmost means and endeavours to preserve and keep the poor people in cleanliness and health"; to pay "a strict attention to their morals and conduct"; to cause "all such of them as were not hindered by sickness or other lawful cause, regularly to attend divine service on the Lord's Day", and to arrange for them "to be taught and instructed in the Church Catechism and Prayers". The Master was himself to bear the sole expense of bringing to justice all such as should "so misconduct themselves as to require the interference of a magistrate". He was, moreover, so to "demean himself to the poor people as not to warrant complaints"—provisos which betrayed the unrest often provoked by the Master's oppressive régime.[1] A further clause requiring the Master to preserve "all the glass windows belonging to the house whole and in good plight", was one commonly inserted in workhouse agreements of the period and again suggests unruly behaviour.

All inmates who were not "incapacitated" were to be regularly employed in "carding, spinning, weaving, or other work, according to their different capacities and abilities", the Master taking "for his own use and benifit the profits arising".

The workhouse bread was to be of specified quality, consisting of two-thirds at least of wheat and the remaining third

[1] Cf. Royston, *infra*, p. 108.

of rye, barley or potatoes, when the average price of wheat in the market of Ely or Cambridge was above 28s. per coomb;[1] when the said price was 28s. or under, the bread was to be made from pure wheat only. Apart from this regulation no fixed dietary was drawn up.

B. PARLIAMENTARY REPORTS OF 1776–8[2] AND 1785–6[3]

Among other questions concerning the working of the Poor Law, which were submitted to each parish by the Parliamentary Committee of 1776, was one relating to the existence or otherwise of a workhouse and "the number of persons which each will accommodate".

Poorhouses of some description did in fact exist in many of the villages which disclaimed the possession of a workhouse, and certain of the workhouses reported were in reality little more than poorhouses at this date. With this qualification, however, a careful examination of the returns, in the light of information to be gleaned from the respective parochial archives, corroborates the evidence given.[4]

In six hundreds[5] of the fourteen into which, exclusive of the Isle of Ely, the rural county was divided, not a single workhouse existed in 1776. In the hundred of Staploe, comprising nine parishes, four parishes had a workhouse, but in no other hundred were workhouses to be found in more than two villages. Fourteen individual parishes were reported to have a workhouse, the inmates in each averaging about twenty-seven in

[1] 56s. per quarter. (Coomb = 4 bushels or ½ qtr.)

[2] *Reports of the Committee on the Laws which concern the Relief and Settlement of the Poor and the Laws relating to Vagrants, and also the State of the Several Houses of Correction, 1775–6.*

[3] Returns relative to the State of the Poor, 1785–6.

[4] The *Report* records six workhouses at Rampton, with no one in residence: this is clearly a clerical error. No vestry records for the period remain, but there certainly were cottages in the possession of the parish at an earlier date. Still more likely there may have been one cottage used for the lodging of six paupers.

[5] Flendish, Papworth, Radfield, Staine, Thriplow, Wetherley.

number. Soham headed the list with sixty inmates; Whittlesford had forty; no other parish had more than thirty—Bassingbourn workhouse was empty.[1]

Whilst the proportion of parishes which had a workhouse was about one in ten in the rural county proper, it was no less than one in three in the Isle of Ely.[2] There were only 331 paupers living in workhouses in the county: in the Isle there were 665—an average of over 60 per workhouse. Wisbech St Peter's housed 150 inmates, March 100, Whittlesey 90, Ely Trinity 80 and Thorney 60.

The Parliamentary Returns for the year 1785 do not give particulars concerning workhouses, but they do specify the amount of money expended in each parish "in setting the poor to work"—which may sometimes merely have meant buying wheels or reels for domestic workers. In the county one-third, in the Isle one-half of the parishes were stated to spend money for this purpose, but the total expenditure in the former case was only £40. 17s. 8d.—an average of about 5s. 9d. per parish; in the latter case the total was £47. 9s. 4d., averaging about 29s. per parish.[3]

It was remarked in a later Parliamentary Report of 1804 that "the materials for employing the poor" were frequently "not furnished by the parish, but by the persons who employ them". This was true to a much less extent in 1776 than at the later date. It is evident that in 1776 the aim of the workhouses of

---

[1] In those parishes where the workhouse was of a considerable size rents were rarely paid. In eighty-seven parishes in the county the payment of rents was a common form of outdoor relief. In all the town parishes, except Little St Mary's, rents were paid for paupers—extensively in St Peter's, Great St Mary's, Great St Andrew's and St Bene't's.

[2] Eleven parishes out of thirty-two.

[3] At Chesterton £8. 10s. 4d. was spent yearly; at Dry Drayton £7. 16s. 1d.; at Burwell £7. 12s. 2d.; at Linton £4. 17s. 0d.; in only three other parishes did the sum exceed £1. In the Isle of Ely the largest sum—£14. 7s. 5d.—was spent at Tydd; £11. 5s. 11d. at Upwell; over £6 at Whittlesey and Sutton; £2. 8s. 1d. at Ely St Mary and in three other parishes about £1.

Cambridgeshire was rarely deterrent and the output was never for long profitable.

The same conclusions with respect to the country generally were reached by the Committee of 1776. It was reported by Sir Cecil Wray "that the present method of regulating the poor in separate parishes and townships is in general ineffectual for their proper relief and employment"; that if the poor were "maintained and employed at one general county expense", not only would settlement disputes in a great measure be avoided, but it would also be possible to establish "proper houses and buildings at such places in each county" as would be best suited "for the reception, accommodation and employment" of the poor, where proper "classing" and inspection could be effected. The necessity of suitably employing "infant and able poor" was emphasised, and the desirability urged of establishing Poor Law Districts and District Houses, administered by Governors and Guardians, after the manner adopted by existing incorporations.

Chapter IX

THE URBAN WORKHOUSES OF CAMBRIDGESHIRE, 1785–1834

The main emphasis of mid-eighteenth century reformers was upon better administration to be achieved through the increase in size of the Poor Law unit. A new wave of interest in this line of progress was manifest during the 'eighties. The famous Shrewsbury House of Industry was established in 1783, "to furnish employment for the poor and compel them to earn their own support". The success achieved at Shrewsbury during the first few years[1] was widely advertised and the mode of organisation copied by other places.

Simultaneously with the renewed interest in administrative reforms there was developing a more humane attitude towards the poor, manifesting itself officially in the legislation of 1782. "The England of 1760–1830", says Mr Fay,[2] "was definitely not what it is often assumed to have been. It was definitely not soft-hearted, and it took little heed of the needs of those who, because they were physically weak, had no power to create a disturbance." There is undoubtedly truth in this assertion: the shadow of war and scarcity influenced the attitude of authority; nevertheless it is impossible to peruse, for example, the voluminous inter-parochial correspondence of this period—arising especially over questions of settlement—without recognising a more frequent note of spontaneous kindliness than in the early part of the century.

The provisions of major significance in Gilbert's Act of 1782[3]

---

[1] By 1791, however, it was admitted that the able-bodied inmates worked "in such a feeble and languid manner that the occupation is any-thing but calculated to preserve, much less generate habits of industry". (Cf. Webb, *op. cit.* p. 223.)

[2] C. R. Fay, *Life and Labour* (1920), p. 91.

[3] 22 G. III, c. 83.

were the grouping of parishes into unions, under an improved mode of administration which replaced the control of the overseer; the finding of work for the able-bodied in or near their own homes, under conditions which almost inevitably involved a system of allowances in aid of wages; and the definite exclusion of the able-bodied from the workhouses, which were to be rendered fitting homes for the aged, the impotent and the orphan.[1]

It is unnecessary to examine the clauses of the Act in detail, for its adoption was not compulsory, and though the proceedings were followed with interest, no Gilbert Unions were ever formed in Cambridgeshire or in the Isle.

It is curious to note the attempts which were made here and there in the county to reorganise the little poorhouses, and occasionally to establish for the first time an organised workhouse, between 1780 and 1834. In these not very numerous instances there was a general tendency to hark back to the principles of 1723—the Act was sometimes deliberately quoted—rather than to accept the idea of the workhouse as an asylum for the impotent. Contradictory attitudes, however, frequently characterised parishes but a few miles apart.

It may have been as a repercussion of the exploitation of child labour, which accompanied the great industrial development of England, that a desire to explore once more the possibilities of rendering the child a productive agent manifested itself in parts

---

[1] By s. 30 infant children were permitted to be sent either to the workhouse or to be placed out with "some reputable person, in or near the parish"—a custom long-established in practice. Maintenance and lodging were, however, by some means to be provided by the parish for unemployed and under-employed persons if need be. According to the actual phraseology of the Act any money earned by the pauper was to be handed over to the guardians, towards the cost of the applicant's maintenance. Any deficiency was to be made up from the rates, but it was hardly at the moment contemplated that such additional sums would be given in the form of money to the pauper himself. Any surplus arising from his earnings was, however, to be returned to the pauper. The transition from these conditions to the later customary allowances in aid of wages was easy.

of Cambridgeshire during the early years of the nineteenth century.

It is desirable to examine in more detail, in this and in the following chapter, the developments in workhouse policy between 1785 and 1834, taking the towns of Cambridge and Royston as examples of urban, and the parish of Bottisham as an example of rural, activity.

A. CAMBRIDGE

The administrative mechanism of the Gilbert plan recommended itself to Cambridge reformers, but with the Gilbertian workhouse they were definitely not in sympathy. In 1785, therefore, a final endeavour was made to obtain a Local Act for the town.

A scheme was drawn up and circulated to the respective parishes and sufficient support was obtained to enable a petition, backed by both university and corporation, to go forward to Parliament. The parish rates, it was stated, had "encreased to a degree so enormous as to become a burthen almost intolerable". If powers were given to build a suitable house "for the reception, employment and better maintenance of the poor, and to regulate the rates made for their relief, it would greatly relieve the inhabitants". The petition was received by the House of Commons and passed on to a Committee, from which, however, it never emerged.

In 1805 a general scheme for the employment of the children of the town was mooted. St Bene't's vestry recorded its profound approval of "so laudable an undertaking", and deputed Mr Gilbert Ives to attend the magistrates' meeting. No common enterprise, however, eventuated. In 1834 the only parish in which there was any pretence of employing workhouse children was Little St Andrew's. Here the children were taught straw plaiting, but the industry was conducted at a loss.

The population of Cambridge increased over 100 per cent. between 1801 and 1831. During this generation several town parishes extended their workhouse accommodation and others agreed to share a common building.[1] The largest workhouse in 1804 was that of Great St Andrew's, with twenty-seven inmates: it still headed the list in 1834 with the same number. St Botolph's and St Peter's had each but four inmates in 1804, and no workhouse was in use at all in Great St Mary's parish, St Giles', St Sepulchre's or Little St Andrew's. In 1834 all the town parishes either had a workhouse or shared one, but Little St Mary's had only two or three inmates—"finding it more beneficial to the interests of the parish to keep the poorhouse empty". Sometimes "disannul'd", sometimes offering free or cheap lodgings[2] to a few paupers, rarely making any pretence of organising work, even at a loss,[3] laxly supervised by a Master or Mistress, such was the picture of the town poorhouses in 1834, as it had been for a century.

Authorities wavered between the advantages and disadvantages of farming-out the town workhouses, but in no case did they contract for the whole poor of the parish. A Mistress farmed the youthful and decrepit occupants of St Edward's workhouse for 2s. 4d. per head, in 1795, but by 1804 the contract system was temporarily discarded by the whole town. Great St Andrew's began farming again in 1809, at 3s. 6d. per head; All Saints' in 1807, at 4s. per head; Little St Andrew's, St Edward's, Holy Trinity and St Clement's were also farming their workhouse poor in 1834.

There was no effective separation between males and females,

---

[1] In 1814 Little St Mary's and St Sepulchre's shared a workhouse, but otherwise managed their poor separately; in 1816 the two parishes shared a new workhouse. From 1823 to 1836 St Bene't's and Little St Andrew's had a common workhouse, and similarly between 1824 and 1836 St Botolph's and St Giles'.

[2] In Great St Andrew's parish, e.g. in 1811, a parishioner was allowed to lodge in the workhouse, but was required "to find himself with board out of his earning". Cf. supra, pp. 89, note, 94, note; infra, p. 115.

[3] The inmates of Great St Mary's workhouse were occupied for a time, in 1829, under a Mistress, in making rods for basket work. A woman had been in charge in this parish in 1821. Women contractors managed the workhouses of St Edward's and Little St Andrew's in 1834.

and illegitimate children formed, in 1834, a large proportion of the workhouse population—fourteen out of the twenty-seven inmates of Great St Andrew's workhouse. This latter building was under the care of a woman in 1834, and was reported as "very clean". Although the house was farmed the dietary was very good—meat dinners thrice a week, hot preparations of milk or broth on the other days, gruel or milk and bread for breakfast, and bread and cheese for supper.

In 1804 the workhouse population of the town numbered only 108, maintained at an annual cost of £1178, as compared with 496 receiving outdoor relief, at a cost of £2478 yearly. Hence the annual expenditure per head was nearly £11 for inmates and only about £5 for other cases. Whilst the workhouse poor had only increased to about 150 in 1834, outdoor paupers had trebled in numbers.

Several parishes were still averse to a general union even at the time of the Royal Commission, but the general consensus of opinion was expressed by the correspondent of St Edward's: "The parishes of this town are small; a union of them would give the means of classification and better education to the children, and would perhaps lessen the litigation of settlements".[1]

B. ROYSTON[2]

In October 1781 the joint vestries of the two parishes of Royston —the one in Cambridgeshire, the other in Hertfordshire— solemnly decided to "enter into an act of union" for local government purposes. A new administrative council was set up, consisting of representative members of the two parishes.[3] The new authority dealt with local government in general, but the essential motive for union was the desire to reform Poor Law administration, and with this end in view the body was so constituted as to conform with the legal requirements of the Work-

---

[1] *P.L.C. Rept.* 1834, App. B 2, Pt. 5, Query 52.
[2] MS. Vestry Books and loose papers, Royston.
[3] Cf. *infra*, p. 244.

house Act of 1723, although going beyond these requirements in certain particulars. It was desired "to join and unite in the maintenance of the poor of the said two parishes, according to the Statute of 9 G. I, c. 7, s. 4". The rates of the two parishes were to be "consolidated at an average of two-thirds, viz. 8*d.* in the shilling for each Pound Rate".

In accordance with the statute it was agreed that "no poor shall be allowed out of the workhouse except casual poor". The arrangement was to stand for three years.[1] Before proceeding further the most careful precautions were taken by both parishes to safeguard themselves severally with respect to possible settlement difficulties, and jointly with respect to powers of compulsion, where two different county jurisdictions were involved.

The joint workhouse was intended not only to maintain, but also to employ the poor, who were farmed-out, in 1782, at 1*s.* 4*d.* per head, the Master being allowed certain additional expenses. The *per capita* basis proved unsatisfactory and three years later a new Master—James Searle, a cordwainer of Wisbech—was appointed at the fixed sum of £260 per annum. The temptation to cut down the number of inmates, by means fair or foul, which this system offered to the Master, was minimised by the proviso which allowed an additional 2*s.* per head weekly whenever the number of residents exceeded fifty. The Master was further permitted "to have and take unto himself the benefit of the said poor peoples work, labour, and service" and to enjoy the use of the house, yard, garden and workhouse grounds free of rent, rates, taxes and the cost of repairs other than of glass windows. The Master was required to provide "three hot meat dinners in every week, of such sort, and such other victuals and drink at all times sufficient, wholesome and proper, as shall be to the satisfaction and good liking of the said Committee, to be from time to time signified". The Master was to supply clothing, to meet burial expenses, legal charges concerned with refractory paupers and medical expenses except in case of small-pox or broken limbs. The Committee reserved to themselves the right to "put

[1] Periodically renewed till 1819.

in or take out from the workhouse any poor person" and to "visit and inspect" at their pleasure.

The workroom was enlarged in 1785 and other rooms were added in 1790 and 1792.

Searle remained in office for some years, but was replaced about 1790 upon the offer of Edmund Cornwell to contract for the house at the lower rate of £212 per annum.[1] The reduction in salary soon showed its effect in the temper of the inmates. A riot broke out in 1792, as a result of which four women were given into custody, but were released on the advice of counsel.[2] In the course of the investigation the disorderly mode of conduct of the house came to light, but in 1792 authorities quailed before visions of the guillotine. Had not "wicked, malicious and evil-disposed persons stuck up divers treasonable and incendiary papers in this town, and sent several anonymous letters directed to some of the inhabitants thereof, threatening to have their blood"![3] The Committee wavered in their practice of offering the house to applicants for relief, rents began to be paid again, and out-relief to be granted more frequently.

At the beginning of 1793 Searle returned to office. Though the salary was not raised above £212, an extra allowance was made for all inmates above the number of forty. The house had been opened with the intention of enforcing work, and some work was carried on till the dissolution of the union. When Searle retired, in 1799, an inventory of the house was compiled: there were in the spinning-room only "4 wool cards—very bad; 2 old chairs and 3 tubs; 13 spinning-wheels and one reel". A picture of the general deterioration and discomfort is conveyed by the dreary catalogue of "long deal forms", eighteen-

---

[1] The Committee agreed to foot certain charges, such as the clothing of children who were to be apprenticed, and the schoolmaster's weekly bill of 1s. for teaching the three R's to the workhouse children.

[2] The Committee on this occasion paid the legal expenses.

[3] A notice, signed by sixty-eight inhabitants, was fastened to the church door in 1792, offering a reward of £50 for information respecting the authors of the threatening letters. (MS. Vestry Papers, Royston.)

gallon caldrons "in bad condition", water casks and wash trays "very bad indeed".

The advertisement for a new Master in 1803 called forth a volume of replies: there was clearly keen competition in the market. The candidates hailed from all over the southern half of England. One was an illiterate bailiff of Soham; one a sack-maker of Huntingdon; another a pathetic cobbler of Wisbech, whose character the Committee would find "unblemished", should they "think well to make inquiration", but who, "having the misfortune to have the leader of his forefinger growing up, was obliged to think of Somethink Else than Cobbling". Several applicants had previously been workhouse Masters: their desire for information on certain points throws light on prevalent customs: "Are you in want of a single man or married? Does your parishioners mean to employ the said person as Superintendent with an annual salary, or do they intend to farm out the poor?—and whether at so much per head per week, or at a certain sum for the whole year? What is the number of poor, and how employed?" asks the Governor of Hillingdon work-house, on the look-out for a better job. "Who is to pay casualties, county rates, yard-landmen,[1] constables' charges, doctor's bills, small pox, broken bones, bastards, appeals against Removal Orders?" enquires an experienced straw-hat manufacturer of Oxford, who has "kept one Poor House on Contract", and has "managed another in Hertfordshire"."What do you pay to your poor out of the house, weekly or monthly?" queries another applicant from Buckinghamshire. Joseph Noakes of Ardingly poorhouse professes a knowledge of the "Manufacture of Wooll, with the Instructing of Youths in Different Branches of Learning", and his wife "understands Cutting and Making of Clothing, and has a competent Knowledge of Cookery". He is leaving his present post "oweing to a Paupers returning home, who it seems will be put in the House as Governor, in return for his Bord, in order to help lower the tax"!

The practice of sending paupers to a distant contractor was

[1] Roundsmen "going by the yard".

common in some parts of the country. Scott[1] instances a parish which sent its paupers "near twenty miles", despatching them by night "in order to elude the public observation and censure". The rigour of the treatment was such that the number of inmates was reduced to eight in a few years. The custom does not seem to have prevailed in Cambridgeshire, though in the early years of the nineteenth century many towns and parishes, including Royston, received the printed advertisements of contracting firms willing to take the poor on such terms.[2]

The elaborate workhouse accounts kept by the salaried Clerk of Royston yield much information.

In 1802 the Committee had reverted to the system of paying the Master a weekly salary for supervisory services, granting him also the use of the garden, with the dangerous privilege of selling the products to the parish "for the yous of the Hous". The inmates at this date numbered only twenty-five to thirty, and, apart from sex, were classified into three age-groups—the old, the middle-aged or young adults, and the children. There were, in January, ten individuals in each of the first two groups, and five in the last. The income from spinning was about £1. 15s. per month, whilst the total expenditure for the same time, including salary, averaged £26. If the Master and his wife be included, the cost of maintenance in the house averaged 4s. 7d. per head per week. According to the Speenhamland scale a single workman was to have his wages made up to the price of three gallon loaves per week. A peck of bread at Royston in the early months of 1802 varied from 3s. 1d. to 3s. 3d., and a gallon loaf, therefore, cost about 1s. 7d. Hence the expense to the parish of completely maintaining a single man outside the house, on this scale, would have been 4s. 9d. The Speenhamland scale, however, allowed only about half the above amount to a wife and to each additional member of the family. The usual allowance to single women receiving out-relief in Cambridgeshire was about three-quarters that of men. There were seven men, fifteen women and five children in the Royston workhouse in March 1802. On the

[1] Scott, *op. cit.* p. 41.   [2] *Vide* Appendix IV.

Speenhamland scale it would have cost the parish about
£18. 10s. 6d.[1] per month to maintain them in their own homes,
whilst in the house it cost £24. 9s. 3d. Since the scales generally
prevalent in Cambridgeshire were considerably less than the
Speenhamland, the difference between the cost of indoor and outdoor relief was in fact still more marked—hence the inevitable
tendency in most parishes to revert to outdoor relief.

The following quantities of foodstuffs were supplied to the
house in 1802, in the course of one month:

164 lbs. of meat (beef and mutton) at 7½d. to 8d. per lb.
70 pecks of potatoes   at 3½d. to 6d. per peck
44 pecks of bread (88 gallons)[2]   at 3s. 1d. to 3s. 3d. per peck
6¼ pecks of flour   at 3s. to 3s. 2d. per peck
4 lb. of butter   at 1s. 1d. per lb.
3¼ pecks of oatmeal   at 3s. per peck
41 lb. of cheese   at 6d. and 7d. per lb.
4 pecks of peas   at 1s. 10d. per peck
2 ozs. of tea   at 5s. 4d. per lb.

The average allowance of meat per person per week, therefore, was 1½ lb., and of bread just over 7 lb.[3] The official county
allowance to vagrants was commonly 1 lb. of bread per day, or
its equivalent, without meat or extras. The cheese allowance at
Royston was only about ¼ lb. per head per week; peas about
2 quarts; flour ½ gallon; potatoes only 1½ pecks; butter was an
occasional luxury, oil being used for cooking. Soup was bought
at the town soup kitchen at 1d. per quart: the supply of this was
more liberal. "The tea-table", said Scott a generation earlier,
"has in particular been inveighed against as the Box of Pandora,
fraught with all the miseries [the poor] suffer." Neither milk nor
tea appeared on the Royston table except on very rare occasions.

---

[1] Reckoning seven men at 4s. 9d. per week, ten women at three-
quarters of 4s. 9d., and five wives and five children at one-half of 4s. 9d.
[2] The gallon loaf weighed 8 lb. 11 oz.
[3] The magistrates' scale for Cambridge, in 1829, was the price of 10 lb.
of bread per head per week.

Though the house was not under contract at this time the diet was far less generous than was customary. During the harvest season the earnings of the inmates increased four- or five-fold, though pauper labour was paid only at about two-thirds the current rate for independent workers. In the best months of the year the total income from work amounted to no more than a quarter of the expenses of maintenance. During the latter part of 1803 a certain John Shepherd started a small manufactory, or School of Industry, where a dozen of the workhouse children were sent during the day to earn 6*d.* per head per week for spinning.

In 1804 £391 was expended on outdoor relief and £296 on workhouse relief, the combined sum being nearly double that in 1785.

In the course of the next decade the great increase in vagrancy converted the workhouse into little more than a tramp ward. The old union was dissolved in 1819.

Chapter X

THE RURAL WORKHOUSES OF CAMBRIDGE-SHIRE, 1785–1834. PARLIAMENTARY REPORTS OF 1804 AND 1834

A. BOTTISHAM

It is interesting to compare with the urban workhouses of two towns so widely dissimilar in many ways as Cambridge and Royston, the workhouse of an energetic rural parish. In 1786 it was decided that the earlier poorhouse at Bottisham was useless from the point of view of work, and that it was therefore necessary to "erect and establish a workhouse, the poor being numerous and at this time very chargeable". The expense was to be met by a rate. Six adjoining cottages were acquired at Lode and the needful alterations undertaken.[1] The old poorhouse was retained, and one or two aged pensioners who were boarded-out with parishioners were left undisturbed. All poor who were capable of work, however, were offered the house, and the payment of rents by the parish ceased.

A Master was appointed at wages of about £1 per month. His duties at this date were strictly supervisory. There were fifteen paupers in the house in 1787.

If the food purchased by the overseer always reached its correct destination the diet was generous.[2] About 3 lb. of beef

---

[1] They were insured with the Sun Fire Office for £200, at a yearly payment of 10s.

[2] For the four weeks ending July 21st, 1787, the beef bill was as under:

"Carried to the Industry House.					£	s.	d.
June 30th. Beef—5 st. 6 lbs. at 3s. 6d. per stone					19	0	
July 9th. ,, 1 st.	,,	,,	,,		3	6	
,, 14th. ,, 3 st. 9 lbs.	,,	,,	,,		12	9	
,, 21st. ,, 3 st. 6 lbs.	,,	,,	,,		12	1½	
					£2	7	4½ "

per person seems to have been consumed weekly. Limited quantities of beans, eggs, milk, pork, potatoes and ale, and considerable quantities of "seconds" and "thirds" flour appear in the accounts. A suspiciously liberal supply of cheese came from the dairy of Mr Watson, the overseer, whilst the barrels of beer were purchased from Mr Rayment, the other overseer. A "bullocks cheak" often provided the house with soup.

The whole earnings of the inmates were claimed by the parish. The yarn spun in the house was sold through the overseer to Thomas Munns, a wool dealer, who allowed from 4d. to 1s. per lb., apparently according to the quality of the yarn, some of which was probably spun by children—the quantities produced by some workers being small and the rate of pay low. The yarn spun in the month of June 1787 amounted to 90 lb. and the sale price to £3. 4s. 11d. The fifteen workers thus earned about 4s. 4d. per head per month—perhaps two-thirds of their food bill. In August the earnings from spinning dropped to £1. 15s. 5d., "because of the above spiners being in other employment". Ben Rawlingson was sometimes put to sheep-minding and Thomas Skipper to bird-scaring on the private lands of the overseer—for which services the parish paid![1]

The monthly income and expenditure in 1787 averaged as follows:

Weekly pensions (not in workhouse)	£3	15	0
Other expenses, including workhouse	28	11	10½
Money earned by spinning	3	7	0

As so frequently happened, the Master soon found it difficult to exact arduous labour from paupers who had no motive for exertion, or from decrepit ancients. The most amenable inmates were children and these tended to form an ever larger proportion of the residents—as many as twenty-one were housed here in 1788. At this date, upon the appointment of a new Master, the parish adopted the plan of farming-out the poor—the workhouse inmates only—at 1s. 7d. per head per week, the Master claiming

[1] Cf. *supra*, p. 90.

any profits arising from work. Outdoor pensioners were receiving about 2s. per week at this time.

Widowers were allowed to pay for the whole or a part of the board of their children in the workhouse, whilst they themselves were at work—a practice common in other parishes. In 1789, for example, Curtis paid at the rate of 2s. 3d. per week for his two children boarded in the house. The picture of the physical condition of the workhouse children is not enhanced by numerous entries such as the following:

Pd. for cutting Hair and Cleaning boys' Heads, 2s.
Pd. to Jno. Knowls towards curing the Boys, 2s.
Pd. Mary Flack 6s. a year to take care of Childrens Heads at House.

Some of the children were given ½d. or 1d. per week as an incentive to work: the item "childrens gift of 6d. weekly" occurs each month for some years.

At the end of 1790 the contract system was abandoned. Mr Crane, the Master, now bought in the provisions and presented his bills to the overseer. Nine-tenths of the occupants were boys at this date. At the same time an agreement was made with two outside dealers to supply the yarn and to take what profit accrued from the inmates' labour. As Crane had no further interest in the industry of the house much yarn was spoiled through lack of supervision and the arrangement was short-lived. Crane was dismissed and the overseer himself, with the assistance of a pauper widow placed in charge of the children, looked after the spinning. At the end of six months the sale of the yarn had realised no more than £4. 5s. 10d. Fewer children were sent into the workhouse, for the system of making allowances to their parents in aid of wages, or of offering nominal work on the roads, was in vogue at Bottisham before 1795. The habit of herding children together in the "ill-contrived apartments" of a parish workhouse, in daily contact with the querulous, the vicious and the sick, was vigorously censured about this period by Nasmith, Chairman of the Isle of Ely Sessions, and Nasmith's dicta were often quoted outside the

Isle. Even where children were the only occupants, "their emaciated forms, with looks of unavailing sorrow or surly discontent" spoke eloquently of the "melancholy gloom within".[1]

By 1798, when Davis was appointed Superintendent, the building had again become in fact what it now was in name—the "parish house". Davis's duties in the house were insignificant and his time was largely occupied as an assistant overseer.

In 1801 the workhouse was converted into a School of Industry, attended both by children residing there and by children living with their parents. Davis was assisted by a Mrs Pottell. As soon as the children were competent they were paid for their labour—at least those who lived åt home—at the rate of 9d. per week. The expenditure on this account came to £3. 6s. 8d. in June. Hence there must have been some eighty-eight children earning wages, and in July about 117. A glut in the yarn-market brought down the number of little employees to twenty-four in September 1802, at which figure it remained for several years. By 1808 there were about a dozen children working in the house. Soon after this date the building ceased to be occupied except on some occasion of temporary emergency.

B. THE COUNTY PROPOSAL OF 1814—AN "ASYLUM FOR THE POOR"

Before comparing the general position in 1804 with that in 1834, an interesting, though tardy, proposal made by the County Bench may be noted. The desperate position of the agricultural labourer at the beginning of 1814 had led to a serious enquiry, conducted by the county justices within their several divisions, into "the manner of employment, the means of support, and the accommodation afforded the poor both for protection and labour". The reports of the justices came up for earnest discussion at the Easter Quarter Sessions of 1814.

The general conclusion was to the effect that "the large sums

[1] Scott, *op. cit.* p. 45.

collected in every parish" in lieu of making the poor "more industrious, comfortable, and happy", had had most lamentable results in a contrary direction. A return to the principles of Elizabethan legislation was the royal road to salvation— "Instruction for Youth, Reformation for the Profligate, Employment for the Healthy, Comfort for the Aged and Infirm". To this end, therefore, the Bench proposed that parishes should

unite together to form an Establishment upon an extensive scale, where Manufactories of straw, hemp, wool, and leather, most useful for common clothing, could be carried on under the direction of sufficient Instructors, in a situation where good Medical Assistance and Religious Consolation could be readily administered—to be called "An Asylum for the Poor"—wishing to make it altogether a place of refuge or desirable resort to all, in the several parishes so uniting, whose misfortunes, infirmities, or indiscretions have reduced them to wants which their labour cannot supply.

The proposal is full of interest: so far from being a place of deterrence, the "asylum" to be erected by the parishes uniting is to be a place of "desirable resort"—where even the profligate shall willingly seek his own reformation! Whilst quoting the Gilbert Act and echoing its humane sentiment, the magistrates deliberately discard the Gilbertian idea of closing the workhouse door to the able-bodied: the institution they envisage is a "manufactory"—a place of employment, of kindly discipline, of education, as well as of comfort.

The expense attending the erection and fitting-up of departments for "labour, support, and instruction" should be met, the Bench suggest, by the parishes uniting "in the proportion of the disbursements to the poor upon an average of three years last past—the money to be raised upon security of the Poors Rates, and to be liquidated one-twentieth part every year, including the interest".

Copies of the proposal were submitted to the overseers of every parish in the county, with the recommendation that vestry meetings for its consideration should be held, after due notice, in accordance with the requirements of "an Act passed 22 Geo. III, intitled An Act for the better relief and employment of the Poor". The overseers were desired to communicate the vestry decisions to the Clerk of the Peace before the next meeting of the Bench. At the July Sessions it was duly reported "that of the parishes which had made returns,[1] a majority was averse to the forming of such an establishment". So ended the final attempt to form unions before 1834.

C. THE PARLIAMENTARY RETURNS OF 1804[2]

1804. Returns for County of Cambs. (175 parishes)		Returns for Isle of Ely (34 parishes)
Total expenditure in all work-houses of county	£9974	£6353
Rate per head per annum	£11	
Total expenditure on out-relief	£44,510	£12,256
Rate per head per annum	£4	
Expense in procuring materials for employing the poor in the house	£16	£1. 7s.
Money earned by workhouse poor and accounted for to the parish	£759	£393

In the nineteenth century, as in the eighteenth, the workhouse played a far more prominent part in the life of the poor within the franchise of Ely than within the county proper. Two-thirds of the total sum spent on workhouses in the whole county (inclusive of the Isle and of the town of Cambridge) was spent within the Isle. In the latter area, moreover, workhouse charges formed half of the total expense of poor relief; whilst in the rest of the county it formed less than a quarter. Of 34 parishes in the Isle 19[3] had a workhouse in 1804; of 127 parishes in the

[1] Thirty-three parishes and one hamlet.
[2] *Returns relative to the Expense and Maintenance of the Poor in England,* 1804.
[3] Nine had been founded since 1776.

county only 18 had a workhouse.[1] The average number of paupers per workhouse in the Isle was 27·5; in the rest of the county it was 14. Whilst there were 522 workhouse inmates in the Isle, in the whole of rural Cambridgeshire outside this area there were but 258.

The only workhouses in which there were more than 20 inmates were as follows:

In the Isle of Ely:

Wisbech St Peter	139	residents
Thorney	73	,,
Whittlesey	65	,,
Ely Trinity	49	,,

In Cambs., outside the Isle:

Soham	55	,,
Burwell	30	,,

Though the *per capita* charges in the workhouse were, on an average, double those of outdoor relief, in the majority of places both in the county and in the Isle the total expenditure on workhouse paupers was far less than on those residing at home. Exceptional conditions were to be found in the following parishes:

Parish	Expenditure on workhouse	Expenditure on other relief
In the county:		
Whittlesford	£207	£156
Soham	753	841
In the Isle:		
Elm	474	227
Outwell	119	24
Thorney	943	386
Upwell	209	159
Witcham	84	52
Haddenham	333	320
Trinity Ely	849	852
Wisbech St Peter	1261	1416

[1] Eight had been built since 1776, though four of the earlier ones had ceased to exist.

Very little money was spent by parochial authorities, either in franchise or county, on the purchase of materials for setting the poor to work, but materials were in some cases furnished by private employers and field labour was also given. The table on p. 121 sets forth the particulars concerning all such parishes as benefited directly by pauper labour; in other cases where money was earned it went to the contractors.

Five parishes in the county and four in the Isle farmed their workhouses in 1804.[1]

There were ten Schools of Industry in the whole of Cambridgeshire. Four of these were in the Isle of Ely and one in Great St Andrew's parish, Cambridge. Only about 140 children were in attendance at these schools, the largest of which was at Wisbech and accommodated thirty children.

D. SURVEY OF THE WORKHOUSES IN 1834

The Reports of the three Commissioners—Cowell, Everett and Power—who conducted enquiries in different parts of Cambridgeshire and the Isle during the years 1832 and 1833, contain scattered information on the subject of workhouses, but it is impossible to compile from the Reports a complete list of the institutions existing at that date.

Of twenty-six parishes investigated in the rural county proper five had what was called a workhouse. Only Orwell was reported as having a "poorhouse", but in 1834 it is probable that other parishes also had mere poorhouses which were not mentioned. In the Isle of Ely sixteen out of seventeen parishes examined had a workhouse, but they had become in most instances "asylums for the old and the children".

Most workhouses within the Isle were farmed in 1834, the contractor being allowed to employ the poor and to take the profits, which, however, "amounted to little", the work being usually the cultivation of the garden or land attached to the

---

[1] In the whole of England the proportion of workhouses farmed at this date was about one in fifty.

Parish	Money expended on materials		Parish	Money earned by paupers and accounted for to parish	
	Out of house	In house		Out of house	In house
	£ s. d.	£ s. d.		£ s. d.	£ s. d.
Chesterton	4 0 8	—	Woodditton	—	45 0 0
Bourn	2 3	1 6 3	Bourn	15 7 6	42 6 0
Longstanton	18 0	—	Over	76 14 8	—
Milton	—	13 6 3	Burwell	—	61 19 8¾
Brinkley	5 0	—	Isleham	—	35 10 0¼
Orwell	1 4	—	Soham	—	115 6 10½
			Harlton	8 3 6	—
			Whittlesford	4 18 0	—
Total for Cambs.	£5 7 3	£14 12 6	Total for Cambs.	£105 3 8	£300 2 7½
Downham	16 7½	15 0 0	Newton	9 2	—
Upwell	4 0	12 0 0	Upwell	32 14 2	—
Total for Isle of Ely	£1 0 7½	£1 7 0	Total for Isle of Ely	£33 3 4	—

workhouse. Almost without exception the workhouses in the Isle were "remarkably clean", being "whitewashed always once, and sometimes twice and thrice a year". The diet was good—meat three days, and cheese or soup the remainder of the week for the midday meal. In a few instances schools were attached, and in some few other cases the workhouse children attended the local Charity Schools. Most frequently, however, children obtained no education, for they were sent out during the day to sift stones, to weed, or to glean, as soon as they were old enough to earn a few pence.

Very few able-bodied paupers were to be found regularly in the workhouses of the Isle. During the winter the idle and vagrant poor tended to drift into the house, whence it was difficult to get rid of them. They were not encouraged to enter, but no differential treatment marked them out from the impotent. Paupers, it was said, took advantage of this reluctance to send them to the house to get their rents paid by the parish. "A man goes to the overseer near rent day", reported Everett, "and says he will let the landlord distrain if the rent is not paid for him, and go into the workhouse. Magistrates usually impose the obligation of providing shelter",[1] and the man gets his way.

The inhabitants of March,[2] alarmed at a rent bill of £400 annually, had just built a new workhouse where a strict regimen was observed—the classes were separated and all were confined to the bounds of the workhouse. A Keeper was engaged who undertook to make the work really arduous and to farm the inmates at a less sum per head than they could be maintained outside. Seventeen acres of good land attached to the house were granted him, free of rates and taxes, and so rigorously did he carry out his agreement that the able-bodied rarely remained. The rent bill dropped to £100 the first year. The enthusiastic Commissioner did not, however, enquire what was to happen to the contractor when his remaining employees consisted only of the sick, the aged and the infants, or how harsh conditions

[1] *P.L.C. Rept.* 1834, App. A, Pt. 1, p. 678. (Everett's Report.)
[2] *Ibid.*

affected these classes. The profits to be derived from the land were very considerable, for it was worth £3. 10s. to £4 per acre. It would therefore pay the contractor to rely upon independent labour and to reduce the number of inmates to a minimum by every device which severity could suggest.

At Wisbech also the workhouse was reported as "not ill-regulated".

In the parishes outside the Isle of Ely the contract system was less in vogue. In general the workhouses partook "more of the class of lodging-houses, there being no employment there". Weekly wages were commonly paid to the Master and a separate allowance made to the inmates. In many of these houses the scenes of filth and promiscuity in 1834 were precisely such as had aroused the eloquent denunciation of Micklebourgh and Scott three-quarters of a century earlier.

Chapter XI

SETTLEMENT AND REMOVAL, 1660–1834

A. THE ACT OF 1662. ITS EARLY WORKING. LATER LEGISLATION

Throughout the whole of the period from 1601 to 1662 "destitution was supported wheresoever it was found, without any such interference with the labour of the poor and with their personal freedom as it was reserved for the restoration of Charles II to sanction, and for subsequent ages to deplore".[1]

The view which thus interprets as a revolutionary break with the tradition of the preceding sixty years the settlement policy inaugurated in 1662 is of course no longer tenable.[2] Legally, it is true, the vagrant poor alone were removable after the Act of 1597, but Sir Francis Harvey had found it necessary, at the Cambridge Summer Assizes of 1629, to admonish justices not to "meddle either with the removing or setling of any poor, but only of rogues",[3] and attention has already been drawn to the growth in Cambridgeshire, during the earlier part of the seventeenth century, of a restrictive attitude towards the stranger on the part of both urban and parochial authorities.

The so-called "Settlement Law" of 13 and 14 Chas. II was indeed an almost inevitable development of the Act of 1601 itself, for since the Elizabethan statute definitely recognised the parish as responsible for the provision of the poor by a compulsory rate, it was certain that should difficulty be found in furnishing the necessary funds, the instinct of self-preservation would raise the query: "Who then are the poor of the parish?" The inefficiency which characterised parochial organisation in the years imme-

[1] Pashley, *Pauperism and Poor Laws* (1852), p. 218.

[2] Cf. The Petition to the Justices of Wilts for Permission to Settle in a Parish, 1618. (Quoted by Brown, Bland and Tawney, *Select Documents* (1925 ed.), p. 382.)

[3] M. Dalton, *The Country Justice* (1630 ed.), p. 98.

diately preceding the Act of 1662 necessarily involved a serious strain upon the rates, with the consequent desire to limit the claimants upon them to the utmost degree. The Settlement Law of 1662 thus became the flywheel around which the Poor Law revolved for more than a century and a half—"turning the question from how to provide for [the poor] into who shall provide for them", and raising thereby "such a spirit of shifting, instead of honest industry in the kingdom, that it has cost many a parish as much to remove one poor person, as it would have done to maintain ten".[1]

By the terms of the statute it became lawful,

upon complaint made by the churchwardens and overseers of the poor of any parish, to any Justice of the Peace, within forty days after any such person or persons coming so to settle, as aforesaid, in any tenement under the yearly value of ten pounds, for any two Justices of the Peace, whereof one to be of the Quorum of the division,…by their warrant to remove and convey such person or persons to such parish where he or they were last legally settled either as a native, householder, sojourner, apprentice or servant for the space of forty days at the least, unless he or they give sufficient security for the discharge of the said parish, to be allowed by the said Justices.

Other sections of the Act gave right of appeal to Quarter Sessions and permitted persons to go for the harvest into another parish, provided they had a certificate of settlement granted by their own parish.

The really vital part of the law was the granting of arbitrary power to remove practically any person of labourer's rank merely in the expectation that he would become chargeable to the rates, according to the capricious verdict of two justices. Whilst doubt may be thrown upon the extent to which able-bodied labour actually was rendered immobile, the Act was in truth the origin of many of the evils which the Poor Law inflicted on the country in the course of succeeding generations.

[1] Thos. Cooper, *Observations upon the Vagrant Laws* (1742), p. 19.

The principle of removal was certainly not new, but if settlement restrictions were severe in the late sixteenth and early seventeenth centuries, efforts to provide work, to control prices and to prevent oppression of one class by another were equally vigorous. In 1662 paternal authority was unaccompanied by paternal care: public opinion on the whole subject of poverty had undergone a radical change.

The Preamble to the Act of 1662 itself states definitely that the main reason for the enactment was the unequal provision of work for the unemployed, whereby parishes which endeavoured to do their duty in this respect were inundated by distressed strangers. Although unemployment was not a widespread menace in rural Cambridgeshire at this date, statutory wages rarely met the needs of a large family. Even before the Act of 1662 it was the unstable position of the married labourer which was the crux of the settlement problem.

A formal Justices' removal order for the year 1665 exists among the vestry papers of St Bene't's parish, Cambridge: evidently the authority given by the Act was occasionally exercised thus early, though no sudden change of policy is manifest. It was not for some five years after the passing of the Act that even the assembled Bench made any close study of its peculiar implications. In 1667 for the first time the wording of their order, in the disputed settlement of one "Margaret Palley, spinster, who endeavoureth to settle herselfe an Inhabitant in the towne of Wivelingham", follows very closely the actual phraseology of the statute.[1] The illegal action of the parish officers complained of in this suit displays their unfamiliarity also with the exact procedure to be adopted.[2] There were ten cases[3] of disputed removal brought before the Court in the

---

[1] Later orders continued to do so, somewhat lengthily, until the procedure had apparently become settled.

[2] They had illegally returned the woman sent to them by a removal order, in lieu of appealing to Court.

[3] The inhabitants of Chesterton, for example, complained that Baker, with his wife and family, had lately come to inhabit in the said "Towne",

PLATE VII

City of NORWICH,
and
County of the same City

To the Churchwardens and Overseers of the Poor of the parish of *Saint Peter Southgate* in the City and County aforesaid, to remove: and to the Churchwardens and Overseers of the Poor of the parish of *Royston in the County of Hartford* to receive and obey

WHEREAS complaint hath been made by you, the churchwardens and overseers of the poor of the parish of *Saint Peter Southgate* unto us whose hands and seals are hereunto set, two of his Majesty's Justices of the peace (one of the Quorum) for the city and county aforesaid, That *William Cooke Labourer and Elizabeth his Wife and Mary and Thomas their Children have* lately intruded themselves into your said parish of *Saint Peter Southgate* there to inhabit as your parishioners, contrary to the laws relating to the settlement of the poor, and that *they are* there become chargeable. And whereas upon due examination upon oath and enquiry made into the premises, it appears unto us, and we accordingly adjudge that the said *William Cooke, Elizabeth, Mary and Thomas are* become chargeable unto the said parish of *Saint Peter Southgate* and we do adjudge that the legal place of settlement of the said *William Cooke Elizabeth Mary and Thomas* is in the parish of *Royston in the County of Hartford*

Roger Herrison Mayor

THESE ARE THEREFORE in his Majesty's name to order and require you the said churchwardens and overseers of the poor of the parish of *Saint Peter Southgate* aforesaid, that you, or some of you do forthwith remove and convey the said *William Cooke Elizabeth Mary and Thomas* from your said parish of *Saint Peter Southgate* to the parish of *Royston* aforesaid, and them deliver to the churchwardens and overseers of the poor there, or some or one of them, together with this our warrant, or order, or a true copy thereof; whereby they are likewise required in his Majesty's name, and by virtue of the statutes in such case made, forthwith to receive the said *William Cooke, Elizabeth Mary and Thomas* into the said parish, and provide for *them as their* own parishioners.

John Browne

GIVEN under our hands and seals the *Nineteenth* day of *September* in the *forty Second* year of the reign of our sovereign Lord *George the Third* by the grace of God of Great Britain, and so forth, King, Defender of the Faith, and so forth, and in the year of our Lord one thousand eight hundred *and two*

Bacon, Printer, Norwich

REMOVAL ORDER, 1802

three years immediately preceding the Act of 1662, and for some three or four years after this date judgments continued to be given with more regard for custom and equity than for rigid legality. In 1665, for instance, it was ordered that Elizabeth Cropley, "a poor child", should be allowed to remain in the parish where she was best known, though this was not in strict accordance with the requirements of the new law. Settlement disputes were still at times referred for decision to two or three local justices,[1] though the subject presently became too thorny a one for such simple procedure.

On the whole the Cambridgeshire Bench endeavoured at first to interpret the law favourably to the circulation of labour. Nathaniel Astwood, in 1664, hired himself for a year to a master living at Croxton and after some six months' service married. His master raised no objection, but the overseer instantly demanded that the man should enter into a bond to indemnify the parish against any possible charge upon its rates. The Court decreed that Astwood be allowed to settle at Croxton without giving security. In January 1665 the parish of Knapwell ousted Mary Lutt from her service there: the Court ordered her to be permitted to return. The magistrates were not so lenient in the case of Thomas Cock who, having purchased a small copyhold at Shelford, proposed to settle in the parish. The Bench adjudged that the man should either enter into bond with the parish or be removed, for it was not till 1723[2] that the possession of an estate gave statutory security against removal.

After about 1665 the Court in fact began to line itself more frequently on the side of parochial authority: it was in this year that the demolition of small cottage property—"the nests of beggars' brats"—was countenanced in no less than eight disputed cases. Nevertheless there are fewer instances in rural

and was "likely to prove a charge". The Bench ordered him to give security, failing which the constables were authorised to take him before two justices who were desired to make out an order for removal to his "place of last abode".

[1] Cf. *infra*, p. 226.   [2] Cf. *supra*, p. 73, note.

Cambridgeshire of this effect of the Settlement Laws than in many counties. Here and there, where the parish was in the hands of one proprietor or of a very limited number who could act, or compel the tenants to act, in unison, the practice was adopted. A flagrant example occurred at a later date.[1] A proprietor possessing nearly the whole of a parish at some distance from Ely hired a farm at Ely, which he managed by a bailiff. He sent his own parishioners to work on this farm, demolishing the cottages left vacant by their transportation. Settlements by hiring were thus acquired, and at the end of the year the labourers were turned off upon Trinity parish, Ely, and their places supplied by a fresh immigration from the employer's parish. It would be difficult to imagine a more effective method of producing casual labour and pauperisation and of discouraging all aspirations towards a settled and prosperous home life.

A bond of £10 was demanded of Francis Kibble, in 1670, before he was authorised by the Bench to settle at Landbeach. This was the sum usually regarded as a sufficient guarantee at this date; hence many folk were in practice enabled to move whom an annual rental of £10 would have prohibited.[2]

Even as late as 1670 settlement procedure had not become stereotyped in Cambridgeshire,[3] but by 1690 a rigid devotion

[1] *P.L.C. Rept.* 1834, App. A, Pt. 1, p. 594.

[2] Wisbech had demanded bonds in the sixteenth and seventeenth centuries. For example, in 1624, "the Bailife deliverd in a bond of Stephen Chapman wth Condicōn that John Chapman shall not be Chargeable to the Towne nor his Wife nor Children". Three other similar bonds were demanded the same year. (MS. Corp. Minute and Order Book, Wisbech.) In 1704 the parish officers of Histon demanded a £40 bond before allowing Elizabeth Hepwell to settle there. This parish was peculiarly insistent upon securing itself against possible charges of various descriptions. (MS. Vestry Papers, Histon.)

[3] In lieu of applying for a warrant to two local justices, the parish of Bourn, for example, in 1670 appealed directly to the Court, which merely issued a warning to Matthew Wiseman, the poor man concerned, that if he did not return with his family to Gravely he would be summoned before the local magistrates.

to law characterised the removals which were taking place with rapidly increasing frequency.[1]

It was recognised by the Legislature, in 1692,[2] that the settlement policy pressed too hard on the labouring classes, and with a view to extending somewhat the means of acquiring a settlement, the statute of that year appointed two alternative modes:

(i) Payment of the parish rates for a year.

(ii) Election to an annual parish office, with due service in such capacity for the whole year.

The whole vestry being aware of a newcomer's intention, it was, of course, easy to prevent settlement under either of the above heads.[3] By the same Act of 1692 certain ambiguities were removed with respect to the acquisition of a settlement by serving apprenticeship in the parish and by formal hiring and service for a full year. Married men, however, were expressly excluded from gaining a settlement by hiring.

Legislation and legal interpretations during the next century and a half introduced numerous modifications in the exact definition of the terms according to which a man was bound to his parish, but the practical effect of such changes was in the main merely to add to the complexity of the law[4] and to increase legal expenses. So complicated did the problem of settlement become that more than a third of the cases taken before the Cambridgeshire Court could not be settled at their first hearing. The chequered career of the Loader family—a mother and three children—may be cited as an illustration of the preposterous extent to which removals and counter-removals were sometimes

---

[1] No Quarter Sessions Records are extant for the years between 1672 and 1689. The large part which Poor Law administration as a whole played in the work of the Bench is evinced by the fact that of 374 entries in the minutes of Quarter Sessions, for the period between 1660 and 1672, 196 concern the poor.   [2] 3 W. III, c. 2.

[3] By an Act of 1689 (1 Jas. II, c. 17) the forty days were to count from the giving of notice to the parish officer, and by a later Act of 1692 (3 W. & M., c. 2) the notice was to be delivered in writing.

[4] In 1834, for example, there were no less than five heads under which settlement by renting alone could be acquired.

carried. Whatever the condition of the victims to begin with, permanent pauperisation and vagrancy were too often, in such cases, the ultimate outcome. The mother died before the final fate of the family was settled, and the children were removed and counter-removed no less than seven times between 1704 and 1708.[1] The incalculable injury inflicted upon the paupers themselves is apt to be lost sight of amid the maze of legalities, and in the actual life of the time the provision of relief did indubitably fall into the background. Uncared-for orphan children, like the little Loaders, snatched from the only friends they had ever known, were tossed hither and thither by those bent only on shifting the burden to other shoulders. Given not even the doubtful training of pauper apprenticeship, to what future could they look but the scrap-heap of destitution? "We shall take no further notice of the child you brought to Royston", callously wrote the vestry clerk of Royston to the overseers of Deptford, and instances of this attitude might be multiplied manifold.

Two exceptions to the above generalisation concerning the effect of later settlement legislation must, however, be noted— the system of certification, presently to be discussed, and the important amelioration introduced by the Act of 1795, whereby removal, except in the case of pregnant single women, was prohibited until the pauper had actually applied for public relief.[2] By a further clause in the Act of 1795 removal might be postponed in case of sickness, the interim expenses being chargeable to the parish of legal settlement.

B. THE RELATIVE ACTIVITY OF THE REMOVAL POLICY AT DIFFERENT PERIODS

An examination of all the cases of disputed settlement coming before the Court of Quarter Sessions for Cambridgeshire between 1660 and 1830 reveals a rapid increase up to about 1730.

[1] MS. Q.S.R. Cambs. 1704–8.

[2] Attempts were sometimes still made to remove before chargeability had occurred, e.g. a case recorded in the *Cambridge Chronicle*, October 1825.

The growing complexity of the law certainly multiplied disputes, but there was probably also an increase in the number of actual removals during these years. The comparative prosperity of the mid-century years partly accounts for a diminution in appeals, but at this date a lawyer was regularly employed by many parishes, and overseers themselves were sufficiently conversant with the law to avoid certain of the ill-considered appeals of early years. After 1796 other influences were at work. The "allowance system" was in full operation, and though the increased pressure upon the rates rendered the overseer doubly anxious to eliminate all who had no legal claim upon the parish, the pauper himself was drugged by a system of relief which paralysed his independence and made him less desirous of quitting his one secure haven. Moreover, the prohibition of removals until actual chargeability had occurred probably did, after 1795, result in some diminution in the number of paupers removed, though the system of certification and the custom of allowing paupers to reside in alien parishes at the cost of the parish owning them as settled inhabitants were already working in the same direction. It is true that the decade 1816–26 witnessed a temporary doubling of appeals in Cambridgeshire, but to post-war depression were added at this date the settlement complexities arising from the disbanding of soldiers, many of whom had contracted dubious marital obligations during the war.

C. THE MODE OF PROCEDURE. ITS MODIFICATION IN PRACTICE

The legal mode of procedure by which appeals were carried through added needlessly to the expense. Upon complaint of the parish officers an examination of the persons concerned was made by two local justices.[1] Immediately the *ex parte* order was

[1] The difficulty often experienced in determining even the actual facts is repeatedly manifest in the records of examinations—the first draft of which is sometimes corrected several times before it assumes its final form. This is particularly true in the case of habitual vagrants.

signed the pauper was removed to the parish of alleged settlement, which only after receiving him became entitled to appeal to Quarter Sessions.[1] If appeal were made and the order successfully quashed, the second parish obtained an order from the justices of the locality for re-removal to the parish which had sent the pauper, which parish might either abide by the decision, or make a further attempt upon some other parish. An order confirmed upon appeal was absolutely binding, but an order quashed determined the issue only as between the two contending parties.[2] Even if quashed for mere "want of form", not till 1732 could the technical error be rectified without repeating the whole elaborate procedure.[3]

In the rebutting by the respondent parish of an alleged settlement it was very common for a third parish to become involved. By a system of due notification the case for all three parishes could have been heard at one sessions. A bill of 1819 clearly recognised the ease with which the futile procedure could be remedied and attention was again drawn to the matter in the Report of 1834, but the "combination of persons interested in creating litigation and expense" held its own till the middle of the nineteenth century.

Before the Settlement Law of 1662 came into being the actual

---

[1] Appeals were nearly always prosecuted by the parish, but in 1750 an individual—John Pitslow—successfully appealed against his own removal from Great St Andrew's, Cambridge, to Littlebury. A similar case occurred in 1804. (MS. Q.S.R. Cambs.)

[2] There are cases recorded among the Cambs. Quarter Sessions orders which appear to be breaches of this ruling. In April 1703, for example, Grantchester appealed against an order granted for the removal of Susan Gryper from Barrington to Grantchester, and the warrant was quashed. An appeal concerning the same two parishes was again lodged the following July against the same order and on this occasion it was confirmed. Seven months were held by the King's Bench to be an insufficient time for new circumstances to arise: in this case only three months had elapsed. There are similar instances later.

[3] Appeals were fairly frequently "quashed for want of form" in Cambs. before 1732. Advantage was taken of the new Act for the first time in 1743.

removal of a pauper had often, in Cambridgeshire, awaited the verdict of the Court, and this sensible practice persisted for some few years later. Thus, for example, in 1663, the three parishes of Willingham, Over and Swavesey were all concerned in the settlement of Anne Baron: the matter was referred by the Bench to three justices of the localities and the woman remained where she was pending their decision.

Normally the legal procedure was followed in later years, but there were exceptions.[1]

After about the middle of the eighteenth century, moreover, in actual practice the merits of the case were frequently considered in an unofficial manner by the parishes concerned before it was decided to bear the expenses of litigation. The overseer of Little St Andrew's parish, Cambridge, for example, writes in 1827 to the overseer of St Bene't's suggesting that the two parishes should jointly submit the case of John Hawes and his family—"a case of some novelty"—to some "eminent counsel", and thus obviate the unnecessary expense of an erroneous removal. St Bene't's overseer replied asking first for a joint conference between the respective parish officers. Several such meetings took place, with the final result that St Bene't's officers were satisfied that the order could not successfully be contested and agreed to receive Hawes and his family. An account for the maintenance of the paupers during the period of investigation was amicably paid by St Bene't's.

In 1784 the parish of Doddington was called upon to receive a certain George Taylor, sent by a removal order from another parish in the Isle of Ely. Upon examination it now seemed that Taylor had served an apprenticeship in St Bene't's parish, Cambridge, but the overseer of Doddington was wary of putting the

[1] At the April Sessions of 1708, for instance, the parish of Kirtling appealed against an order for the conveyance of Ann Freak and her five children from Stetchworth and the case was respited till the following July. At this date it was again respited, "Ann Freak and her children in the meantime to remain at Stetchworth until next Sessions". Apparently, therefore, the family remained at Stetchworth throughout the proceedings. There are other similar instances.

parish to the expense of a mistaken removal and wrote to St Bene't's asking for an investigation to be made into the alleged service. "Sir," replies the overseer of St Bene't's, "I waited on Mr Sharpe a Barber and Peruke Maker in our Parish with your letter. He says George Taylor never was an apprentice to him, nor served him in any shape, and likewise says he knows not any thing of him. Gentlemen, I Judge you are imposed upon by this man."

Correspondence of this nature bulks large among vestry papers after about 1750.

The more alert urban vestries were beginning to exercise caution even at an earlier date. In 1717 Great St Mary's prohibited the lodging of any appeals without full discussion by the vestry, and a little later forbade the overseers even to apply for removal orders without such discussion. St Bene't's vestry issued similar instructions about the same time.

Many parish officers adopted the practice of bringing all paupers arriving by a removal warrant before the justices for full examination, and in very many other cases a most careful magisterial investigation took place, which was by no means always followed by the issue of a removal order.[1] Nevertheless there were many occasions on which the examination was merely nominal. The case of Widow Samwell illustrates this fact and at the same time exemplifies the brutality to which the settlement policy all too often led. The widow was employed in St Edward's parish, Cambridge, and managed to maintain herself and two children until one of them was stricken with small-pox and she was compelled to relinquish her job. In dire distress she sought the overseer, who hurried her to the nearest justices. She was put through a perfunctory examination and it was determined that her place of settlement was Battle, in Sussex. An order for her instant removal thither was made out. A waggon was chartered, the owner undertaking to deliver his human freight within three

---

[1] The statement that a warrant was "usually issued as a matter of course", upon complaint by the parish officers, is far too sweeping. (Webb, *op. cit.* p. 327.)

days. Jolted in an unsprung vehicle, along roads notorious for their impassable condition, the wretched family were exposed to the full blast of a February day. When the waggoner pulled up for the night, on the hither side of London, one of the children was dead. The miserable cortège was hurried along the following day. Upon its arrival at Battle the parish officers were compelled to bury the dead child and to provide shelter and medical attendance for the survivors. It became evident, however, after investigation, that Battle was not legally responsible. The atmosphere cleared immediately, for by this date—it was at the close of the eighteenth century—expenditure incurred under an erroneous removal was recoverable. The inoculation of the remaining child was ordered, and groceries and clothing were provided on a scale far more generous than would have been allowed by Battle authorities to their own legal poor. St Edward's officers were notified that an appeal was impending, the accumulation of evidence began, and the lawyers were happy.

Attending the parish officers on the paupers being delivered; Consulting if adviseable to appeal,   6s. 8d.

Upon agreeing to an appeal, delivering notice to ye Officers of St Edwards,   6s. 8d.

Drawing notice and copys,
Attending the Officer next Monday,   3s. 4d.

Writing a letter to Mr Pemberton, Clerk of the Peace, for information as to the Sessions being held, and to recommend a gentleman to conduct the appeal,   3s. 4d.

Making inquiries in the parish of Battle, if any person of the name of Samwell lived in the place as a Servant, or if his parents ever lived in the parish. Searching Parish Registers of births, marriages, and burials,   13s. 4d.

And so the fees mounted. At this point, however, St Edward's officers awoke to the reality of the hornets' nest which buzzed about their ears, and finding their position untenable before the law, hastily desired the officers of Battle to withdraw the case and promised to receive the paupers back again without the intervention of the Court. The total expenditure on the transport to Battle, medical attendance and burial, maintenance during the sojourn at Battle, lawyer's charges and re-transport to Cambridge, would have maintained the family at home for more than two years and might easily have been avoided had a careful investigation been made in the first instance. In any case the sickness of the child would have justified the examining magistrate in suspending the order according to the Act of 1795.

D. SUSPENSION OF ORDERS. EXPENSES

Previous to 1795 overseers' accounts often record the death of a pauper occasioned by his deportation from some other parish.

Elizabeth Pamplin, a sick woman, was removed in 1758 from Kirtling to Weston Colville by order of sessions. The latter parish perforce had to receive her, but promptly lodged a counter-appeal. The lawyer's expenses run thus:

Warrant to defend the appeal,	£0. 3s. 4d.
Writing a letter to Mr Rushbrook to inform him when the sessions were to be held,	£0. 0s. 0d.
Postage of his answer,	£0. 0s. 4d.
Pd to the Clerk of the Peace for Subpoena,	£0. 2s. 6d.
Drawing notice for officers of Weston Colville to produce the pauper,	£0. 6s. 8d.

At this point the account abruptly terminates by the laconic note: "but the pauper was dead".

The power to suspend removal orders in case of sickness certainly was used after 1795. The parish of legal settlement, however, frequently betrayed a pressing desire to curtail the suspension period within the strictest limits, for expenditure by the non-responsible parish was apt in such cases to be lavish. Joseph Young, for example, "Pleance, his wife, and fore Children", were ordered to be removed from Upwell to Littleport. The wife was near her confinement and the magistrate consequently suspended the Warrant. Eighteen days later the child was born. The doctor's bill amounted to £1. 2s. 6d. There is no record of repeated medical visits and the case was apparently quite normal, yet the family remained at Upwell for nearly four months before the suspension was cancelled. Apart from the doctor's bill, the groceries together with the money allowed to the family amounted to 17s. 9d. weekly. According to the scale in vogue for settled parishioners the allowance for a man with his wife and five children would have been 16s. 6d. per week.

Many heavy doctors' bills were incurred in similar circumstances. An account for numerous "decoctions" and visits, amounting to about 3s. 6d. per day for several weeks, was presented by a certain Dr Crispin of Ware to the overseers of Royston. It was hardly surprising that the doctor was still clamouring for its payment some eleven months later, having sent in repeated accounts in the interim.

The simple removal of a pauper cost on an average several pounds in the mid-eighteenth century. The Court charges to be met by Burwell in consequence of a settlement appeal, in 1802, came to £27; an appeal prosecuted by Royston, in 1781, cost £9. 12s. 10d., representing about the average expenditure in such cases. For the county as a whole removal affairs, in 1776, engrossed one forty-ninth of the total Poor Law expenses; by 1785 the proportion had risen to one twenty-eighth; in 1804 it was one thirty-fifth. In the university town itself the economies practised between 1785 and 1804 were more effective, the relative proportions having fallen from 1 in 19 in 1785 to 1 in 650 of the total expenditure upon the poor in 1804.[1]

E. WHO WERE REMOVED

It has sometimes been asked whether, prior to 1795, expulsion really did commonly take place before the pauper sought public

[1] E. M. Hampson, "Settlement and Removal in Cambs. 1662–1834" (*Camb. Hist. Journ.* vol. II, no. 3, 1928).

relief. In a large proportion of Cambridgeshire cases the parish did not wait for such a contingency to arise. In some parishes the distinction between those persons who had and those who had not yet fallen upon the rates is clearly marked. Where circumstances demanded it, the printed formula "likely to be chargeable" is deleted and replaced by the phrase "hath already been chargeable".[1] Evidence to the same effect abounds in the correspondence between overseers and men faced with the prospect of removal. In the archives of the county there are many cases recorded in which honest, industrious labourers, in actual employment, were adjudged by the magistrates "likely to be chargeable".

Thomas Hampson, a young wheelwright of Royston, was examined before the magistrates in 1735. He was a native of Henbury, in Staffordshire, and had served his full apprenticeship in the neighbouring parish of Lee. He had then obtained journeyman work in Rutland, but soon after his marriage with a widow there had been threatened with removal to Lee. Hampson, who had not yet lost his independence, departed on his own initiative, and accompanied by his wife arrived at Royston. As an able mechanic he succeeded in gaining weekly employment—a form of terminable service by which Royston customarily defended itself against settlers. The man soon came under the notice of the vigilant overseer, and after examination was ruthlessly despatched to Lee, although he was in actual employment at Royston, whilst there was not the slightest guarantee that work would be procurable in the village he had quitted over a twelvemonth before.[2]

It was certain classes of people, however, that the law hit most directly. Newcomers of a shady character, in obvious duresse or ill-health, and—more important perhaps than any—married men with families, were the prey upon which the vultures swooped mercilessly.

---

[1] Hinxton was an exception. During the mid-eighteenth century this parish removed only those who were "now chargeable".

[2] MS. Vestry Papers—Justices' Examinations, Royston.

So long as he was not allowed to gain a settlement, a single, or professedly single man, of able body, was in fact by no means necessarily an unwelcome newcomer, for there was always the possibility of his marriage to some drug on the parochial market, who thereby acquired the settlement of her husband and could be removed when occasion arose. Occasion did often arise, in the judgment of the parish, so soon as there were signs of a family. Sometimes even this event was not awaited and removal of the newly-wed couple took place immediately; in other cases no steps were taken until a second child had arrived. Hampson had been welcome enough before marriage. Jasper Fell, a Barkway labourer aged twenty, found temporary work at Royston. "Married yesterday to Mary Hemingford", recorded the justice who gave the order to move on. John Brown, another Barkway labourer, came in 1702 to the parish of Swaffham Prior and there fell beneath the spell of a woman with a bastard child. The overseer lay low till the wedding was safely accomplished, then promptly procured a warrant for the removal of the pair to Barkway.

It is impossible to peruse the numerous records of folk brought for examination before Cambridgeshire justices without recognising the extent to which labour did circulate in spite of the Settlement Laws.

In the years between 1660 and 1831 some 945 appeals against removal orders came before the Cambridgeshire Quarter Sessions. Of these cases less than one-eighth were concerned with unmarried men, whilst no less than one-third related to men with families—or over a half if married men without children be included. Within a few months of marriage the overseer was dogging the steps of the labourer: more than a third of the married men who were removed had not yet become parents, and in the majority of the remaining cases they were removed as unable, or likely to be unable, to maintain their families so soon as the third child was on the way—striking testimony to the inadequacy of labourers' wages to meet the needs of a family.

The following statistics are compiled from the records of Quarter Sessions of the county from 1660 to 1831:[1]

Total no. of Appeals	Men only	Women only	Men with wives only	Men with families	Average no. of children in family before removal
884	105 ($\frac{1}{8}$–)	179 ($\frac{1}{5}$–)	154 ($\frac{1}{6}$–)	294 ($\frac{1}{3}$)	2·4

It will be seen that women—single or widowed—also form a markedly important group.

One natural result of the discouragement offered by the Settlement Laws to legitimate marriage was a serious increase in immorality. The legal place of settlement of a bastard was, until 1744, that of birth. Frankly brutal efforts were in consequence made to pass on pregnant single women before the birth of the child should settle it upon the parish. Of examples of this policy the overseers' account books are full.

Some 1155 removal orders, covering the period 1665 to 1834, have been unearthed in this county. By far the larger proportion of these relate only to the last forty years of the period. More than a third concern pregnant single women. This unfortunate class was specifically exempted from the terms of irremovability expressed in the Act of 1795 and consequently forms a large proportion of the total number of persons who suffered removal after this date. The question of bastardy will, however, be considered later.

F. THE DISRUPTION OF FAMILY LIFE

As the eighteenth century proceeds one is struck by the increasing frequency with which men fall under the ban of the Vagrancy Law for the offence of running away and leaving their families chargeable to the parish. The tie of family life had been loosened at all points.

[1] For 115 years of this period the records are complete. (Cf. E. M. Hampson, *op. cit.*)

Men resident in distant places wrote asking assistance from the overseers of their parishes of legal settlement, openly threatening if it were refused to send their families home, whilst they themselves 'listed or adopted the life of the roads. "This is the last time that I intend wrighting", says George Ingrey to the Royston Committee, in 1806.[1] "I am Determined of what I Mean to Do, and that is if we Dont have a Letter or Some Relieve I Certainly will Send them Holme to the Parish. I will go into the Army again for I think it is a Nuff to Make a man Do what he whould Never think off." In some cases overseers, backed at times by the Bench, even encouraged men who were actually at work, but unable to maintain their families, to remain where they were whilst the family returned to the place of legal settlement. The undesirability of such a policy from the standpoint of family life hardly impressed an age accustomed to the wrenching of young children from the arms of their parents.

Among appeal cases alone—representing but a fraction of the removals which took place—there are seventeen clearly recorded instances in this county where families were broken up as a result of the various members having acquired different settlements. Any child above the age of seven was capable of acquiring an independent settlement through apprenticeship; bastard children were in the first instance settled in their place of birth; whilst step-children took the settlement of their own father. "Nurse children" below the age of seven, though chargeable to the parish of settlement, were not legally removable from the parent, but in practice there are not a few instances where infants were separated in spite of legal rulings. In 1833 Mary Mayes was removed from Little St Andrew's parish, Cambridge, to Little St Mary's, but her five-weeks-old baby was ordered by the Court to remain in the former parish.[2]

[1] MS. Vestry Papers, Royston.
[2] MS. Q.S.R. Cambs. 1833.

G. ENCOURAGEMENT OF FRAUD AND OF CASUAL EMPLOYMENT

William Rayment of Mildenhall, as early as 1665, was censured by the Court for visiting his aged parent at Isleham, it being alleged that by this means he was seeking to gain a settlement with his mother. The poor, "from causes peculiar to their circumstances", said Scott, "are more frequently subjected to involuntary separation, but natural affection of relations is common to the rich and to the poor, and will as frequently produce visits to its absent object".[1]

It was of course true that the fraud, collusion, and open bribery practised by parish officers found their natural response in the subterfuges of the poor. Children, for example, professed themselves hired to parents who were actually in receipt of parish relief.[2] Servants deliberately broke the year's contract with a master by taking a week-end holiday without leave. It was the masters themselves, however, who had taught this artifice to the poor.

At the annual hirings, for example, held at Sturbridge Fair, James Wye,[3] sporting the badge of his calling, took his place beside other yokels awaiting engagement. The usual questions were put, the earnest money given and the bargain clinched. "Take your holiday, my man," says Farmer Bullen of Trumpington, "and come to me this day week without fail." The simple Corin seeks his waiting Phyllis and hies him away to the fair, little dreaming that his wily master has by this means curtailed the year's service by a few days and thus prevented any settlement within the parish. Numerous instances of this practice might be adduced.

"Hath served in divers places, but never for a full year", is the frequent comment of the recording justices. The fashion of casual hiring by the week became increasingly common in the course

---

[1] Scott, op. cit. p. 16.
[2] A case is recorded in Great St Mary's MS. Vestry Book in 1769.
[3] MS. Vestry Papers, St Bene't's, Cambridge.

of the eighteenth century. Thus were the Elizabethan statutes, which aimed at fostering steady and continuous labour, frustrated by the settlement policy.

Artifice was equally common with regard to the payment of rates and the leasing of £10 tenements. "I paid the rates upon the house," writes John Stone, endeavouring to prove his settlement at March, "but the overseer hath recorded them under the name of Widow Helme, who held the house before me and now is deceased. The officers refuse me to examine the books—they keep all close against me."[1] A married woman of the name of Lee was removed, in 1821, by a warrant from St Giles', Cambridge, to St Sepulchre's, on the ground of having acquired a settlement in the latter parish by renting a £10 house—a fairly common occurrence in the nineteenth century. It was argued before the Court that the rent was only £9. 19s., since the landlord returned one shilling per year.[2] Many settlements were obtained in Little St Andrew's parish, Cambridge, whilst the extension of Downing College was in progress. The overseers of other parishes collusively paid the £10 rent for sundry men in order to get them settled in Little St Andrew's.[3]

Monetary inducement to quit the parish was sometimes offered to poor folk and brazenly recorded by the overseer— 20s. was thus paid to a poor woman by the officers of Great St Mary's in 1682.[4] Having failed in an appeal to Sessions concerning Mary Newman, the overseer of Meldreth in 1728 entered up the sorry tale of expenses incurred for lawyers' fees at the trial, for "wine with the counsellor", and for frequent libations of beer. He closed the account with the lugubrious item: "Lent to Mary Newman in the towns name, to prevail with her to goe a way off from Meldreth, 4s. 6d.—and she hath not gon"! The overseer had for once met his match.

[1] MS. Vestry Papers, Littleport.   [2] *Cambridge Chronicle*, Nov. 1821.
[3] An Act of 1819 prohibited such collusive action.
[4] S. 41 of Gilbert's Act of 1782 asserted that such "enticement" was frequently practised by parish officers, and penalties ranging from £5 to £20 were in consequence imposed.

H. CERTIFICATES

A question of essential import in estimating the restriction upon mobility resulting from the settlement policy is the extent to which the system of "certification", legalised by the Act of 1697,[1] was really operative.

"The system", says Pashley,[2] "appears in truth to have done little more than increase the power of the parish officers over the poor." An examination of the way in which the system worked in Cambridgeshire must considerably modify this conclusion.

The parish granting a certificate made itself responsible, usually only to the parish accepting it, for the persons named. Occasionally in this county the certificate was addressed in general terms "To all whom these presents may concern".[3] The Settlement Law of 1662 had itself provided for the granting of "testimonials" to permit married householders temporarily to leave the parish during seasonal demands for labour elsewhere— a practice common in Tudor times.[4] The "Certificate Act" of 1697 extended the privilege of mobility to unmarried persons and contemplated prolonged—possibly permanent—settlement in the new parish. Even this policy was no novelty. Various parishes in Cambridgeshire had organised a very similar system before the Act came into being. At a General Vestry meeting at Great St Mary's, in 1675, for example, it was

resolved and agreed that William Cole and Rebecca his wife, now Inhabitants of All Saints parish, and late of this parish, shall be no charge nor burden to the said parish of All Saints, and in case they or other of them come to want, so as they cannot maintaine themselves, then they shall be taken in as our poore, and received into our parish as Inhabitants againe, witnesse our hands the day and yeare above written.

---

[1] 8 and 9 W. III, c. 30.   [2] Pashley, *op. cit.* p. 240.

[3] A certificate was issued by Linton to the two parishes of Swaffham Bulbeck and Bottisham.

[4] They were frequently used at Wisbech in the sixteenth century and are mentioned in Tudor statutes.

PLATE VIII

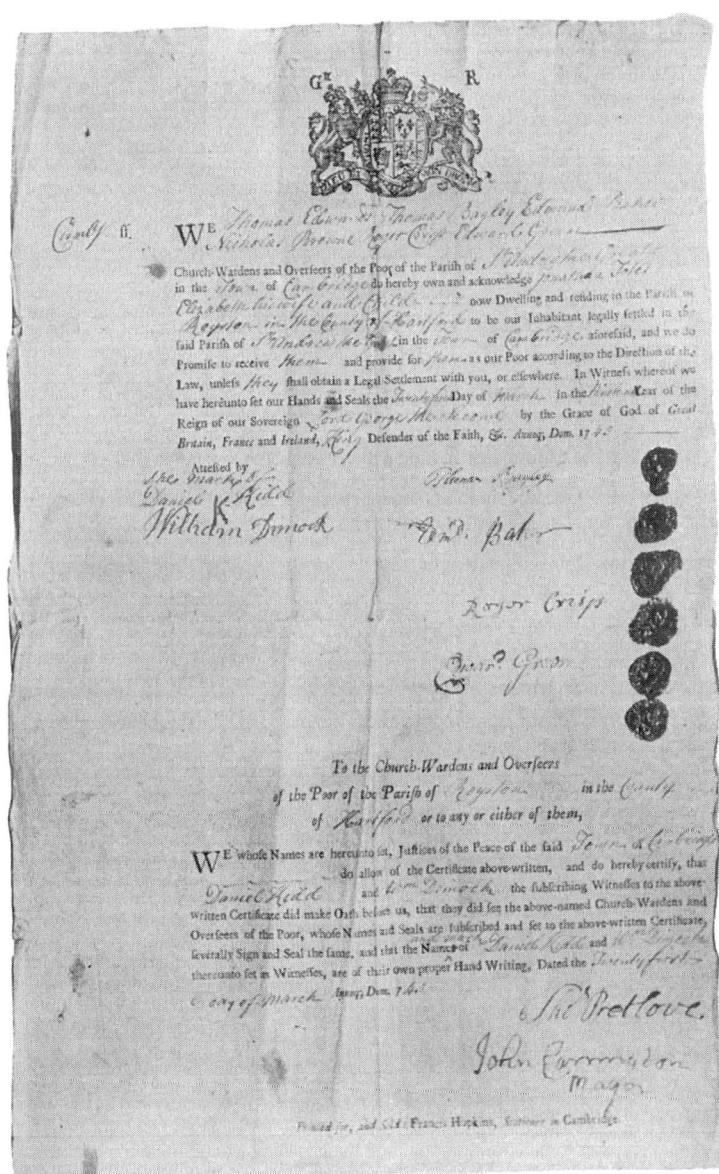

CERTIFICATE OF SETTLEMENT, 1745

Twenty-three signatures were appended. A similar certificate was granted by the same parish in 1685, and by Little St Mary's in 1690.

A certificate granted to St Botolph's, Cambridge, in 1698, mentions the statute of the previous year, and from 1700 onwards many such documents were in use. Plainly advantage was taken of the Act very promptly in a county already familiar with the principle.

According to the Act no person armed with a certificate was to be refused admission to a parish, nor was he to be removed thence until he became actually chargeable. Attempts were nevertheless made to eject certificated persons: in 1748 two Cambridge magistrates signed a warrant for the removal of Thomas Bryant and his family from Holy Trinity parish to St Edward's. Upon appeal the order was quashed, "it appearing upon the face of the said order that the persons were certificate persons, not having become chargeable to Holy Trinity".[1]

Exceptional terms were inserted in some certificates. Bexwell, in Norfolk, undertook to receive back merely "upon request" from Littleport the persons named in the document. St Botolph's officers had no great faith in the binding character of certificates, for in 1737 they demanded that bonds of security should be given with a certificated person coming to their parish. Baldock, in Hertfordshire, granted certificates to Cambridgeshire parishes on several occasions in the latter part of the eighteenth century, but the guarantee of responsibility was only for one year.

Unfortunately for the holder of a certificate he was excluded from gaining a settlement even by hiring or by any of the alternative modes open to other men, and by an Act of 1713 any servant or apprentice bound to him was likewise precluded from obtaining a settlement on account of such service. Of the added vexatiousness which the intricacies arising from the widespread use of the certificate system involved, parish documents and Court records speak eloquently. Although designed to facilitate movement the system often worked in an exactly opposite

[1] MS. Q.S.R. Cambs. 1748.

direction. John Townsend, for example, found himself up against the regulation at Christ's Hospital, whereby all employees were as a matter of routine required to bring settlement certificates. He had been provisionally appointed a beadle. The post was a permanent one, but in lieu of pensioning its ancient servants, the hospital preferred, when the time came, to return them to the parish which they had probably quitted half a century before, to spend their declining years among strangers, amid the squalor of an eighteenth-century workhouse. Townsend, a native of Great St Mary's, Cambridge, had served his full apprenticeship to Luton Markham, Commander of the *George Augustus*, but had recently broken down in health and had been obliged to quit the service. The commander was now deceased and the parish in which he had resided when not at sea refused to give a certificate to the apprentice because the boy had always slept on board. The wife of Commander Markham had used her influence to procure the post at the hospital and she now writes a pressing letter in support of the youth's application to the overseers of his native parish—Great St Mary's. She begs the parish to grant a certificate, "otherwise as Quarter's Day draws near, he will lose the advantages at Christmas, which are very considerable, besides the salary of the ensuing quarter". He is, she says, "a poor, honest, single young man, having no fortune but some good friends who have taken much pains to get him his place. Your compliance will prevent him being burthensome to *any* body, being a place for life". Time passed without result, and the young fellow, bewildered by the strange working of Providence in the guise of "Axes of Parliment", made a last effort to set the wheels in motion through the good offices of his sister at Cambridge. He writes:

To Mistress Townsend,

        At Meades Coffee House at Cambridge.

Dear Sister,

     Pray do gitt this thing singed, for by Axe of Parliment I seems to have no rights to be a Habitant anywheres, unless I be sined for. Mr. Peck has don what he can, but I am like to lose my employment.

From your loving Brother,

John Townsend.[1]

Notwithstanding such serious drawbacks, the general effect of granting certificates does seem to have been a beneficial modification of the harsh removal policy. The use of certificates, both in Cambridgeshire and in the neighbouring counties, was clearly very general before 1795. After this date some parishes—Bottisham for example—used them only to rid themselves of women "enceintes". Other parishes issued certificates on behalf of paupers in temporary difficulties who were resident in some distant parish, undertaking to repay the expenditure of the alien parish rather than incur the serious risk of prolonged unemployment if the pauper were brought home. Great St Mary's vestry, in common with most of the town vestries, usually required a copy of the removal order to be transmitted in such cases, before issuing a certificate. Some authorities refused to give certificates at all—the officers of Hatton Garden, London, in 1803 explain to their confrères at Royston that certificates are never given.[2]

In certain parishes of the county lists were compiled of the certificates received up to date. The freest use seems to have been made of the system in the period between 1740 and 1780. At Royston the climax was reached between 1740 and 1744. In 1777 the vestry of Great St Mary's apparently considered that the issue had been somewhat too facile, for it was ordered "that certificates should be granted only in vestry, and signed by a majority".

By far the largest number both of certificates and of removal orders were concerned with parishes within the county—of 70 certificates collected at Linton only four related to distant

---

[1] MS. Vestry Papers—Justices' Examinations, Great St Mary's, Cambridge.
[2] MS. Vestry Papers, Royston.

parishes; this was about the average for parishes which were not very near to the county borders. At Royston 70 out of 105, at Littleport 52 out of 76 certificates related to internal parishes, and of the remaining certificates in these two border places only four or five were issued to or by distant parishes.

I. MAINTENANCE IN ALIEN PARISHES

Apart from the granting of formal certificates the system of maintaining paupers in alien parishes, without insisting upon removal, even though the paupers had become chargeable, did much to mitigate the severity of settlement regulations. Sometimes the assistance was given directly to the pauper, after enquiry made of the employer or the local clergy; sometimes it was given through the officers of the parish where the pauper was then living.

As early as 1619 Great St Mary's vestry was reimbursing the parish of Chesterton in this manner. In 1662 the overseers of Hardwick allowed "12d. per weeke" for the maintenance of Ellen Grastock at Kingston. In 1703 Great St Mary's agreed "that the sum of 40s. be remited to Robt Chalice, one of our poor parishioners now resideing and inhabiting in Dunmow in Essex, for the payment of his rent". By the second decade of the eighteenth century the practice was common, though it was not till sixty or seventy years later that the payments to "non-residents" formed a considerable item in parochial accounts. It is clear that by this date overseers were impressed by the heavy charges incurred merely for transport, and were realising that removal almost invariably meant the sale of the pauper's few possessions and the jeopardising of his chances of surmounting what might prove to be only temporary misfortune. In not a few cases, therefore, where the pauper was situate at a considerable distance, much really thoughtful correspondence took place between the respective officials, before deciding whether removal, reimbursement, or the sending of relief directly, should be the policy pursued.[1] Each procedure involved risks peculiar to itself, and parishes differed considerably in the attitude displayed.

All the town parishes of Cambridge paid considerable sums annually by the late eighteenth century, on account of non-residents, and were on the other hand repaid for their own expenditure on paupers legally settled elsewhere. "I believe our Gentlemen will not be against anything in reason," writes the Master of the workhouse at Lynn, in 1781, to the overseer of St Bene't's, Cambridge, "only be as sparing as you can. I shall mention it to Alderman Thos. Bagg, who will be at your Fair. Therefore it will be proper for the woman to apply to him." The difficulty of transmitting sums of money and of investigating the circumstances of non-resident paupers and the economy with which relief was being given by officers not in control of the purse-strings, is exemplified by this letter. "Some of our parishioners always attend Stortford Market and will let you have the receipt for your paupers money then", writes the vestry clerk of Sawbridgeworth in 1776. The fear of careless expenditure was of course a well-founded one. Throughout the period from 1781 to 1834 Soham regularly maintained paupers elsewhere, but never at a higher rate than allowed to home paupers. Great St Mary's vestry was prepared to go to law, in 1766, over the unreasonable bill presented by the officers of Fenstanton, but other parishes paid unduly heavy charges many times rather than face the expense of legal proceedings. "Be as sparing as you can"—naturally this is the key-note of correspondence on the subject. Justices, overseers, employers, philanthropists, paupers[2] themselves take up the pen to plead with distant overseers on behalf of those who are loath to leave their homes and friends, to be returned to the cold welcome of a parish they may not even remember.

[1] After 1795 the removing parish was legally responsible for the cost of transport and had therefore one strong incentive to avoid actual removal.

[2] After about 1780 many Cambridgeshire paupers could write, though fewer women than men.

"Gentlemen," writes Wm. Wrosun to the officers of St Bene't's, "I worked a weak att my masters and Lay Bad four days again. my family are all most Stavd naked and if you do not pleas Send us sumthing we must come home." He points out that he has a job there awaiting him as soon as he recovers.[1]

The payment of rents on behalf of paupers situate in other parishes was peculiarly open to abuse on the part of rapacious landlords. "I send to you respecting Frederic Bentin", says the overseer of Beccles. "Their Rent is due for the year at Michls. next, and if not paid they will have their things taken a way. Then they Must Come home to you for they are in Gret distress. The woman is a very Industrous Woman but one child is not a year old."[2]

Certain parishes definitely refused relief to non-residents. Isleham turned a deaf ear even to such moving supplications as the following, penned apparently by a kindly landlord, on behalf of "a poor lame old man called Adam Raynor, whose wife endeavoureth to support them both. He says he could manage with but an extra shilling a week. He is honest and sober and his wife has regularly worked here many years. I understand you have a workhouse and are by no means compellable to relieve the poor man without him coming to you, but 'twould bring his gray hairs with sorrow to the grave". The man was nevertheless despatched to the workhouse at Isleham, whilst his old wife was left to pine in artificial widowhood.

The desperate fight against circumstance which poor folk were prepared to put up in order to avoid the dreaded break with all they held dear is exemplified over and over again in the obscure vestry annals of this county. "There is often an unaccountable affection for some particular habitation", says Scott, with rare sympathetic insight. "Such things", he adds, "are of little import in reality, but they are of much in idea; and in idea exist many of our sublimest pains and pleasures."[3] Sentiment had little place in the mid-eighteenth century attitude

[1] MS. Vestry Papers, St Bene't's, Cambridge.
[2] *Ibid.*   [3] Scott, *op. cit.* p. 47.

to poverty, though there is a more frequent manifestation of a humanitarian spirit in the closing years of the century. "W^m. Rawlinson is almost Naked and is afflicted with ye Rhumatism", writes an overseer of Waltham to an overseer at Cambridge. "He is quite willing to come to you if you wish it. I don't know how to advise you. They are miserable poor. My heart is wrung for them." Here is a genuine desire to meet the needs of the case sympathetically. In the earlier part of the eighteenth century Royston was very chary of granting relief to non-residents. In 1802 frail little Elizabeth Hudson was left orphan by the death of her mother at Avening, near Gloucester. Her father—like so many fathers of the period—was missing. The legal settlement of the child was indisputably at Royston, but the overseer of Avening wrote to Royston quoting the dying mother's urgent request that the child she had struggled for years to support independently—at such cost to them both—should not be sent away from the only friends she had ever known.

"The child", says the overseer, "has been very poorly this Winter. I am afraid she will be but of a weak Constitution, having suffered considerable from want while her mother lived, she being often so ill and never would apply to you for help, having always such a fear of being brot away from her native place to Royston. We have put the child to weaving, but are obliged to deal gently with her on account of her feeble frame and very slender make. We have taught her to read, write and sew very prety, so that we hope in a yer or twos time she will (if well) be able to get her bread in an easier way if not able to follow the loom."

To the credit of Royston on this occasion the child was permitted to remain at Avening.

Of the many important social problems which circle around the settlement policy, none perhaps are of more lasting moment than those concerned with pauper apprenticeship and with the damaged prospects of the married labourer. To an examination of these questions the next two chapters are devoted.

Chapter XII

PAUPER APPRENTICESHIP

A. APPRENTICESHIP AND SETTLEMENT

The reigning theories of discipline, together with the growing tendency to regard him as an actual wage earner, made the lot of even the independent labourer's child no easy one from the late seventeenth century onwards, and it may be that the life of the pauper apprentice in rural parishes was but little worse than that of his non-pauper fellow.

The medieval system of apprenticeship had been adopted by Elizabethan legislators as the best mode of affording a national scheme of technical education which would prevent poverty by providing each child with the tools of a livelihood. Whilst it was no part of the Elizabethan aim to offer industrial training which should raise the labourer's child out of the ranks to which he supposedly belonged, pauperism was a sore in the body politic. Sufficient training, industrial and moral, to avoid collapse below a certain level of efficiency must therefore be secured. If such were the purpose of apprenticeship, perhaps over the country as a whole no branch of the Elizabethan Poor Law departed, during the eighteenth century, more widely from the original conception, as a result of pressure upon the rates and of the loophole which apprenticeship seemed to offer to the parish officer under the Settlement Laws.

It has been shown[1] that the apprenticeship clauses of the Poor Law had from the outset encountered opposition, and that much stimulation by the Privy Council had been necessary before masters could be induced to accept undesirable children. During the Restoration period the whole organisation of industry was breaking down. So far as the meaner occupations were concerned, the Settlement Laws gave to the decadent apprenticeship

[1] Cf. *supra*, chap. iv.

system a new fillip just at a time when society was becoming less and less static. Even had there been no rate-reducing motive on the part of the overseer, the prolongation of a system based on ignoring the need for mobility was bound, if effectively enforced, to result in overcrowding certain fields of labour, with all which that implies.

The Act of 1662 granted to the apprentice the right to consider himself a settled inhabitant of the parish in which he had been indentured—the locality, that is, with which in general he had most ties. The intention of the Act was liberal. Practical disputes soon made it necessary to determine exactly how and where the forty days' residence applied. It was ruled that the apprentice should be settled in the parish where he chanced to have slept for the last night of his apprenticeship, provided that he had slept there forty nights *in toto*. He might, however, gain a settlement anywhere else during the whole term of service by sleeping in the parish for forty days, and many were the complications which arose. Any child above the age of seven was enabled to acquire a settlement independently of his parents, and it became increasingly the aim of parish officers to secure that the children for whom they were responsible should be thrown at the earliest possible moment into the arms of some other parish. This policy became more marked after the Act of 1692 emphasised the right of settlement which apprenticeship gave.

Some 918 Cambridgeshire indentures, ranging between the years 1631 and 1830, have been examined. Seventy-eight refer to the period before 1692, and of these sixty-six were made out to masters in the same parish as that to which the child already belonged; six were to neighbouring parishes and six to parishes at a considerable distance. The effect of the settlement policy became obvious in the post-1692 period. Of the indentures for these later years 258 bound the child to a master in the same parish, 576 dispatched him to neighbouring and six to distant parishes. Parishes differed considerably in the extent to which they used apprenticeship with a view to securing a settlement elsewhere: only six of the nineteen indentures which are preserved at Meldreth, for instance, placed out the child in a different parish; on the other hand, only six of the thirty-four at Burwell bound him in the home parish. From the worst evils, however, associated with the apprenticing of pauper children far away from kith and kin, in the great industrial regions where no supervision could possibly be exercised, Cambridgeshire was practically free.

Compulsion could only be exercised in the particular parish where the overseer held sway; hence, if apprenticeship were to be secured in an alien parish it must be to persons to whom a child, or his premium, represented a remunerative speculation—

> They in their want a trifling sum would take
> And toiling slaves of piteous orphans make.

The moral and economic suitability of the master tended to become of secondary consideration so long as the child was fixed upon another parish. The unwillingness of suitable masters to take pauper children is evident from the occasional payment, after 1698, of the £10 penalty for refusal; it is betrayed also in the considerable number of cases pleading to be excused the burden. Some parish authorities compiled lists of eligible householders who were required to take apprentices by rota. This was the practice at Shepreth, but Mr Philip Hale refused in 1663 to have a pauper girl on his hands for twelve years or more. The Court ordered him to accept the child and to repay the parish the interim charges of maintaining her. John Wright, a gentleman farmer of Thriplow, refused to take Roger Taylor as his apprentice in 1661. The Court ordered the farmer to accept the boy, but directed the parish officers to provide his clothing and fixed the termination of the service at the age of twenty-one in lieu of the statutory age of twenty-four. The youth was, however, of more use to his employer between the ages of twenty-one and twenty-four than at any other period and the fiat of the Bench was flatly set at nought by the farmer, who declined to have any dealings with the boy. After a third hearing Wright's influence was sufficient to persuade the Court to rescind its own order and to direct that the boy be apprenticed to a tradesman who would teach him a craft.[1] This attitude of the gentry is typical and probably accounts for the fact that remarkably few children were apprenticed to husbandry in this agricultural county.[2] A small premium was less of an inducement to men of this class than it was to the struggling craftsman.

It was the difficulty thus experienced by parish officers which led to the enactment of 1698,[3] whereby contumacious refusal was penalised by a £10 fine. The penalty was frequently paid in Cambridgeshire for the first few years after the Act was passed, but land-owning interests were strong, and before the middle of the next century a system of placing-out pauper children for a few months at a time with the inhabitants in turn had developed in many rural parishes. The sympathy of the landed justices naturally encouraged the practice, and regular apprenticeship was more and more confined to petty trades. In 1748, for instance, Thomas Bidwell, a farmer of Barnwell, applied to be excused from taking as an apprentice the girl sent to him by the overseers of Barnwell. The Court cancelled the indenture and ordered "that Mr Bidwell do take the child to keep and provide for her for two calendar months, persuant to the parish agreement for that purpose, and so as his turn shall happen to be with the other farmers of the parish aforesaid".[4]

B. NON-INDENTURED APPRENTICESHIP AND OTHER FORMS OF SERVICE

Other methods of placing-out children "after the manner of an apprentice", without formal indenture and for various terms, were evolved in the course of the eighteenth century, but in such

[1] MS. Q.S.R. Cambs. 1661 and 1663.

[2] Out of 918 cases 36 children only were apprenticed to husbandry. By the interpretation of the Courts, even in Tudor times, service in husbandry had been exempted from the compulsory apprenticeship regulations, but so too had trades of an unskilled character.

[3] 8 and 9 W. III, c. 30.

[4] MS. Q.S.R. Cambs. 1748.

cases no settlement was acquired. In 1745, for example, young Edward Jeames was placed out by the overseer of Shelford "with Mr Jno. Aylmer, for yᵉ year, the Parrish finding him with Cloathes". Another Shelford lad was put out for six months to one farmer and then for three months each to two other farmers —the parish again finding his apparel. William Pool served with his uncle, a carpenter of Newton, "in the quality and nature of an apprentice for four years, but not by indenture". John Morley of Littleport, in 1724, "for the Consideration of the Sume of £3", by a "Bargaine and Contract made with the sd. Church-wardens and Overseers", agreed to "take, maintaine and keep as a Servant, Anne Carvell, being a poor Childe of the afsd. Parish, for the Terme of Three Years", providing her "with meat, drink, cloathing, washing and lodging", and at the end of the said term "giving unto her meat and convenient Cloathing, as good in every respect as she now is Cloathed withal at the time of her entry into Service". Morley pledged himself, under a bond of £6, to perform the contract.

Other children were hired out for wages as soon as they were old enough, by the day, by the week, or for a few months at a time. Thomas Pukey was sent by Royston early in the nine-teenth century to a neighbouring parish for a year, "for the wages of 5s. a year, and 6d. earnest. To be Cloathed by the Parish".

C. THE TEACHING OF A TRADE

The contention[1] that pauper apprenticeship was never intended, even in Elizabethan days, as more than a legalisation of the customary boarding-out system seems hardly supportable. In practice this is indeed what apprenticeship frequently became, but the whole code of Elizabethan poor-relief is intimately bound up with that evolved for the regulation of industry, and it seems clear that the purpose of even pauper apprenticeship was to

[1] J. O. Dunlop, *op. cit.* p. 251.

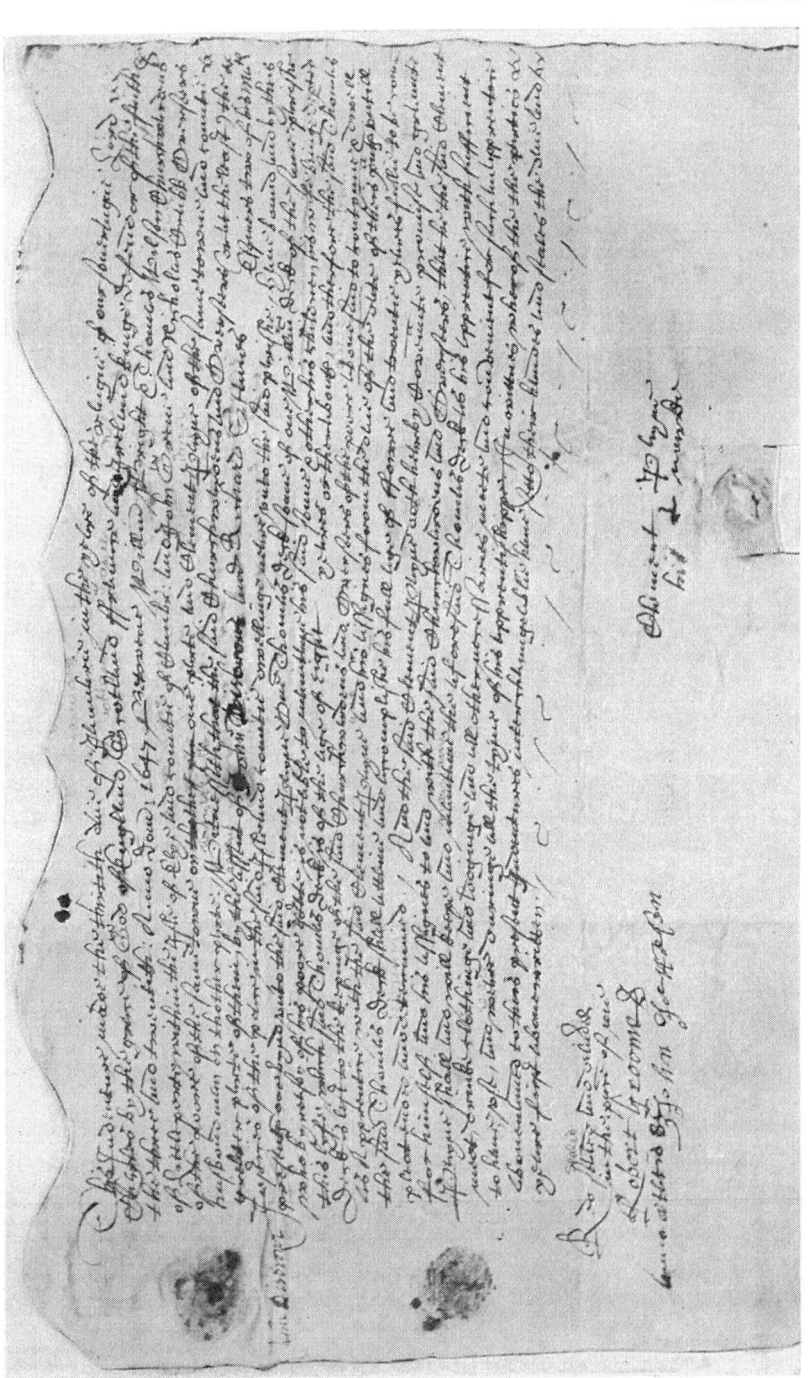

PLATE IX

FORMAL INDENTURE OF A BOY
but no stipulation *re* Teaching

supply a training for the humbler walks of life.[1] So far as boys are concerned the Cambridgeshire indentures usually specify the trade to be taught. Neglect to carry out this obligation occasionally forms the plea before Court for the cancelling of a pauper binding. In the less skilled crafts, with comparatively little definite teaching a lad must usually have been enabled to acquire sufficient aptitude to earn his own living, in accordance with the aim of Elizabethan legislation. The real crux of the matter lay in the over-stocking of the market in low-grade occupations.

The officers of Teversham were ordered by the Bench, in 1665, on their part to pay the promised premium of £5, whilst the employer was required to give an undertaking that he would teach his apprentice the trade of a blacksmith.

"Refusing to instruct him in his business and to provide necessaries for him, and turning him out of doors", were successfully urged as grounds for vacating the indenture of John Greystock, a poor child apprenticed by the overseers of Dry Drayton to a cordwainer of Cambridge in 1748.

William Sewell, bound to a tradesman of Clare, in Suffolk, by the overseers of Bottisham in 1723, was to be "instructed as a fell-maker or glover"; John Miller, apprenticed to a tailor of Cambridge, was to be taught the tailor's craft. Similar terms were made in the case of most, though not of all boys actually indentured. A few girls were apprenticed to trades such as weaving or stay-making, but the great majority were either bound to "the art and mystery of housewifery", or the indenture merely stated that the child should be "wisely used".

Cordwaining or "cordwinding" claimed far more pauper

[1] The anonymous author of *An Ease for Overseers* seems to bear out this contention. Writing in 1601 he says: "There be many Overseers that without respect of facultie, honestie, or abilitie of the masters, are readie to thrust out poore mens children for apprentices, when either the masters, not being able to receive them, will by some device or hard intreatie provoke the apprentices unlawfully to depart; or els the apprentice shall consume his time without experience of his trade: if they be thus posted off it will nothing at all benefit but rather increase the charge of the parish".

apprentices than any one other trade—if real skill were acquired as cobblers and shoemakers it is astonishing that no fuller use was made of it by Masters of the workhouses to which too many pauper apprentices eventually drifted. The remaining apprentices were fairly evenly divided among the different types of petty craftsmen and shopkeepers.

It needs little imagination, however, to conjecture the type of training likely to be offered by an ignorant, impecunious master, concerned only with the obtaining of a premium. Even in the skilled crafts the slackening of the master's sense of responsibility for his servant was frequently commented upon by moralists of the eighteenth century. "The children of this town", said Professor Whiston, advocating in 1705 the establishment of Charity Schools in Cambridge, "are troublesome and thievish, profane and wicked, mischievous and insolent, and no wonder, for they that have not much better training than the brutes that perish cannot have much more sense of virtue and vice, of right and wrong, than the brutes have."[1] Pulpit oratory is not the only evidence of this state of affairs.

D. THE PREMIUMS OFFERED. ILL-TREATMENT. PRECAUTIONS ADOPTED

The premiums offered varied very greatly: much depended on the extent to which benefactions were available to supplement the rates. Thirty shillings to five pounds formed the customary sums during the seventeenth century; three pounds to twenty pounds during the eighteenth and early nineteenth centuries. Only such parishes as Soham or Burwell, however, with wealthy endowments, paid so high a figure as twenty pounds, for this was about the average premium paid in the latter part of the eighteenth century in this county on behalf of non-pauper children apprenticed to such trades as tailoring. Benefactions had in many cases increased greatly in monetary value in the course of the eighteenth

---

[1] W. Whiston, *A Sermon preach'd at Trinity-Church in Cambridge,* 1705.

century; rarely, however, were steps taken during this corrupt age to raise the premiums offered[1]—malversation of the funds was exceedingly common. Sometimes a larger number of children were placed out, but the change in the value of money meant that benefactions were increasingly used to bind children only to the lowest-grade occupations.

Some writers have pointed out the careful distinction drawn by parish officers between non-pauper children whom they apprenticed out of voluntary funds and children apprenticed out of the rates. Such a discrimination might well be expected in view of the attitude towards poverty very generally manifested during the late seventeenth and eighteenth centuries. Cambridgeshire overseers undoubtedly gave first consideration to the children of those whom they regarded as having undeservedly come down in the world—and sometimes they stretched that interpretation to satisfy personal interests—but quite certainly they made wide use of voluntary funds for the benefit of pauper children also.[2] The real advantage as an apprentice which the child of the poor but independent labourer frequently enjoyed over his pauper contemporary was the possession of parents or friends able to interfere on his behalf.

"£10 is too little encouragement", said Hanway in 1766, to induce suitable masters to take children "at a tender age".[3] In very many instances the sum given corresponded only to the cost of the child's bare maintenance for one, or for a couple of years. Strong temptation was offered, therefore, to the petty master to exact long hours of drudgery from the child in return for his keep. Girls were often apprenticed in this county at the

---

[1] Wisbech Corporation did order in 1822 that the sum of 50s., customarily given as "consideration money", should be increased to sums varying from £3. 10s. to £7. 10s.

[2] By the Act of 1610 (7 Jas. I, c. 3) benefactions for the apprenticing of children were to be applied to "the poorest sorts of children". On the other hand, the rates were sometimes drawn upon for the apprenticing of non-pauper children. The son of the workhouse Master was in several Cambridgeshire instances improperly so apprenticed.

[3] J. Hanway, *op. cit.* p. 103.

early age of nine or ten, boys not usually till twelve, or even fourteen or fifteen. Bastard children of both sexes were commonly bound out at seven or eight years of age.

Cases of cruelty and neglect did occasionally reach the ears of the Bench, usually through the absconding or bankruptcy of worthless masters. Rarely otherwise could the cry have been heard of the down-trodden little drudge, accustomed to the acceptance of his lot as the result of an inscrutable Fate. A few of the older or sturdier ones indeed succeeded in running away and went to swell the stream of vagrants and to risk the horror and contamination of an eighteenth-century gaol. Richard Stubbing, a tailor of West Wickham, was summoned before the Bench in 1670, for "having much abused Jeremiah Teversham, his apprentice, by immoderate beating and not allowing unto him necessary meate, drinke, and cloaths". The apprenticeship was cancelled and Stubbing ordered to repay forty shillings of the premium and to return to the boy all his clothing. There were four cases of definite ill-treatment which by some means penetrated to Quarter Sessions between 1660 and 1670. At no period between 1700 and 1800 was sufficient interest taken in the sufferings of the pauper child for his grievances to be brought to daylight even so frequently as during the earlier decade. That his grievances were lighter in the eighteenth century it is impossible to suppose:

> None put the question—"Peter, dost thou give
> The boy his food?—What, man! the lad must live".
> None reason'd thus—and some on hearing cries,
> Said calmly, "Grimes is at his exercise".

By the close of the seventeenth century the urgency of the settlement problem deadened sensibility to other aspects of apprenticeship. The type of master to whom overseers were prepared on occasion to send children is evident from the appeal of the overseers of Dullingham, in 1768, against the apprenticing of a boy by the overseers of Cherryhinton to Joseph Sanfield of Dullingham, who was a regular pensioner of the parish. The indenture was cancelled and one-third of the £5 "consideration money" ordered to be returned.[1] Where valuable apprenticeship trusts existed most careful precautions had often been taken by the benefactors to ensure the well-being of the apprentice—a fact suggesting an intimate knowledge of the evils which had arisen. Soham, for example, required testimonials from the minister of the parish to which the proposed employer belonged. Wisbech St Peter's usually exercised considerable care: the following advertisement was inserted in the *Cambridge Chronicle* in 1787:

The Churchwardens and Overseers of the Poor of Wisbech St Peter's, in the Isle of Ely and County of Cambridge, take this method to inform the public that there are at this time in the Poor-House of Wisbech aforesaid a number of very healthful Boys and Girls, from 13 to 15 years of age, whom they are desirous of putting out as Apprentices to respectable people; and as the Churchwardens and Overseers purpose to give premiums with each of them, no person need apply but such as produce testimonial proofs of character and situation.

The premiums at Soham, and in fact in thirty of the thirty-six parishes of which the indentures have been examined, were customarily paid only in instalments—in one instance in five annual instalments,[2] in many cases in two instalments, still more commonly in three, and on one occasion no premium at all was given until after the first year's trial. Payments were generally made annually, but at Meldreth in 1706, with a girl bound to a shepherd, the premium of £11. 10s. was paid in triennial sums over a period of nine years. On the rare occasion when a child was apprenticed as far afield as Lincolnshire, the overseer of Meldreth obviously recognised the risk involved, but the

---

[1] MS. Q.S.R. Cambs. 1768.

[2] Elizabeth Turner, in 1694, was thus apprenticed by Great St Mary's parish, Cambridge, to John Pinder for seven years. The sum of 20s. was paid down and a similar annual sum promised for the next four years. In this parish no indentures were permitted to be drawn up without the consent of the vestry. (Great St Mary's MS. Vestry Book.)

stipulation that the paltry extra sum of five shillings should be given at the end of the third year, "if the child be well used", could only have served as a sop to the parochial conscience. Some opportunity of investigating the manner in which the bargain was being performed was, however, afforded by the method of deferred payments.

The parish of Littleport actually required the employer to give security to the extent of £12 when a poor boy was apprenticed to him in 1651. A similar demand was made at Histon in 1674 and again in the early eighteenth century.[1] This method of safeguarding the parish was sometimes adopted in later cases when no formal indenture was signed.

Entire disregard concerning the character of the master can hardly be laid to the charge of Cambridgeshire parishes as a whole, but little investigation into the condition of the labour market can be placed to their credit. The apparent relief of the rates was achieved at the expense of future unemployment and poverty, and was after all but a tit-for-tat policy between parish and parish.

E. THE PERIOD OF SERVICE

During the course of the eighteenth century the number of apprentices who absconded increased; advertisements offering rewards for their capture became a familiar feature of the *Cambridge Chronicle*. It was, however, lusty youths of eighteen or twenty years of age who alone dared run the gauntlet. The evil of retaining young men in servitude till twenty-four years of age, in trades requiring little skill, was animadverted upon by Hanway in 1766. The law was amended in 1778 and the age limit for boys reduced to twenty-one. Before this date in Cambridgeshire the terms were often shorter than the statutory requirement. More than half the indentures for the years between 1631 and 1778, however, nominally adhered to the legal age of twenty-four in the case of boys and twenty-one or marriage in the case

[1] Cf. *supra*, p. 128, note 2.

of girls. Seven years was not an unusual limit for apprenticeship of either sex. On the back of a Bottisham indenture nominally retaining the boy in service till twenty-four, was added the note, "to be released in 7 years". At Kirtling before 1778, with one exception, all boys were bound for the legal term: in this one case the master entered into a £20 bond to liberate the apprentice at twenty-one. In the late eighteenth century the service sometimes terminated at nineteen. A Duxford girl was, in 1654, bound out till twenty-four years of age, and some indentures— contrary to law—prohibited the marriage of girls no less than of boys before the expiration of their term. The Act of 1778, however, made compulsory the inclusion in the indenture of the phrase "or marriage", where girls were concerned, and the Act seems to have been observed in Cambridgeshire.[1] A considerable number of girls were apprenticed only till eighteen.

From the middle of the eighteenth century the tendency in all directions was towards less rigidity and shorter periods of service.[2] The Industrial School and the workhouse, and from 1795 onwards the gravel pit and the "rounds", took the place of apprenticeship for many children. In an indenture of 1821 the parish officers of Bottisham arranged that the master should "during the first year of the said term provide and allow unto the said apprentice towards his maintenance the sum of one shilling per week, and for the remainder of the said term half the sum he earns at his said trade", the parish supplementing the means of maintenance by a grant of two shillings a week for the first year.[3] A somewhat similar agreement was made on behalf of an apprentice at Royston in 1819.

---

[1] Attention was drawn to the Act by the overseer of Bottisham.

[2] Wisbech found it necessary, in 1809, to insist that "Thorloe's charity" should not be "applied to apprenticing for less time than till 21". (MS. Corp. Minute and Order Book, Wisbech.)

[3] An indenture of 1825 bound a non-pauper youth of Bottisham for three years only. During the last 2½ years the master was to pay his apprentice "one full moiety of the wages usually paid to journeymen in the said trade". A premium of £10 was given. (MS. Vestry Papers, Bottisham.)

From such sources of information as the paupers' accounts of their own careers, when examined by the justices, it is obvious that many children, especially after the early years of the eighteenth century, were never apprenticed at all, and of those who were formally bound—non-pauper as well as pauper—very many failed to complete the full period of service.

Summarising the position it would seem that though the results were serious enough, the evils of apprenticeship pressed less hardly upon the Cambridgeshire child than they did upon many of his contemporaries.

Chapter XIII

BASTARDY

A. SETTLEMENT POLICY AND BASTARDY LEGISLATION

A large family was a menace to the rates. This fact lay behind the drastic removals of married men endeavouring to settle in a new parish, and accounted also for the attempts made in some localities to curtail housing accommodation. A marked increase in immorality was in part the natural result of such frustration of the legitimate desire for a normal married life. The only remedies of the age were jeremiads against "the vice and idleness of this present time", combined with brutal efforts to pass on the ever-increasing burden of illegitimate children to some other parish. Since the place of settlement of a bastard was primarily that of birth, the first glimpse of a pregnant single woman, however precarious her condition, was enough to bestir the overseer to marshal for the fray every weapon which either law or fraudulent ingenuity could devise to get the woman beyond the confines of his parish; or, should he fail in this, to pursue the putative father with the utmost vigilance. The exceeding frequency with which unpleasant entries occur in both constables' and overseers' accounts of this county shows how serious were the obstacles placed in the path of normal marriage.

In June 1721 the overseer of St Botolph's, Cambridge, "paid to Doll Carter, she being near her time, £2. 17s. 6d. by which we got ridd of her"—an entry which seems well classified under the heading "Extronardy Disbustments"! Poor Doll Carter, however, figures a few days later at Shelford, where the overseer records: "Pd for removing the woman Carter out of a field, 4d.; Pd for Dr. Warrick to attend her, 4s. 6d." Then follow the usual gruesome details of funeral expenses.

Of bastardy *qua* bastardy the law took no cognisance, but the begetting of an illegitimate child likely to be chargeable to the parish was an offence against the Act of 1576,[1] which allowed two justices, after examination, to order a payment to be made weekly or otherwise by both parents, under penalty of imprisonment. "The great dishonour of Almighty God", so piously alluded to in the preamble to an Act of 1610,[2] was of small consequence provided the offender could afford to enter into "a bond harmeles" to indemnify the parish.

In order to secure the parish against absconding fathers the Act of 1662 allowed distraint on the goods of defaulters—many of whom at this date were evidently of a social grade above that of the pauper. It was apparently considered that the father escaped too easily, for by the further Statute of 1733, on the unattested oath of the woman before a single justice, any man charged by her as the father could be arrested—without even a hearing of his defence—upon application by the overseers or by any substantial householder, and forthwith committed to prison unless he negotiated a bond for the child's maintenance, or at least entered into a recognisance to appear before the next Quarter Sessions.

In practice Cambridgeshire justices did sometimes summon the man before them to investigate the "cause and circumstances", although not required to do so by law. Moreover, they did not invariably commit him to prison for non-payment of security or for lack of recognisance. Even before 1733 it was not an unknown practice for women to swear to men falsely in order to extort money. In a Cambridgeshire Quarter Sessions' case of 1706 the woman herself cited two co-respondents—at her preliminary examination she named Roger Jotherton; before the County Bench she admitted that the culprit was really William

---

[1] 18 Eliz., c. 2.
[2] 7 Jas. I, c. 4. This Act increased the penalty imposed upon the woman to one year's imprisonment in the House of Correction. For a second offence imprisonment was to be continued until sureties were forthcoming. An Act of 1810 (50 G. III, c. 51) reduced the term of imprisonment to one varying from six weeks to one year.

Ellis, but as Ellis had suddenly developed a patriotic fervour for military service, Jotherton had seemed the more profitable defendant. In several other cases brought before the Court the charge was successfully rebutted by the reputed father. There is nothing to show that the general moral standard of women in Cambridgeshire fell immediately as a direct result of the Act of 1733. It is not until the end of the century, when economic conditions were such as to urge women to desperate deeds, that a rapid increase in immorality is obvious and attempts to extort hush money become fairly frequent. Of bastardy cases coming for one reason or another to the notice of Quarter Sessions between 1660 and 1749 there were 30 cases; between 1757 and 1771 there were 37 cases; between 1796 and 1830 there were 365 cases.

B. THE EXACTION OF PENALTIES. THE SOCIAL STATUS OF OFFENDERS

Very few women were imprisoned for immorality in this county after 1660—"it being an expense without the least benefit".[1] During the period 1660 to 1760 there were only three instances recorded of commitment of men for financial inability to enter into "a bond harmeles". Poor men did not, however, go scot free during these years, if they were in a position to pay even some portion of the child's maintenance. John Reeve of Burwell, in 1754, acknowledged before the magistrate his responsibility for the boy born of Alice Rendal, a single woman. No security was demanded of the man, but he was made to sign a formal agreement to pay the small quarterly sum of six shillings until the child should attain the age of seven, and to refrain from "cohabiting with the sd. Alice Rendal", who undertook to nurse the infant herself. A poor man of Great St Mary's parish was allowed, by agreement of the vestry in 1763, to pay only one guinea down on promising to leave the parish.

[1] Reply of Harston to Commission of 1834. (*P.L.C. Rept.* 1834, App. B 1, Pt. 5, Query 47.) Cf. also *ibid.* App. A, Pt. 1, p. 678. (Everett's Report.)

Between 1760 and 1770 a more determined stand was made. Some thirty cases of bastardy were brought before the Court, and in ten of these cases men were imprisoned for failure to discharge their responsibilities. In several other instances the men involved were obviously of humble position, for they found it easier to accept the alternative of marriage with the woman than to produce the sums demanded.

In the years between 1796 and 1834 the number of men committed for failure to indemnify the parish increased to eighty-nine. The growth in the number of offenders who did manage to offer security was, however, still more rapid. About one-third of the putative parents brought before the Court were described as labourers—in 153 instances they belonged to this class; in twenty-three to the class of servants, apprentices, shop-assistants or grooms; and in eighty instances to the slightly higher grades of tradesmen and artisans. There were, however, no less than 160 cases in which the culprits were yeomen farmers, millers, gamekeepers, publicans, apothecaries, undergraduates or gentry. During the years of stress and strain in the early nineteenth century parish authorities in this county concentrated on the pursuit of such men as it was profitable to catch.

C. MAINTENANCE ORDERS. FRAUD AND PERJURY

In the earlier years of the eighteenth century the weekly sums charged upon the parents towards the maintenance of their illegitimate offspring had commonly been fixed by the Cambridgeshire Court[1] at 2s. for the father and 6d. for the mother

---

[1] In the earlier years of the eighteenth century it was usual in Cambridgeshire to demand the same sum as security whether the offender were rich or poor. Some failed to make good their undertaking to the parish and in due course their sureties were mulcted to the extent of the sum pledged: £25 contributed by three friends as security on behalf of an offender of St Bene't's parish was forfeited in 1770. A similar proceeding possibly explains the entry which Ashby finds difficult to account for in the case of Tysoe, a parish in Warwickshire. (Ashby, *One Hundred Years of Poor Law*, p. 94. Vinogradoff, *Oxford Studies*, vol. III, 1912.)

(when she did not herself nurse the child), without any consideration of the social status of the parent: in the later years larger sums were often assessed upon wealthy parents than upon poor. In certain Cambridgeshire parishes the whole sum received from the man was passed on to the woman—at Harston, for example, one mother received the 4s. weekly paid by a prosperous merchant who had misconducted himself. In other cases the parish benefited—theoretically at least—by the difference between the sum usually paid to unmarried mothers and that received from the father. The parish of Bourne, for example, received £29 from putative parents, in 1830, and paid out only £22. This position was, however, exceptional, for bastardy payments were a source of peculiar temptation to unscrupulous overseers. The parish accounts of Soham were the subject of a detailed investigation before the Court in 1793: an error of £3. 9s. was detected in a bastardy item amounting to £8. 13s. 6d. In 1763 Anne Brand of Chesterton complained to Quarter Sessions that no allowance at all was being paid to her on account of her illegitimate child: investigation proved that on promise to hush up the affair the father had paid down a lump sum which had lodged in the overseer's pocket. Elizabeth Plaw of Whittlesford took her plaint in 1800 to the Rev. Andrew Pern, a clerical justice. Three and a half years previously she had been delivered of a base-born child, to whose parentage she had duly sworn before the magistrate. The overseers of Whittlesford had, however, refused to execute the warrant issued against the father, and had taken advantage of the woman's probable ignorance to threaten her with imprisonment if she spurned their offer of a shilling per week. She had recently learnt that others in her position were receiving 2s. 6d. weekly. Suspecting that the overseers had benefited by a private arrangement with the father, the justice ordered the parish to allow the usual sum or to procure the father, "which", the justice added significantly, "may easily be done since you know where he is!"[1]

Compounding with the officers in a lump sum, and thereby

[1] MS. Maynard Collection, Saffron Walden Museum.

freeing himself of all further responsibility, was in certain districts of the county a very common practice on the part of the reputed father. Soham had followed this custom when possible all through the eighteenth century—twenty-seven guineas were paid down on one occasion. The parish, however, discovered the ease with which defalcations occurred and this, added to other objections, led to a query being raised in the King's Bench. The resulting opinion was printed and affixed to the back of the overseers' account book as a caution to future officers. "Such an agreement", runs the verdict, "places parish officers in a situation which the Legislature did not mean to do, and which public policy forbids...for if the money be received immediately, the benefit is to those persons who are then living in the parish, while the burden may be thrown on future generations; whereas the Act meant that those who were to bear the burden should have the benefit of the indemnity." £10 down was the amount generally demanded by St Bene't's parish in the mid-eighteenth century—at Isleham it was only £5. Either sum was quite inadequate to recoup the parish for the expenses of lying-in and for the maintenance of the child for seven or eight years. "The custom of giving small sums", said Jonas Hanway in 1766, "seems to have introduced the opinion that a parish child's life is worth no more than 8 or 10 months' purchase."[1]

Where the woman benefited to the full by the larger sums assessed upon men of means, her financial position—and possibly that of widows with children assisted according to the magistrates' scale—was better than that of childless women.[2] In such cases strong temptation was offered to a hard-pressed woman either to seduce some guileless youth or to give false

---

[1] J. Hanway, *An Earnest Appeal* (1766), p. 38.

[2] In 1833 fewer parishes in Cambs. paid over the whole sum to the woman than had been the case ten years earlier. A difference of 1s. per week was commonly made in the allowance to a woman if the man were in a good position, but it was generally acknowledged that it rarely paid a woman on this scale unless there were several children. The reformers of the time clearly exaggerated the influence of financial profit, though it weighed in certain cases.

evidence respecting the man concerned. Even when the parish was the main beneficiary it was to the interest of the overseer to induce the woman to swear to some man well able to foot the bill. Benjamin Howard was brought before the County Bench, in 1822, as the well-to-do reputed parent of a child born of Sarah Higgins of Whaddon. It was clearly proved that the mother was guilty of "wilful and corrupt perjury".[1] Many women received sums of £20 or £30 as hush-money at Royston at the end of the eighteenth century.[2]

D. NINETEENTH-CENTURY PROSECUTIONS.
THE EFFECT OF FORCED MARRIAGES

Equally insistent were the attempts of parish officers to encourage women to saddle some non-parishioner with the offence. In such case, if the man were too poor to find security, the threat of imprisonment could be used to induce him to marry the woman, who could then be safely removed to her husband's parish. In 220 out of 332 cases of bastardy brought before the Court between 1800 and 1832, for which the necessary particulars are recorded, the man was not settled in the same parish as the woman. Among these 220 were numbered the majority of the 89 cases in which imprisonment was inflicted upon men unable to indemnify the parish and unwilling to be forced into wedlock. During the decade of acute economic depression from 1810 to 1820 the very rapid increase in immorality induced parish authorities to make a final trial of the deterrent effect of imprisonment: of the 72 men brought before the Bench and condemned to gaol during these ten years 51 were impecunious labourers, some of whom certainly were involved with women of their own parish. With the exception of this interval poor men were rarely prosecuted in Cambridgeshire during the nineteenth century, unless their settlement were in another parish.

[1] *Cambridge Chronicle*, April 25th, 1822.
[2] MS. Vestry Books, Royston. Cf. also *P.L.C. Rept.* 1834, App. A, Pt. 1, p. 592. (Cowell's Report.)

The evidence afforded by parochial documents points to the same conclusion. Numerous romantic accounts of the search for and capture of fugitive fathers enliven with grim humour the vestry annals of the county. "Whether Mr Bumble was able to ingratiate himself with Mrs Corney or not, he often did a good stroke of business for his parish in the matrimonial market."[1] Rarely, however, do vestry accounts refer to men belonging to the same parish as the women, unless the men were in a financial position to reimburse the parish without the embarrassment of marriage.

	£	s.	d.
Spent won we Went to honsey[2] to thak the Faler oup	0	1	6
Spent won we wos ther	0	0	6
For My journey to Chambridg	0	2	0
Payd for the Lysence	1	7	6
Spent at Dullingham	0	0	6
Payd to Mr Daves for Marring of tham	0	7	6
To the Order	0	4	0
To Mr Greaves Signing the order	0	2	0
To My Journey to Dullingham	0	2	6
To My Journey to Barnwell to remouef them	0	2	0
Expens thar	0	0	6
	£2	10	6

Thus did Isaac Ashman, overseer of Bottisham, relate the victorious capture of an offender, his marriage, and the removal to Dullingham.

In 1728 the parish officers of Meldreth dashed in pursuit of a "fornicator", Bernard Quilton, a settled inhabitant of a distant parish. After many hardships, supported by frequent libations, they secured and conveyed the culprit as far as the lock-up at Kneesworth. Completing the return journey to Meldreth on the morrow they found Mr Willows, the vicar, awaiting the party with marriage license prepared. "Offering the woman with one

[1] W. M. Palmer, *Meldreth Parish Records* (1896).
[2] Horningsea.

hand and a warrant with the other, the overseers gave the man the option of going to church or to gaol", and thankfully dumped down the fees with a sigh of relief that their mission had been successfully accomplished for £2. 13s. 8d.

"Can you keep a look-out for John Clark?" writes the overseer of Littleport to a friend at Terrington. "John Clark", comes the reply, "is at Lodgings at his Brothers which I have carefully examined after and find that he may be easily taken. He begins to shew himself by going out to Work. It is generally thought that he do not intend to have the girl."

Sarah Gear was a disturbing element in Royston life from her early years. Heavy expense was incurred on her account in the pursuit and prosecution of Thomas Fagg, a wealthy publican of Holborn. Though the Court drastically reduced the town's claims from £23 to £12, Fagg was ordered to pay a weekly sum of 5s. This sum was handed over to Sarah Gear on condition that she maintained the child herself. In 1793 the town was thrown into a panic by reports from the French capital and by unrest within its own borders, and with much trepidation did the overseer venture to draw attention again to Sarah's condition. For some reason of her own she flatly refused to swear to the man suggested by the overseer, and in lieu of committing her to the bridewell the officer attempted subterfuge. He approached the suspect, a certain Henry Gayford, an inn-keeper of Waltham, and offered him a substantial bribe if he could persuade the girl to join him at Waltham. Apparently Gayford's advances were acceptable to the gentle Sarah, and when she received the offer of service at the said inn, she calmly demanded that the Royston Committee should rig her out with clothing and pay her fare. They acquiesced without a murmur. A couple of years later Sarah was back at Royston, accompanied by her second unfortunate offspring, Gayford having quitted the inn and departed into the blue. She continued to be a source of perpetual expense to the parish for the next four or five years, till John Skipp, an eligible young bachelor from Barkway, coming to seek his fortune at Royston, fell in with the bewitching Sarah. With a watchful eye the overseer fanned the flame, put no obstacle in the way of the man's sojourn in the town, and probably even used his influence to help him to find a temporary job. In due season it became clear that the adventuress had again carried the day, but this time the Committee were prepared to exert their power and to force the young man into the bonds of matrimony. The fees were paid by the parish, the ring provided and the knot tied on Tuesday; on Wednesday the overseer presented a removal warrant, and the newly-wed couple found themselves promptly launched on the road to Barkway. Only a year later the irrepressible Sarah was again on the hands of Royston. Her lawful marriage had resulted in the desertion of her husband and she had returned to her former haunts. Now, however, her settlement was incontestably at Barkway, and with a sigh of satisfaction as he reflected that the youngest child had been born under the pious influence of wedlock, the overseer once again sped her out of the town to seek what ventures she would further afield.[1]

There are many records in Cambridgeshire of forced marriages between very youthful parties in the period between 1800 and 1834, for the hopelessness of the future outlook offered little inducement to restraint. Such marriages were frequently followed by the husband's desertion. The legitimacy of the offspring might sometimes be secured, but only too often did it mean their upbringing in an atmosphere which it is impossible to consider moral.[2]

E. IMMORALITY AMONG THE LABOURING CLASSES

It has been shown that offenders of a social grade above that of the labourer loomed large in the pages of Quarter Sessions during

---

[1] MS. Overseers' Accounts and Papers relating to evidence taken before the justices. (Royston.)

[2] The illegality of much parochial expenditure under this head was pointed out by the Cambs. Bench in 1831, when the overseers of Soham were prosecuted for irregularities. (MS. Q.S.R. Cambs. 1831.)

the critical period between 1796 and 1834.[1] It would, however, be a great mistake to assume that male immorality was mainly confined to these classes: it was rampant also in the labourers' ranks, but the sexual irregularities of poor men, as has been seen, did not come into the limelight unless the burden could be saddled upon other shoulders.

There were twenty-seven bastard children on the hands of Soham parish in 1829; in 1833 there were thirty-one. Ten of these thirty-one children were living with their mothers, who were allowed weekly sums varying from 1s. 6d. to 7s. In certain of these cases clearly the father was in comfortable circumstances. The remaining twenty-one children were lodged in the work-house: these children were probably the fruit of illicit intercourse between parishioners too poor to arouse the exertions of the overseer. In other parishes of the county the proportion of the bastardy expenses which arose from immorality among the very poor of both sexes seems to have been somewhat less. But of £277 expended by Soham on bastard children only £62 was refunded by the putative parents. In the case of fifteen parishes investigated by the Royal Commissioners in 1833 the position was better: the total sum spent on bastardy amounted to £1983 and of this £1093 was recovered. The indemnity of the parish had nevertheless not been secured though every other interest had been sacrificed to it.

F. SUGGESTED REFORMS

"Can you suggest any, and what, change in the laws respecting bastardy?" asked the Commissioners in 1833.[2] Various parishes proposed minor changes in procedure with a view to curtailing the period of warning which allowed defaulters to escape before the warrant could be issued. "Take the subject out of the hands of the parish, and allow the mother to sue the father for direct payment", replied an official of Over, anticipating with unusual

---

[1] Contrast Ashby, *op. cit.* pp. 84, 96.
[2] *P.L.C. Rept.* 1834, App. B 1, Pt. 5, Query 49.

acumen the reforms of a much later generation. "The best change would be to repeal every statute relating to bastardy", wrote the vicar of Harston, "to have a County Asylum for mothers during the time of nurture; the children educated and taught some useful employment; and the mothers given some religious instruction and induced to emigrate for their benefit." The thorough-going reformer of Waterbeach probed nearer to the root of the matter than any other correspondent: "The most effectual method of preventing improvident marriages", he suggested, "would be to give children a good education, and to put it in the power of both sexes by persevering industry to accumulate a sufficiency to begin the world with comfort". The general sentiment of the Commissioners themselves, however, was expressed in the replies from Histon and Foulmire:[1] "The whole expense should fall upon the mother—if the woman knew that there would be no provision for the child there would be few bastards".

---

[1] Usually so spelt at this date; the modern spelling is Fowlmere.

Chapter XIV

RELIEF OUTSIDE THE WORKHOUSE, 1660–1782

A. THE PENSION LIST. BADGING THE POOR

Apart from workhouse enactments and statutes relating to settlement the changes in the general Poor Law between 1660 and 1782 were of minor importance. In local administration attention was to a still greater extent concentrated upon the chess-board problems of removal. Relief must, however, be given to those whose claims were indisputable, and for these the dole and pension continued for more than two centuries the most ubiquitous form of assistance.

The unlimited power exercised by overseers in the selection of persons for the pension list was recognised by an Act of 1692.[1] Such persons, it was stated, were frequently chosen "upon frivolous pretences and for private ends", and were retained upon the list "notwithstanding the occasion or pretence of their receiving collection hath ceased". It was therefore enacted that the list of recipients should be drawn up at a public meeting of the vestry, held yearly or more frequently, and that no other person should receive "collection" except by order of a justice or of Quarter Sessions.

In order further to safeguard the rate-payers against an unwarranted growth of the pension list, an Act of 1697[2] required that all persons in receipt of public relief should wear badges openly upon the right sleeve.

It was the general opinion that in the course of the ensuing twenty or thirty years justices in their turn had grown careless, and in many instances ordered relief without due investigation. Hence, in 1723,[3] magistrates were required by law to

---

[1] 3 W. & M., c. 11. [2] 8 and 9 W. III, c. 30. [3] 9 G. I, c. 7.

examine the pauper on oath and to assure themselves before issuing an order for relief that application had first been made to the overseer, who had more immediate opportunity of knowing the circumstances. The reforms inaugurated in 1692 were certainly called for in Cambridgeshire. Mere summary entries, such as the following, defied investigation but were still the only form of accounts kept by many parishes:

Whittlesford, 1652: Given to several people, 4s. 6d.

Sawston, 1673: Given this year to poore not able to work, £41. 13s. 3d.

After 1692, however, in perhaps the majority of the larger parishes a regular annual investigation of the pension list was instituted and was maintained with some show of thoroughness for the next thirty or forty years. In 1693, for example, Linton vestry assembled and compiled the following pathetic schedule of paupers entitled to the weekly collection:

	li.	s.	d.
Tho. Smith and his wife being very Ancient and decreppid are to receive weekly	00	01	00
Widd. Chapman Being Aged and past worke	00	01	00
Arthur Parish being adged	00	00	04
Widd. Redgwell old and hur worke done	00	01	00
Widd. Wright aged and lame	00	00	08
Widd. Casboult Beinge bed Read	00	02	00
Widd. Beeres ancient	00	00	04
Mary Brand beinge lame of a fistula	00	02	00
Eliz. Jackson beinge old and lame	00	00	08
Widd. Digines beinge lame	00	01	00
Widd. Dockrill poor widd. ouercharged with children	00	01	06
Ann Elett poor and ouercharged with children	00	00	06
Widd. Bell the like	00	00	06
Jo Baritt and his wife old and theire worke done	00	00	06
Ann Richmon beinge lame	00	00	04
Mile Cole for Sabroakes Child	00	02	00

	li. s. d.
Tabersons wife ouercharged with Children and husband run away	00 00 04
Old Skiner decrepid and past labour	00 01 00
Luke Hady An Iddot	00 00 06
	00 17 02

No able-bodied men were included in the above list, but widows, as at all periods and in all parishes, were conspicuous. It is, however, to be noted that at this date, in contrast to the position which obtained in not a few parts of the county a century later,[1] even "ancient" widows and certain of those "ouercharged with children" were clearly expected to earn some part of their living. The type of pauper qualified for inclusion in the yearly "collection list", or "calendar", was very similar in all parishes which took the Act to heart and regularly weeded out the recipients. The rates of allowance had increased, but in other respects the list drawn up at Easter 1728 by the vestry of Bottisham corresponded to that of Linton:

		1st month	2nd month	3rd month	4th month
Widow Gebson at	2s.	IIII	IIII	IIII	IIII
Gorge Rite	2s.	IIII	IIII	IIII	IIII
Widow Granfel	1s.	etc.			
Alse Longe	1s.				
Widow Mansell	1s. 6d.				
Wid. Piper	2s.				
Wid. Crane	2s.	IIII	IIII	IIIO	O
Doll Curtes	1s. 10d.	etc.			
Ann Whiten	2s.				
Roberd Daye	2s.				
Mary Souell	1s.				
Edward Gelsen	2s.				
Rich Smeth with Eaten boye 1s. 6d.					
Will Kene with Eaten boye 2s.					
Frances Meler with Eaten garl 1s. 6d.					
Alse Hesell 6d.					
		£1. 5s. 10d.			

[1] Cf. *P.L.C. Rept.* 1834.

Slight alterations in the names year by year suggest that up to about 1730 or 1740 some real supervision was exercised by the Easter vestry. The names of the paupers who passed muster at Bottisham were entered in a register, and against each name the overseer had merely to record by strokes the number of weekly payments made.

The weekly pensioners cost Linton in 1693 about £45 per annum, representing a rise of over 10 per cent. since 1686—and this after careful elimination of improper cases. Magisterial influence was strong in the Linton district, though it was exercised here mainly through the vestry, of which the leading local justices, Millicent, Sclater, and Richers, were active members. Notwithstanding close supervision the number of pensioners persistently[1] grew, and at the Easter vestry meeting of 1710 it was consequently ordered that weekly payments be made in public at the close of the Sunday evening service; that "no addition be made to the weekly collection"; that no money be paid for "by-collection"—casual relief—except under written orders "from John Millicent Esq., Thos. Richers Esq., or Thos. Sclater Esq., or five of the most substantial inhabitants, or three of them with the two churchwardens"; and that "the vouchers for what is so disbursed be produced at the passing of Overseers Accounts". Two years later a Linton vestry of fifteen members, including the three magistrates, repeated the above injunctions and added sundry very significant ones. No purchase was to be made of "cloths or other necessaries for the poor except by written order of one or more justice, or of five of the most substantial parishioners". No overseer whilst in office was himself to supply clothing or other goods to the parish poor, unless he would guarantee to "sell them as cheap as any other person of the said parish"![2] Orders made at the monthly meetings of the vestry were to be disallowed unless duly signed by those present.

---

[1] Cf. Wisbech in 1677, *supra*, p. 63.

[2] At Meldreth, in 1732, the overseer, Jonathan Stockbridge, himself provided the carriage of coals for the poor, at the cost of the parish, though his charges appear to have been reasonable.

The attempts to limit relief at Linton had been supplemented in 1697 by a prohibition of door-to-door begging, under pain of losing the regular allowance. Children were the worst offenders in this respect. In 1703 it was further ordered that persons on the approved list, "and all others y^t shall come into the weekly Collection for the future shall wear a badge on the right arme, and those persons that shall refuse to weare the same shall bee forthwith taken out of the Collection". Badges had frequently been worn by institutional poor in Tudor times.[1] In 1682 Great St Mary's vestry agreed "that all the men and women that do or shall inhabit in the Almes houses by Gt St Marys Church, and that receive weekly collections, shall have every second year, the men one blue carsey coate, and the women one blue carsey wascott as their upper garment, with a badge on the right arme, S.M.G." This it might be supposed was to prevent the selling or pawning of the parish clothing; but it was further ordered that "all those that the parish pay rents for shall be obliged to weare the said coats, if the parish so requires it". In 1684 £9. 18s. 6d. was paid for "cloth, coates making, and for mending the Badges". This was of course before the Act of 1697. In many Cambridgeshire parishes the wearing of badges was insisted upon between about 1700 and 1730; after that date it seems to have died out, though the Act was not repealed till 1810. The overseer of Meldreth, for example, paid for badges in 1708, 1714, 1717, 1720 and 1723; Bottisham provided "Bagges" in 1727 and again in 1730; St Botolph's, Cambridge, in 1712.

Abuses crept in even where magistrates were most alert, hence it is easy to surmise what the conditions must have been in less active parishes. At Linton the calendar was restrained within reasonable limits only with difficulty.[2]

[1] They were suggested by the Statutes of 1557 and 1563. Wisbech badged the regular pensioners in 1680: 180 badges were made and a stamp was designed to facilitate their manufacture in the future. (MS. Corp. Minute and Order Book, Wisbech.)

[2] Particulars are available at Linton for certain years. In 1694 there were 20 names on the list; in 1697, 31; in 1701, 26; in 1705, 29; in 1710, 34; in 1712, 27; in 1724, 18; in 1729, 33; in 1731, 27; in 1733, 25.

In the latter part of the eighteenth century the relative expenditure upon what were classified as casual charges or by-expenses, as distinguished from the registered collection, or weeklies, grew rapidly. Between 1760 and 1770 in most parishes of the county one notes the by-expenses beginning to preponderate. Even in the first thirty years of the century the same trend is well marked: in 1693 the by-expenses at Linton amounted to less than one-fifth of the whole disbursements to the poor; in 1731 they formed over one-third. The overseer's account for the first half of the year 1731 was as follows:

1st Overseer:

	£	s.	d.
By 28 weeks Registered Collection	50	2	8
„ Occasional Payments during that time	12	19	4½
„ Incidental Expenses laid out for the poor	5	15	0
„ Expenses in Clothing for use of poor	8	14	9½
	£77	11	10

No less a sum than £131 was spent at Linton, in 1731, on poor-relief—including £8. 13s. 7d. on a settlement appeal. In 1693 the total had been but £58. This rate of increase was above the average, but in every parish examined the advance in expenditure was marked.

One item on the credit side of the Linton balance-sheet of 1731 should be noted: "To Goods sold of Alice Hooper, 14s. 8d." The practice of refusing relief unless the meagre possessions of the pauper were pledged to the overseer was not as common at this date as it became later, but Linton affords by no means an isolated example. "To break up their little domestic establishment, to seize...I know not by what authority, on the furniture and moveables which they have, perhaps by unrelenting industry and parsimony during a long course of years, been able to get together, to do this, Gentlemen," said Nasmith, addressing the Grand Jury for the Isle of Ely, "is irretrievably to break the spirits...to drive men to despair, and to make them callous and indifferent as to future destiny."[1] Inventories of paupers' goods taken over by the parish constantly appear among vestry papers.[2]

Magisterial intervention was not very common in the smaller villages of the county, but in one or two of the main parishes in each hundred the history of Linton repeats itself. In some cases the overseer found his activities so seriously hampered, not only by the justice but more often by the vestry, that he shirked accepting office whenever possible: not infrequently one finds a woman elected as overseer.

B. RELIEF IN KIND

The following summary of his half-year's expenditure was made by the overseer of Swavesey in 1737:

		£	s.	d.
To ye weekly bill ye 1st Qtr.		9	5	0
Do 2nd Qtr.		12	6	3
To ffewell		8	17	0
First By Bill		1	18	9
Second By Bill		1	18	$2\frac{1}{2}$
To Mr Cutcheys Bill		1	5	$6\frac{1}{2}$
To ye repairs of ye Town House			11	6
To ye Rents		6	10	9
To Abatements			19	6
To Carrying Mary Bensted to Landbeach per Order, and Expenses		1	0	0
		£44	12	6

[1] Cf. Scott, op. cit. p. 48: "It is really cruel to treat as criminals, whose property is confiscated, those who...have no crime but inevitable poverty".

[2] In 1812, for example, the overseer of Meldreth made the following note:

"Inventory of Old Grace household Goods:

1 Box Reale and wheal and tea kittle

2 Borsketts 2 pans wood Dish.

3 Basons Chamber pot hutch New Bed Cord hoe and staff.

Bed and Bedstid and Sundry".

For an inventory made at Bottisham in 1783 see Appendix v.

The "by" bills, for which invoices were now presented to the vestry and preserved among the records, included casual payments during sickness, the purchase of wheels and reels for sundry paupers, clothing expenses, repairs to shoes, etc.

Relief in kind took various forms, of which "ffewell" was perhaps the most important. Bequests specifically devoted to the purchase of coal for the poor were enjoyed by the majority of Cambridgeshire villages, but it was usually necessary also to draw upon the rates. In some cases the coal was distributed freely to certain families during the winter; more often supplies were purchased wholesale by the parish and retailed below cost price to the poor. "Secole" was obtained from Newcastle, being conveyed by coasting vessels to Lynn and thence by river to Cambridge. During periods of warfare much difficulty was often experienced in maintaining the supply. In 1702, for example, a petition to Parliament was sent by the corporation of Cambridge, complaining that through "want of sufficient convoy...the ships and vessels cannot be secured...against privateers, which at this juncture do so infest the coasts thereabouts that no vessel dare venture by sea. By reason thereof the price of Sea Coal is advanced to one third part, and is likely to be raised to a much greater rate unless it be timely prevented".[1]

In many of the Fen parishes, before enclosure, the poor were able to dig turf freely. In other parts of the county it was often necessary for the parish to purchase turf for cheap retail sale. A quantity was bought and carted to Meldreth, in 1719, and sold at a reduced price to the poor. Forty bushels of coal were similarly bought and retailed in the same parish in 1726. In December 1777 Sawston purchased at a cost of £1. 2s. 6d. 3000 of turf as well as a quantity of "coles" for free distribution to certain parishioners. "Thirteen thousand of Turfe at 3s. 6d. the thousand" were bought by Whittlesford in 1724: part of it was given and part sold to the poor.

The county was not well timbered, and the serious shortage of wood was obvious as early as 1697, when Linton threatened

[1] Cooper, *op. cit.* IV, p. 52.

to "put off the collection" any family whose children were caught breaking up hedges for firewood. The warning was repeated in 1710, and in 1756 prosecution was threatened.

Apart from the fitting-out of apprentices, clothing formed in almost every parish a considerable item of chargeability.[1] Beds, bedding, and other articles of furniture were loaned at times from the workhouse store. Hoes and spades were sometimes given, and very frequently reels, wheels and cards. In almost every inventory of paupers' household goods, wheels and reels are catalogued, and entries such as the following are common:

1694: Pd. for a Linnen wheel for George Macer   3s. 6d.
1706: Pd. for a pair of Cards for Hugh Johnson   2s. 2d.
       Pd. for a Wheel for him   2s. 6d.

Cows, horses, and hogs were now and again provided by the parish. The overseer of Duxford, in 1724, "Bought Widow Dover a Cow, £4. 2s. 6d.", and gave "Widow Campin mony to buy a hog, £0. 13s. 6d." The overseer of Great Shelford, in 1712, "bought a Cow for old Andrew" for £2. 18s., and "exchanged" a cow on behalf of Cock at a cost of 3s. In 1734 Fuller Wooten of the same parish was compensated "for Loss of a Cow, £2. 2s."[2] Great Shelford was fortunate in possessing

---

[1] Overseers' bills of the following description are to be found wherever parish papers are preserved:

"Meldreth, 1696.
                                             s. d.

3½ yards of course cloath for a coat and breeches for Aynesworths boy   8 0
For making of them   2 10
For a pair of shoes for him   2 10
For a pr. of shoes for Hunts girl   2 6
For a pr. of shoes and pattins together   2 6
For a pr. of stockings he bought her   1 0"

Bottisham parish paid, in 1765, "for a Coat and weastcote, 9s. 6d.", but the following year the overseer, Abraham Cutchey, was a tailor, and the cost of similar garments rose to 13s. 6d.

[2] In 1745 the overseer of Great Shelford paid to Stephen Northfield "for the loss of his Hoe, 5s." (MS. Vestry Book, Great Shelford.)

charities which were freely used to supplement the rates. In 1745 "Jno. Faircloth and Daniel Corney, Churchwardens of Gt. Shelford, bought Wid. Thorn a horse, by the Consent of the Parish, for which hors they gave £2. 3s. out of the rent of Rich. Cocks House. The said Hors cost £3. 3s., the other pound they gathered in the parish for the said Wid. Thorn". Here and there one thus finds churchwardens and overseers in their distinctive capacities still working in harmony and combining voluntary and compulsory funds in the fashion of an earlier century, though it was "deserving" widows or orphans who benefited most by voluntary charity. The tendency of the age was more typically manifested in the benefaction of Alderman Mott who, in 1762, left small sums of money for distribution to such poor of Cambridge as were "not receiving collection".[1]

Some few parishes gave doles of wheat, meslin, barley or rye. Bottisham[2] frequently made allowances such as the following:

1727: Paide Roberd daye 1 Peack of wheat	1s. 4d.
„ „ „ 2 „ „ meslin	2s. 1d.
„ Widow Swan 1 „ „ wheat	1s. 4d.

A bad harvest raised the price of corn so seriously as to produce a tumult at Cambridge in 1757. Profiteering was suspected, and a mob composed largely of women broke open a granary in the town and carried off fifteen quarters of wheat, belonging to a farmer who had that day refused to sell at 9s. 11d. a bushel. The following day a further twenty-seven sacks of flour were triumphantly appropriated by the rebels. Similar conditions threatened in 1768:[3] the Vice-Chancellor sided with the consumers and ordered the corn-market to be opened at 11 a.m. and to be kept open till 1 p.m., declaring that the late hour of opening recently adopted by dealers prevented much corn from coming to market and resulted in the price being "enhanced to the poor".

[1] *House of Commons' Reports of Committees*, Supplement I, Charitable Donations (1786–8), p. 104.
[2] MS. Vestry Books, Bottisham.
[3] Cooper, *op. cit.* IV, pp. 297, 353.

An allowance of a peck of rye (valued at $7\frac{1}{2}d$.) granted in 1741 by the overseer of Stetchworth to an able-bodied man, nominally on behalf of his family, is an interesting anticipation, such as has been noted occasionally even at earlier dates,[1] of the widespread policy pursued later in the century. In 1763 John Reeves of Bottisham received a grant of 2s. on similar grounds.

C. EMPLOYMENT. THE SURVEYORS' RATE. INCREASE IN POOR-RATES

Except in connection with workhouse projects it seems to have been unusual to maintain a parish "stock", in accordance with the Act of 1601, during the eighteenth century, though the practice was revived here and there, as will presently appear, in the following century. Occasionally the Bench issued an order to some negligent parish to provide work for an unemployed man, "or else to give him relief". Parishes did at times employ able-bodied paupers in "field-keeping", in breaking and sifting gravel, and in carting stones during the middle years of the century. In 1764 several men were so employed at Whittlesford at 4s. or 5s. per week. Sawston, in 1777, set men "gathering stones for the parish" at 5s. per week, or cutting willows at 6s. Independent agricultural labourers received not more than 6s. in this part of the county during the 'sixties and 'seventies. As early as 1717 Meldreth set a man to work "gathering stones" for several days in the week, and made up the insufficient wages so earned by "6d. extra".

In 1757 a payment of £3. 3s. 8d. was made by the Highway Surveyor of Linton to the overseer, "for use of labour of paupers to gather stones", and from this date onwards an annual sum, increased greatly in amount by the nineteenth century, was handed over from the one officer to the other. Two-thirds of the money earned by labourers on the road was, in 1834, paid as

[1] In 1614 the Town Bailiff of Wisbech ordered the parish officers to allow a man relief "for his children". (MS. Corp. Order and Minute Book, Wisbech.)

relief by this parish. Great Gransden was the only village in the county of which it was reported in 1834 that the Surveyors' Rate was applied to improving the roads "at fair wages". "In this county generally", said Cowell in 1834, "the Surveyors' Rate is disused, or at least disbursed exactly as the Poor Rate in paying parish wages, whereas it ought to be applied to the fair remuneration of actual labour properly superintended."[1]

Most indeed of the practices so widely prevalent between 1795 and 1834, and so justly condemned by the Royal Commissioners, had their origin in earlier years.

Calculations based on statistical returns to Parliament for the years 1776, 1785, 1803 and 1834 give the following rates of increase in the total disbursements to the poor:[2]

	1776–1785	1785–1803	1803–1834[3]
	%	%	%
Town of Cambridge	50	47·5	45[4]
County of Cambs. (excluding Isle of Ely)	51·7	110	89
Isle of Ely	32·6	125·4	110

[1] *P.L.C. Rept.* 1834, App. A, Pt. 1, p. 590. Cf. also *ibid.* pp. 241, 251. Certain parishioners of Soham appealed to Quarter Sessions against items of this nature in the overseers' accounts in 1831. (MS. Q.S.R. Cambs. 1831.)

[2] For the Parliamentary Returns for the respective hundreds of the county, see Appendix VIII.

[3] The population of the whole county increased 61 per cent. between 1801 and 1834.

[4] That is to say there was a rise of 50 per cent. between 1776 and 1785, a further rise of 47·5 per cent. between 1785 and 1803, and a still further increase of 45 per cent. between 1803 and 1834. The increase of population, especially between 1811 and 1821, has to be borne in mind, and also the inflated prices during the French Wars.

Chapter XV

RELIEF OUTSIDE THE WORKHOUSE,
1782–1834

A. DEVELOPMENTS, 1782–1796

The increase in expenditure upon poor-relief between 1776 and 1785 was clearly marked in every district of Cambridgeshire. It was to "casual" charges, moreover, that an ever larger proportion of the poor-rate was devoted, and among those to whom irregular payments were thus made were steadily growing numbers of men and women who must obviously have been temporarily unemployed or under-employed. The sum of 2s. 6d. per week, for example, allowed to a blind man by the parish of Histon in 1740 could barely have supported him unless he were living with relatives, but the grants of 1s., 1s. 6d. and 2s. made at the same time to various other men must clearly have been insufficient for complete maintenance. It was evidently expected that these small doles would be eked out by casual employment. Here in essence, therefore, was the system of supplementing wages out of the rates. Gilbert's Act of 1782 recognised the hardship endured by poor folk unable to obtain the all-necessary addition to their parish doles, and gave legal sanction to the principle of aiding the able-bodied out of the rates, without requiring them to enter the workhouse, should insufficient employment be available.

Although no Gilbert Unions were formed in Cambridgeshire, it was from about this date that magisterial interference on behalf of the able-bodied poor began to be of more frequent occurrence. The spring of 1782 was very late and corn was reported dear.[1] Early in 1783 the justices of the hundred of Whittlesford met in

[1] Extracts from a Whittlesford farmer's diary, describing the seasons 1771–85. (MS. Maynard Collection, Saffron Walden Museum.)

conclave, with a view to systematising the relief to be granted to the unemployed of this district. They decided that "every man who has a family, and behaves himself seemly, be allowed the price of 5 quartern loaves per week, with 2 quartern loaves added for each member of his family".

In 1785 the crops were again seriously deficient, and an outbreak of small-pox in the villages of south-east Cambridgeshire added to the local distress. The scale of 1783 had aroused opposition, hence a modification was made. It was simply agreed to make up the wages of married labourers to 6s. per week.[1] The system is seen in operation in the following communication, addressed in January 1787 by Edmund Fisher, a magistrate of Duxford, to the overseers of the neighbouring village of Whittlesford: "Mark Runham of your Parish has been with me this Day to complain that the Surveyor will pay him only 10d. a Day for his Labour. If that be the case you must make it up a Shilling; as it is agreed by the Justices that every Labouring Man who has a family, provided he behaves well, and does not neglect his Work, shall have 6s. a Week".[2]

During the 'seventies of the century the number of workless labourers set to gather stones at Sawston was never more than two or three at a time, even in the winter. In 1785, during many months of the year, there were four or five, and in the years which succeeded such entries as the following become more and more frequent:

1786: Pd. John Taylor	4	days work	4s.
Pd. John Brown	6	,, ,,	6s.
Pd. Wm Flack	5½	,, ,,	5s. 6d.

From 1790 onwards there were occasions when men were not even set to work at all, though at first the relief granted was less than when they were occupied in breaking stones. Items

[1] It is not clear whether any additional allowance was made for children in this second agreement. (MS. Maynard Collection, Saffron Walden Museum and MS. Vestry Papers, Whittlesford.)

[2] MS. Maynard Collection, Saffron Walden Museum.

of the following nature occur "1790: James townsen, no work 2s."

In 1792 the Roundsman System was adopted in the Sawston area. Men were sent round the village with a ticket, and employment given at what rate and for what time the farmer thought fit. The parish then made up the wages to a shilling per day, or gave the whole sum of one shilling if no work had been obtained, usually recording the transaction thus: "1792: Gave Harras for going after work 1 day, 1s."

It is hardly surprising to find that by 1794 the number of able-bodied men more or less regularly on the rounds at Sawston had increased to twelve. In this year the minimum maintenance rate was raised to 7s. per week,[1] and an allowance for children was added.

In 1792 the first entry of a similar character was made by the overseers of both Bottisham and Burwell. In this district also the wages were made up to one shilling per day, when actual work was done either for individual farmers or in the parish gravel pit. If men merely went the rounds unsuccessfully 2d. a day was deducted:

> 1792: John Bensted 2 days worke   2s.
> John Mathes 2 days no worke   1s. 8d.
> Jorge Morgan 2 days no worke   1s. 8d.[2]

In 1794 the rate at Bottisham was raised to 1s. 4d. per day and the deduction of 2d. now ceased.

The Roundsman System, in one form or another, was particularly common at this date in the Isle of Ely.

It was in 1795, however, when to the distress occasioned by ruinous harvests was added the terror of revolution, that discussion of the agricultural labourer's position was in every

---

[1] It was dropped again to 6s. in 1796. A scale on the basis of the price of bread and the size of the family was in operation here throughout the first three decades of the nineteenth century. In 1804 no less than twenty-four families were so relieved in addition to certain other paupers. (MS. Vestry Books, Sawston.)

[2] MS. Vestry Books, Bottisham.

mouth. Should the justices be called upon, as in earlier days, to fix wages in accordance with the cost of living, or should the existing allowances out of the rates be amplified? Were the justices alive to the opportunities for profiteering? By what means could the consumption of corn be curtailed?

Subscriptions were raised in Cambridge to provide the poor with bread at the reduced price of 6*d.* the quartern loaf.[1] The result was that consumption increased, the shortage became more pronounced, and the market price rose still higher. Petty food riots broke out in the town. The mob seized a lighter laden with flour; the county magistrates, assembled for the July Sessions, in considerable trepidation ordered the flour to be conveyed to the Town Hall. The Deputy Mayor sent for the owner, paid him for the flour, and assured the populace that it should be used to enable them to have bread at 6*d.* the loaf. The next day measures were taken by the authorities to prevent the "regrating" of meat and other market offences, a reduction in prices was promised, and quiet was restored.[2]

The sale of flour and bread below cost price was, however, tabooed as a degrading form of charity by certain of the more independent workers of the Eastern Counties. The neighbouring town of Bury St Edmunds declared itself in favour of fixing wages according to a sliding scale. Arthur Young, impressed by the arguments of the Suffolk magistrates, circularised the newly established Cambridgeshire branch of the Board of Agriculture on the subject of a minimum wage. The Cambridgeshire Bench met to consider the position. They turned down the proposal to regulate wages and substituted suggestions for systematising grants from the rates. "Relief to the labouring poor in husbandry", the Bench agreed was very necessary. An allowance, therefore, of "3*d.* per head for every such person until next harvest would not be more than adequate". In parishes where wages exceeded 7*s.* per week a "proportionable deduction" in this sum should be made. Justices were requested to communi-

---

[1] Weighing 4 lb. 4 oz. (Cooper, *op. cit.* IV, p. 454.) Cf. *infra*, p. 211, note 2. [2] *Ibid.*

cate this opinion to the vestries within their respective divisions, recommending them to meet and arrange concerted measures, which should be submitted for magisterial approval.

At the same time farmers were gently admonished and advised "that a rise in wages of the labouring poor would be expedient", since such rise had taken place in neighbouring counties and the necessities of the poor were no less in Cambridgeshire.

At the next meeting of Quarter Sessions the magistrates endeavoured to cut down the consumption of bread corn and, to their credit, set the example by pledging themselves to use only standard bread[1] in their own families, and to prohibit the use of flour in other articles of domestic consumption—"earnestly recommending" others to follow suit. Millers were "recommended" to abstain from grinding, and bakers from baking, any finer quality of flour. Parish officials were urged to apply charitable subscriptions "in meat or other articles of food", rather than in wheaten flour. Dealers guilty of forestalling, engrossing, regrating or offering prices above the market rate were to be rigorously prosecuted. At an adjourned Sessions it was demonstrated that the purchase of growing crops was a common, though concealed offence, and the Clerk of the Peace was instructed to take immediate legal proceedings.[2]

Meanwhile the Minimum Wages' Bill had been defeated by the eloquence of Pitt, and the famous meeting of the Speenhamland magistrates had, in 1795, set the seal upon the alternative policy of the bread scale—the making-up of the labourer's wages on the double basis of the price of bread and the size of his family.

In 1796 the principle of granting outdoor relief to the ablebodied was ratified by Parliament.[3] A single justice might at his

[1] The flour to weigh three-quarters of the weight of the wheat, and to consist of "the whole produce of the grain, the bran or hull thereof only excepted".

[2] MS. Q.S.R. Oct. 1795.

[3] By 36 G. III, c. 23. (In 1815, by the Act of 55 G. III, c. 137, two justices might grant an order for six months, and renew it indefinitely though the amount of relief was limited.)

discretion order such assistance for one month, and in company with a colleague might renew an order from month to month indefinitely.

B. THE BREAD SCALES

Scales were drawn up at divisional meetings for particular parts of the county at different periods between 1783 and 1821, and were in general use by 1800. No common county scale seems, however, to have been adopted in Cambridgeshire till 1821.

The Speenhamland scale fixed the minimum weekly income of a single man at the price of 3 gallon loaves,[1] and allowed an additional $1\frac{1}{2}$ gallons for each member of his family. In terms of the present day this allowance has been calculated as approximately 14s. 7d. per week for a family consisting of man, wife and three children—"about one-half of what a parsimonious Board of Guardians would to-day (1926) regard as a bare subsistence!"[2]

The Cambridgeshire scale of 1821 ran as follows:[3]

A single woman, the price of			3	quartern loaves per week			
„ „ man	„	„ „	4	„	„	„	„
A man and his wife	„	„	7	„	„	„	„
Ditto and one child	„	„	8	„	„	„	„
„ and two „ [ren] „		„	11	„	„	„	„

A man and his wife and four children and upwards, at the price of 2 quartern loaves per head per week.

It will be necessary to add to the above income in all cases of sickness or other kinds of distress, and particularly of such persons or families who deserve encouragement by their good behaviour, whom parish officers should mark both by commendation and reward.

By Order of the Magistrates
Assembled at the Shire Hall,
Cambr. 15th Dec^r., 1821.

---

[1] The gallon loaf weighed 8 lb. 11 oz. and was equivalent to rather more than 2 quartern loaves.   [2] Webb, *op. cit.* p. 182.

[3] *P.L.C. Rept.* 1834, App. A, Pt. 1, p. 584. (Cowell's Report.)

Whilst the Speenhamland scale allowed the price of 9 gallon loaves, or about 18½ quartern loaves, per week, for a man with a wife and three children, the Cambridgeshire scale allowed only 11 quartern loaves. A single man in this county was expected to maintain himself completely on the price of less than 2½ lb. of bread per day, whilst even the county prisoner, in 1789, was given 1½ lb. of bread, or its equivalent, in addition to shelter.

It is not clear whether or not the county scale of 1821 was adopted by the town magistrates of Cambridge, but in 1829 they drew up a scale independently of the county.[1] Its wording was identical with the scale of 1821, except that the allowances were in each case ½ quartern loaf more than in the county. Systematic rates-in-aid of wages were, however, formulated by individual parishes of the town at an earlier date. The exact terms of one for St Bene't's is preserved in a vestry minute of 1816:

Agreed by a majority of officers and parishioners that the under-mentioned Wages should be given to the Labouring Poor when at work for the parish, and what to pay them out of Work:

Single Man, at work per day		1s. 0d.
out of work		6d.
Man with 1 child, at work		1s. 4d.
out of work		8d.
„ „ wife and 1 child, at work		1s. 4d.
out of work		8d.
„ „ „ and 2 chln., at work		1s. 4d.
out of work		8d.
„ „ „ and 3 chln., at work		1s. 6d.
out of work		9d.
„ „ „ and 4 chln., at work		1s. 6d.
out of work		9d.

Signed 2 churchwardens, 3 overseers, 12 parishioners.

The quartern loaf was selling at 11¾d. in Cambridge in 1816,[2]

[1] A copy of the scale is to be found pasted on the back of one of the MS. Vestry Books of St Bene't's parish. Reference is also made to it in *P.L.C. Rept.* 1834, App. A, Pt. 1, p. 241.

[2] *Cambridge Chronicle*, 1816.

hence the unmarried man at work for St Bene't's parish for six whole days could purchase just over six quartern loaves; if entirely unemployed only three. There was certainly little temptation offered here recklessly to increase the size of the family with a single view to improving the financial position: a man with a wife and three children could purchase, on a full week's work, only about nine quartern loaves—two loaves less than on the county scale of 1821.

Though apparently widely adopted in rural counties[1] the bread scales were not accepted without a dissentient voice. In 1800, and again in 1807, Whitbread struggled in vain to press a Minimum Wages Bill through Parliament. The proposal of 1807 was considered by the County Bench at an adjourned Sessions, but failed to gain any influential support. Effective criticism of the scales was indeed delayed till the war came to an end. A House of Commons' Committee reported against the system in 1817, yet four years later, utterly ignoring the disastrous results upon both pauper and independent labourer, which twenty years' experience had everywhere revealed, Cambridgeshire drew up its first general county scale.

From the 'twenties onwards, as conditions all over the county became more rigid, it is noteworthy that the number of labourers committed to the county gaol under the Vagrancy Law for "refusing to work for the customary wages" rapidly increased —and this notwithstanding the drastic treatment meted out to the Ely and Littleport rioters a few years before. A "riot and conspiracy to raise wages", among the agricultural labourers of Kirtling in 1822, and a similar disturbance at Sawston in the following year, heralded the disorders which were to follow a decade later, when allowances in many parts of the county were even lower than in the 'twenties, and when the position of the independent labourer had in consequence become insupportable. "The system of paying wages out of the poor rates, from its effect in reducing the wages of labour," said the Report of 1834, "had compelled men of independent minds and industrious

[1] There seems to be still need for detailed investigation on this point.

habits, from the absolute impossibility of maintaining their families on their earnings, to apply for relief."[1]

House of Commons' Committees condemned the scales with increasing vehemence in 1822, 1825 and 1828, but the alternative proposal to fix a minimum wage was again rejected by Parliament in 1827.

The high price of bread and the growing tension manifest led the Cambridgeshire Bench to appoint a Committee, in 1828, to consider "the allowances to be made by overseers to persons applying to them for the relief of themselves and families". The Committee reported in favour of the scale, but actually suggested a reduction of the existing grants. "The best criterion towards determining what is requisite for the support of a man and his family", said the Committee, "is the current price of bread. The regulations made on this supposition by the Magistrates on the 15th Dec., 1821, have been in general most beneficial: yet it appears that the scale as there laid down does not correctly determine the allowance for the support of a large family, when the prices of bread and flour are high, inasmuch as potatoes and the necessary household articles seldom at the same time rise proportionably." On these specious grounds the Committee recommended that, uniformly throughout the county, magistrates should so far depart from the scale of 1821 as to substitute for each quartern loaf the sum of $10\frac{1}{2}d.$, for such time as the price of the loaf remained above $10\frac{1}{2}d.$, and that they should at all times take into earnest consideration "the character of the applicant". The Committee further urged that overseers should be "attentive in seeing to the actual employment" of persons applying for relief—not at this date with much hope of its being profitable, but "as task work, whereby the industrious man may be distinguished from the idle one, and his earnings be made proportionate".[2]

The recommendations were not, however, adopted. The magistrates of the Royston division asserted the impossibility

[1] *P.L.C. Rept.* 1834, App. A, Pt. 1, p. 682. (Everett's Report.)

[2] MS. Q.S.R. 1828.

of enforcing a scale. Many had been the skirmishes. The town had finally adopted Sturges-Bourne's Act of 1819 and had established a Select Vestry which consisted mainly of tradesmen, representative of town interests. The new vestry had determinedly resisted "the keeping up of a large standing army of paupers for the benefit of the landlords and farmers of neighbouring parishes, who in Spring, harvest and fine weather would take them off the rates at 6*d*. and 1*s*. a day, and send them back again in shoals in Winter and bad weather".[1]

In these circumstances the Bench played for time and appointed a further Committee of investigation.

The stress laid upon "good behaviour" and "deserving character" was typical of these years. With barns to preserve and grocery stores to maintain, magistrates and overseers tended no doubt to be

> Liberal of their aid
> To clamorous importunity in rags,
> But ofttimes deaf to supplicants, who would blush
> To wear a tatter'd garb, however coarse,

but the "deserving" came too often within the category of the "servile, tale-bearing, dust-licking, canting and hypocritical", animadverted upon by the penetrating Denson of Waterbeach.[2]

The Committee reported in January 1829[3] to the following effect: The administration in many parts of the county was "neither in conformity with the letter nor spirit of the legislative enactment of the 43rd of Eliz."

In scarcely a parish in the county did the churchwardens take any part in the execution of the Poor Laws. Monthly meetings were almost universally discontinued and the whole distribution of the parish funds left to one overseer. In direct violation of the Acts of 1692 and 1723 applicants were continually relieved by

---

[1] *P.L.C. Rept.* 1834, App. A, Pt. 1, p. 585. (Cowell's Report.)
[2] J. Denson, *A Peasant's Voice to Landowners* (Camb. 1830), p. 46.
[3] MS. Q.S.R. 1829.

the "Acting Overseer" (as he was now called) upon his sole authority, and his accounts were passed without comment. The able-bodied poor were frequently relieved with money without any work being required of them, or were herded together in a gravel pit to labour or to loiter to the entire demoralisation of their habits.

The Committee desired in consequence to advocate the following measures:

(1) The adoption of the Act of 59 G. III. The appointment of Select Vestries would encourage an able body of parishioners to meet frequently, to examine closely every applicant for relief, and to scrutinise strictly every item of expenditure.

(2) The exaction of work from all able-bodied paupers to whom relief was granted. For this purpose the suggestions of the 59 G. III, c. 12, should be put into practice. A portion of land should be acquired or set aside for cultivation by pauper labour. Only by way of loan should any relief to the able-bodied be given, except in return for labour.

(3) A better system of parish account keeping would enable magistrates to see at a glance which items were improperly included. The method devised by Mr Metcalfe of Foulmire, and published by Messrs Shaw,[1] rendered accounts at once "intelligible and perspicuous".

[1] The system was adopted by many parishes in other counties. Expenditure was classified under the following heads:
  (1) Aged and infirm, constantly on the parish: (a) Resident; (b) Non-resident.
  (2) Widows and children.
  (3) Men and boys working for the parish.
  (4) Tools and materials to set the poor to work, clothing, fuel and food.
  (5) Lunatic, occasional, and casual poor.
  (6) Medical assistance, funerals, repairs of poorhouses, rents for the impotent.
  (7) Bastard children and legal expenses connected therewith.
  (8) Law expenses and removals.
  (9) County rate, parish constable, militia, etc.
Some Cambs. parishes bought the printed book for entries under these

The recommendations were based on the more important of the two optional Vestry Acts which became law in 1819,[1] and which aimed particularly at curbing the power of both acting overseers and individual magistrates. The section of the Act which empowered vestries to provide poor parishioners with allotments, at reasonable rents, was not endorsed by the Committee.

heads. Many overseers, however, found it to their interest to demur at the expenditure of 6s. on the book! Other parishes nominally adopted the classification, but it is by no means easy to determine by what criterion the overseer included or excluded many items. The heading "lunatic, occasional and casual poor" proved particularly unsatisfactory. Very many parishes included in this class those temporarily unemployed. "I met with very few instances", said Everett in 1834, "in which I could make the accounts in the overseers' books correspond with the printed returns to Parliament for that year, or ascertain what description of items had been deducted from the gross amount." "The usual jumbling mode of accounts", was his very just description of the Bottisham books in 1834. (*P.L.C. Rept.* 1834, App. A, Pt. 1, pp. 256, 685.)

[1] 59 G. III, c. 12. By this Act parishioners were empowered to nominate five to twenty substantial householders, who, after approval by a magistrate, should constitute together with the vicar, churchwardens and overseers, a Select Vestry. The Select Vestry was to meet fortnightly or oftener, to examine applicants for relief and to give detailed directions, thus taking the real control out of the hands of both overseers and magistrates. Only after refusal by the Select Vestry, and after cross-examination of the overseers, could two magistrates grant relief for one month. In case of dire emergency one justice might order immediate relief until the next meeting of the Select Vestry or, if there were no Select Vestry, of Petty Sessions.

By s. 12, with the approval of the Vestry, the parish might take a farm, not exceeding twenty acres in extent, paying to the labourers upon it "reasonable wages for their work".

By s. 13 the parish was empowered to let out land to the poor in allotments, at a reasonable rent, the lessee taking the produce of the land and the parish applying the rents to the provision of winter fuel for the poor. (This provision was reaffirmed with minor modifications by 2 W. IV, c. 42.) Not more than a shilling rate was to be expended on allotments or parish farms without the consent of a stipulated majority of the Vestry.

S. 29 allowed relief to be granted to the able-bodied by way of loan.

On the subject of the able-bodied the Bench were converted: they proceeded to circularise parish authorities on the "unpolitic and pernicious practice of making up wages out of the poor rate". The result was merely an abandonment of any uniform system and a return to the endless diversity which had previously characterised relief.

At the time of the Royal Commission of 1832–4 the bread scale of 1829 was still in general use in the town of Cambridge, and within the Isle of Ely also a general scale was operative.[1] In the Linton district an allowance of 1s. above the old scale gave disastrous encouragement, in the view of the Commissioners, to "the best fed and most comfortable and thriving population of paupers in the county of Cambridge".[2] At Gamlingay the rates were 3s. per week for men—whether employed by a private individual or only by the parish—with additional allowances of 2s. for a wife and 1s. for each child, beginning with the first.[3] At Littleport no allowance was given to single men if privately employed at all; for a married couple the rate was 5s., and 1s. 6d. each was added for the first two children; where there were more than two children the allowance for the man and wife fell to 4s.— hence upon the appearance of a third child the family income was increased by only 6d. a week.[4]

In rather over a third of the parishes interrogated in 1833 the use of the scale was said to have been abandoned,[5] but the reply from Foulmire somewhat modifies the statement: "the Magistrates' scale of 1821 was acted upon for years. Though now formally rejected by the justices, it is virtually recognised as the scale of relief".[6]

The official attitude adopted by the Bench in 1829 did

---

[1] The date at which the scale for the Isle was drawn up has not been discovered, but in 1829 an allowance of 1s. 6d. per child was granted to labourers whose wages were below 4s. weekly. *P.L.C. Rept.* 1834, App. A, Pt. 1, p. 593. (Cowell's Report.)

[2] *P.L.C. Rept.* 1834, App. A, Pt. 1, p. 246.   [3] *Ibid.* p. 243.

[4] *Ibid.* App. B 1, Pt. 2, Query 24.

[5] *Ibid.* Query 20, pp. 49–72.

[6] *Ibid.* App. A, Pt. 1, p. 54.

encourage individual reformers now and again to appeal against the allowances given to men in private employment. Soham in particular came much into the limelight, although the practices of the overseers of that parish were those commonly adopted elsewhere. The first appeal to Quarter Sessions against the Soham rates in 1829 was unsuccessful, but the following year three rates were quashed. In 1831 two further appeals were made, as a result of which sundry payments to unemployed men at Soham were declared illegal.

C. ROUNDSMEN AND THE LABOUR-RATE

When the bread scale fell into disrepute many agricultural counties revived one or other of the earlier methods of "billeting-out" the poor, or adopted a labour rate.

Where a labour-rate was agreed upon, the number of settled labourers within the parish was estimated and their total wages' bill calculated. A rate to cover this amount was then levied, usually on the basis of the poor-rate. The persons so assessed agreed to pay the allotted sum in wages or to hand it over to the parish. Large farmers usually approved of the system, though it tended to prevent movement. A few parishes in Cambridgeshire—more particularly in the Isle of Ely, where on the whole the average size of the farms was greater—adopted a labour-rate round about 1831.[1] It was usually discarded, however, after a very short trial, on the grounds explained by the vestry of Haddenham: "The tradesmen and small farmers oppose a plan which settles upon them more labour than they can employ".

A modification of the Roundsman System was sometimes, though not very commonly, tried in this county. Pauper wages were fixed by the parish, and each occupier agreed to take a certain quota of unemployed labourers, according to some basis of assessment. The employer in this case had every incentive to

[1] An Act of 1831 (2 and 3 W. IV, c. 96) legalised the practice between 1831 and 1833, if a sufficient majority in favour of it could be secured in the vestry. (*P.L.C. Rept.* 1834, App. B 1, Pt. 3, Query 28.)

exact genuine work—in fact sweated labour—but he frequently found himself obliged to turn off independent workers in favour of the pauper contingent. In 1829, for example, the unemployed of Royston were distributed among the occupiers according to acreage. Two men fell to the lot of a certain Mr Nash, who was compelled in consequence to discharge two of his regular employees. One of these, John Watford, "a steady, industrious, single man, who by long and rigid economy had saved about £100", was a parishioner of Barkway. Barkway employers, however, would only offer work to those whose wages were partly paid by the parish, and Watford's savings debarred him from parish assistance. Finally he bought two horses and a cart and "obtained a precarious existence as a corn-carrier between London and Cambridge—ridiculed for not spending his money at a public house and thus enabling himself to gain work".[1]

In those parishes where scales were superimposed upon the Roundsman System the result was to produce almost universal pauperism. The attitude of Barkway was typical:

A man could not get any help from the rates unless he was destitute, and unless he got help from the rates he could not obtain employment, for a farmer would not pay a man 10s. a week when he could employ the roundsman at half that sum. Free movement from village to village was checked by the Settlement Laws. Nor were the labourers the only victims; the yeoman and small farmer, who spent little on wages, had to pay part of the wages bill of their richer neighbours.[2]

"Turn men" had been a very familiar feature of Cambridge-shire life between 1795 and 1820, but the system was dying out here at the moment when it was being revived elsewhere as a result of the abandonment of the bread scales. With the small occupiers and shopkeepers the Roundsman System, like the labour-rate, was never popular, for these classes could not profitably employ their full quota.

[1] *P.L.C. Rept.* 1834, App. A, Pt. 1, p. 591. (Cowell's Report.)
[2] *Ibid.* p. 339. Cf. *ibid.* p. 254.

The bread scales lingered on till 1834 in various parts of Cambridgeshire. By that date direct payments "to make up the wagges" of men employed by private individuals were not customary: relief was granted theoretically either "on account of large families" or to men at work only for the parish. Practically, however, the allowance began in many cases with the first child.[1] Married men, moreover, were usually given preference where employment was limited. Hence in actual fact the rates were still largely used to supplement the wages given by individual farmers.

Notwithstanding the admonitions of the Bench in 1829, some parishes made no pretence in 1833 of offering any labour to unemployed men, whom they simply relieved according to a fixed rate. Where work was offered—whether in the county proper or in the Isle—it was most commonly in the gravel pit or on the roads. With the demoralising effect of such pretended occupation the Poor Law Report resounds. Frequently the attitude of the overseer towards unemployed men was surly, overbearing and even cruel; at other times it was utterly reckless.[2] The paymaster for one end of the straggling village of Bottisham was himself a pauper! A typical conversation at Bottisham between the debonair type of overseer and the unemployed labourer, theoretically at work on the roads, is recorded by the Commissioners:

Overseer. Well, Master Fletcher, what's yours this time?

Pauper. Well, Tom, you know I reckon 10ᵈ a day's 5s. 2d.; that's what you gave me last time.

O. Why! you wasn't on the road when I came yesterday morning.

---

[1] At Linton not till the fourth child; at Chatteris and Comberton not till the fifth; and at Fulbourne not till the sixth child, but these parishes were exceptional. (*P.L.C. Rept.* 1834, App. B 1, Pt. 2, Query 24, pp. 49–72.)

[2] So Metcalfe of Foulmire described it. He was a discriminating and well-informed witness before the Commission of 1832–4. (*Ibid.* App. B 1, Pt. 4, Query 43.)

P. Well, you may take off half a day if you like; let's have no words about it.

O. Well, but you wasn't there in the afternoon either.

P. Wasn't I? Well, take off a day, man, can't you? He is paid for the other five days. They go to the road at 9 till 11.30, and 2 to 4. It is impossible to watch attendance. No work is done, for the roads are in excellent repair.[1]

At Gamlingay £615 out of a total Poor Law expenditure of £1434 went to paupers working for the parish. An attempt had been made to employ men in draining the unenclosed lands, but here, as elsewhere, the scheme was defeated by the protests of those whose lands were already enclosed, who objected to contributing to work in which they had no personal interest. Having failed to provide useful labour, the parish set the paupers to "task" work—the collecting of stones from the surface of the cultivated lands. The men were paid at a piece-rate of 2*d.* per bushel; they worked until the sum allowed by the scale had been earned. The stones would have sold for about 1½*d.* per bushel, but this would have deprived the parish of further means of employment; hence a number of lads were regularly engaged, "some with their hands, some with large sticks by way of bats, in returning the collected stones to the impoverished acres", in preparation for the next day's task![2]

D. OTHER SCHEMES OF WORK AND RELIEF

(1) *Allotments and Spade Labour*

Here and there less degrading methods of assisting the distressed labourer prevailed.

The outcry against the use of agricultural machinery led to the occasional reintroduction of spade labour. It was held that the crops benefited to some extent, but except where—as at Papworth—the whole village was in the hands of one or two

---

[1] *P.L.C. Rept.* 1834, App. A, Pt. 1, pp. 247–8. (Power's Report.)
[2] *Ibid.* p. 243.

occupying owners, who were themselves the principal rate-payers, the expense was prohibitive to employers. At Linton, between 1829 and 1832, the farmers agreed to pay for the digging of 100 acres at the rate of 13s. per acre—3s. per acre above the cost of ploughing. The difference between the 13s. and the actual cost of spade labour was paid by the parish.[1] A similar arrangement was made in several other parishes.

The effects of the Industrial Revolution were beginning to be felt by 1830 even in distant Cambridgeshire, and spinning was ceasing to be a profitable by-employment. It was in these circumstances suggested that the statutory powers given by the Act of 1819, and by Hobhouse's Act of 1831, to parochial authorities to let out land to cottagers in small allotments should be exercised. Between 1831 and 1833 the movement gained much support—especially from the vigorous pen of Denson, who calculated that on half-acre plots[2] self-respecting labourers could, and did, clear a profit of £3. 10s. yearly, which just enabled them in many cases to keep their heads above the stagnant parochial waters.

In about one-third of the villages of the Isle of Ely farmers were in the habit, in 1833, of letting a little land to labourers for half the year, for a crop of potatoes. The farmer ploughed and manured the land in return for half the produce.[3]

"Until you enable a poor man to benefit himself", said Denson, "you will do nothing to the purpose." The granting of allotments was generally admitted to be good for the labourers' morale, but the diminution of the rates was less marked than Denson would allow.

(2) *Manufactures and Public Utility Works*

At Linton a small hemp factory was started in 1832, offering employment to a few women and children as well as to men.

---

[1] *P.L.C. Rept.* 1834, App. A, Pt. 1, p. 246. (Power's Report.)
[2] Denson disapproved of smaller allotments than one acre. (Denson, *op. cit.* pp. 25, 64, 73.)
[3] *P.L.C. Rept.* 1834, App. B 1, Pt. 2, Query 24.

A similar little wool factory at Foulmire, for which women and children working at home supplied the yarn, dragged out a precarious existence between 1790 and 1800. At Little Gransden, and other villages on the Bedford and Essex borders, straw-plaiting was introduced as a domestic industry about 1790 and continued to offer remunerative employment for the next fifty or sixty years.

Soham was the fortunate beneficiary of valuable charity lands, left in 1674 in the hands of trustees,[1] partly for the purpose of providing employment for those in need. A free-school was also maintained out of the charity. In February 1795 it was decided to devote a proportion of the funds to the encouragement of home-spinning, and the schoolmaster—"passing rich on £40 a year"—was invited to earn an extra guinea yearly by supervising the distribution of payments to the spinners.

Apparently the benefaction was used to augment the inadequate wages paid by private woolmen. The arrangement made in 1795 was as follows:

5d. per lb. for every Pound of Yarn spun by such necessitous poor Persons as are exhibited in a List at this meeting, and approved of by Feoffees present, shall be given in addition to what is now given by the Woolmen, which is now only 7d. to the shilling, in order to encourage the sd. poor to work by making the Work a Shilling for a Shilling, for the better support of the sd. Families in this very inclement Season. And in case the Woolmen shall either rise or fall in future per lb., with respect to Spinning, then in that case the Feoffees do hereby agree to give such a Sum in addition to what the Woolmen give per lb., as shall make the Spinning work a Shilling for a Shilling to the sd. Spinners.[2]

Evidently the woolman's "shillingsworth" was a well-known amount,[3] and by this mode of making up wages the woolman

---

[1] On the division of the commons, in 1685, 116 acres of moorland had also been allocated to the use of the poor. The profits were to be devoted to providing work, apprenticing children and paying a schoolmaster.

[2] MS. Feoffees' Accounts, Vestry Papers, Soham.

[3] Compare medieval piece-rates. Cf. also Heaton, *The Yorks. Woollen and Worsted Industry*, p. 336.

was faced with exactly the same temptation to reduce the wages' bill as was the farmer.

In 1798 the Feoffees dropped the spinning project and devoted their funds to the equally pernicious scheme of supplementing the wages paid by the Highway Surveyors for the digging of gravel and the repairing of the roads. This plan was followed till 1810, in which year the spinning was revived. No less than 122 wheels were bought by the Feoffees and sundry repairs to reels executed. The services of the schoolmaster in this sphere were dispensed with, and the allowances to the domestic workers were paid through the medium of four village agents, three of whom were women, who augmented their own slender incomes (perhaps acquired as spinners themselves) by earning a small commission. Certain of the transactions at the beginning of 1811 are indicated by the following items:

	£	s.	d.
Mr Wheeler of Cambridge for 2 Sp. wheels 10s.			
Carriage 1s. 6d.		11	6
Mr Norman of Ely for 72 Sp. wheels at 4s. and 1 Reel			
6s.	14	14	0
Jos. Levett of Soham for 36 Do. at 5s. Mending Reels			
etc.	9	13	7
Mr Lucas of Soham for 12 Do. at 5s. Do.	3	8	10
Extra wool paymts:			
Through			
Wd Peck for allowce for 145 lbs. yarn Sp. at 4d.	2	8	4
Jesse Peachey ,, ,, 32 ,, ,, ,, ,,		10	8
Miss Smith ,, ,, 36 ,, ,, ,, ,,		12	0
Hannah Sharp ,, ,, 43 ,, ,, ,, ,,		14	4

A rather curious order was issued by the Trustees in 1811: "If any person or persons putting out wool shall presume to give more per lb. for spinning than what is given by the Feoffees of this Feoffment, in addition to what the Woolman gives, so as to make the Spinning more than a shilling for a shilling, such person shall be excluded from the benefit of the additional sum given by the Feoffees". It may be that the agents either gave to their spinner friends, or retained for themselves, a larger sum than the Trustees thought proper, to the detriment of other spinners. By thus raising the rate above "a shilling for a shilling", less shillingsworths were spun than ought to have been for a given sum, and fewer individuals were aided to the extent intended.

The agents had grown to nine in number by 1814, but had fallen to seven in 1816. In 1818 there were only three. For some years more and more of the distributing and paying had passed through the hands of one agent, a certain Wm. Hull. Between 1819 and 1822 there were only two agents, who displayed a keen rivalry. In 1819 the woolman's rate had—not unnaturally—dropped to 4*d.* per lb., and 8*d.* per lb. was made up by the Feoffees. Hull and Lucas evidently found their middleman profits considerable. Between 1822 and 1830 women agents occasionally gained a small commission again, but the main business was in the hands of the two men. By 1830 the Feoffees found themselves paying an ever larger proportion of the spinners' wages, and in this year the whole project was dropped. The possibility of its continuance was discussed again in 1831, but in 1832 it was finally abandoned.[1]

At Histon, in 1799, a considerable quantity of raw wool was bought and stored in the Town House for distribution to home workers, but here the overseer managed the business without the mediation of agents. A sum of over £20 was expended by the parish during the one month of April in payments for spinning, but no record survives of the price obtained for its sale. In August, whilst harvesting was at its height, only £7. 12*s.* was paid out for spinning.

This method of assisting adult workers soon petered out, but in 1812 a project for the employment of children was set on foot.[2] The combined vestries of Histon St Andrew and Histon St Ethelred proposed to set up "a manufactory of stockings, spinning, or any other trade, art or mystery", for the employ-

---

[1] MS. Feoffees' Accounts, Vestry Papers, Soham.

[2] Cf. Royston and Bottisham, *supra*, pp. 112, 116.

ment of children actually chargeable to the rates. No manufactory or Industrial School in which all the children could be concentrated seems to have been started, but three widows were selected as "teatchers", and a stock of worsted for the children to spin and knit was purchased by the overseer, who himself arranged for the sale of the finished product. Coal, forms, and tools were supplied by the parish, though the rooms used were the unwholesome cottages of the women teachers, to whom 3d. per child was allowed weekly for instruction. From July to October no payments were made to the children, but by that date presumably they had acquired some proficiency, for the parents were allowed a flat rate of 1s. per week for each child's work. The number of little employees increased to forty-two by November, and to fifty-six by the end of the year, though it fell off somewhat when spring offered opportunity for casual employment in the open air.[1]

Similar little Industrial Schools were tried in other villages during the first two decades of the nineteenth century, but they failed to pay their way and gradually lapsed.

The Select Vestry of Wisbech approached the corporation, in 1827, with a view to enlisting their interest in a public improvement scheme which should offer employment during the ensuing winter. A canal,[2] cutting off the bends in the river between the town and "Kinderley's Cut", was much needed for the improvement of the harbour, and it was finally resolved to undertake this work at the joint expense of the port and harbour dues and of the poor-rate. The corporation, however, were distrustful of inexpert parochial supervision, and stipulated that the direction of the work and the selection of a Superintendent should be left in their hands. A joint committee composed of members of the corporation and of the vestry was appointed. When the work had been got under way it was found that more hands could usefully be employed; hence an invitation was extended to the vestries of neighbouring parishes to join in the undertaking,

[1] MS. Vestry Books, Histon.
[2] It was known later as "the Paupers' Cut".

provided that the supervisory duties remained under the direction of the corporation, and that two-thirds of the wages of the workers were paid by such parishes as took advantage of the employment offered.[1]

(3) *Cheap Flour. Voluntary Subscriptions. Soup Kitchens*

The sale of flour, coal, and occasionally other commodities at reduced rates was, as has been seen, a long-established practice, sealed in fact with the approval of Tudor tradition. It was revived in seasons of depression down to the end of our period. Sometimes the wholesale purchases were made by aid of the rates; sometimes voluntary subscriptions were raised for the purpose.[2]

In 1801 bread touched the fabulous price of 1*s.* 9*d.* the quartern loaf at Cambridge. It was during the years between 1795 and 1817 that the public purchase of flour was most common. Parish officers were by no means always alive to the best bargains, and private dealers at times reaped huge profits at the expense of the parish. "I bought Rey this Time Twelve Month at 50*s.* per Q^r", wrote Wm. Blow, a farmer and corn-merchant of Whittlesford, in 1802. "I could have sold it 122*s.* per Qr. The poor had there Flower, Good Rey, for 2*s.* 6*d.* per peck. Parish pd. the Difference to me, which was 1*s.* 9*d.* per peck. It was a Blessing to the Poor and good to me. I bought 320 Quarters."[3] The transaction was hardly a blessing to the rate-payer![4] The overseer, however, endeavoured to save on parish allowances, by dint of crediting

---

[1] MS. Corp. Minute and Order Book, Wisbech.

[2] In July 1795 the corporation of Wisbech determined to "join with such of the respectable inhabitants of the town" as were desirous of purchasing a sufficient quantity of wheat to secure a regular supply during the winter, to be retailed cheaply to the poor. The Bank of Wisbech came to the rescue and loaned £500 on the security of the corporation seal. The loss on the subsequent sale was met partly by subscriptions and partly by a grant from corporate funds. (MS. Corp. Minute and Order Book, Wisbech.)

[3] MS. Maynard Collection, Saffron Walden Museum.

[4] Apparently Blow made a profit of £1376.

the pauper with having received the full value of the flour.[1] The paupers at once complained to the Rev. Andrew Pern, the local magistrate, who was kept well occupied at this time in check-mating overseers of the district. The magistrate worked out the scale, as it applied in several typical cases, and sent the examples for the enlightenment of the overseer.

Nath. Horlock: Family consists of man, wife and 6 chn.—two above 10 years old.

	£	s.	d.
Man earns		9	0
Wom. and Chln.		1	0
One Son		6	0
Second Dr		3	0
3 Pecks of Flour at 2s. 6d., which is sold for 4s., is a saving of 1s. 6d. per Peck		4	6
Half Peck			9
	£1	4	3

Nunn: Man, Wife and 4 Chln., all under 10 years.

	s.	d.	
Man earns	9	0	
3 Pecks of Flour	4	6	
Allow^ce in Money	4	6	Must be pd by Overseer.
	18	0	

Grey: Man, Wife and 4 Chln., all under 10 years.

	s.	d.	
Man earns	9	0	
3 Pecks Flour	4	6	
Allow^ce in Money	4	6	must be pd. by Ovs.
	18	0	

[1] At Sawston, in 1801 and at later dates, a similar policy was being pursued. Entries such as the following occur:

	£	s.	d.
1801, Pd. to make up there allowance		15	
Money instead of flour	1	13	1½
1817, Joseph Flack instead of flour	1		

(MS. Vestry Books, Sawston.)

To the Overseer of Whittlesford,

I have sent you the statement I have made of some of your poor People, who have complained to me this Morning, and I am sorry to see that two of them are in so much distress—for instead of improving their situations, they are rendered worse by taking away their allowance in Money and selling them Flour at a reduced Price—I desire that 4s. 6d. pr week be added to Nunns and Grays Families from the Time the Flour has been allowed.

You may form a Calculation for the rest of your Poor upon the Plan I have sent, and spare yourself and the Poor and me a great deal of Trouble.

Jan. 5th, 1801.   A. Pern.[1]

Entries of the following nature appear in many parish books about this time:

Ickleton, 1805:
For Flour sold to the Poor:

		£	s.	d.
From April 13 to Apr. 15				
5 stone at 3s. 6d., sunk 1s. per stone,			5	0
Apr. 17 to May 14				
51¾ stones at 3s. 4d., sunk 10d. stone,		2	3	1½
May 15 to June 11				
36¾ stones at 3s., sunk 6d. stone,			18	4½
		£3	6	6

Bottisham, 1796:
Pd. Mr Harris bill for flower, sunk 1s. per stone, 102¾ st. £5. 2s. 9d.

Sawston, 1810:
Taken of the poor for Flour and bran, £195. 0s. 7½d.

Kirtling, 1801:
Pd. to make up there allow^ces, Money instead of flour, £1. 13s. 1½d.

Bottisham, 1796:
4 weeks, 74 children at 6d. each, £7. 8s. 0d.

The last item referred to flour allowances granted on the ground of a family—a system which prevailed at Bottisham for

[1] MS. Maynard Collection, Saffron Walden Museum.

some ten years. In 1800 the number of children had increased to 171 in January and 180 later; the flour allowances rose in February to 9*d.* per head. Entries of this year make the position clearer:

3rd January: 171 children at 6*d.* per head, £4. 5*s.* 6*d.*
13th   „   Pd. 51 children at 6*d.* not being flower enough, £1. 5*s.* 6*d.*
Feby: Pd. Edward Piper his Child for 2 weeks, By the Justice Order, 1*s.* 6*d.* 90 Stone of Flower for the Children at 1*s.* 6*d.* per Stone, £6. 15*s.* 0*d.*

In 1801 potatoes were stored for retail sale to the poor: "Cash received for Potatoes bought for the Poor of Bottisham, £15. 15*s.*"

Food riots broke out at Cambridge in 1800, and were again followed by corporate and university measures to prevent profiteering. "The illegal practice of forestalling having of late been carried to a shameful and alarming length in this place", ran the Vice-Chancellor's notice, "it is determined…to bring every such offender to immediate and condign punishment." The Senate voted £200 for the prosecution of "monopolisers", and public notice was given that the market "for higlers and those who buy to sell again" would not in future open before 12 o'clock, and that before that hour it would be open to other inhabitants only. A less altruistic resolution than the earlier motion of the county magistrates was passed by the heads of the university, agreeing to abstain from pastry and to limit their own consumption of bread, but relegating "the use of substitutes" to the "poorer classes".[1]

Subscriptions were raised in the town to enable provisions to be sold cheaply and to establish Soup Kitchens.

Village kitchens and soup shops were among the most popular forms of philanthropy advocated by the "Society for

---

[1] *Cambridge Chronicle*, Sept. 20th and 27th, 1800. See also Cooper, *op. cit.* IV, p. 467.

Bettering the Condition of the Poor", established in 1798. Kitchens were set up at Cambridge, Wisbech and Royston, and in many of the larger villages of the county—sometimes financed, as at Cambridge in 1800,[1] entirely by voluntary means; more often supported partly at least by the rates.[2]

They were rarely open continuously but were revived when seasons were bad. Between 1800 and 1802, 1814 and 1817, and again between 1830 and 1833, soup shops were very popular with the charitably disposed of this county, who delighted in circulating recipes for the making of vegetable broths which could be sold at 1d. per quart in 1800, and usually at 2d. in 1816. Sometimes the soup was distributed freely.

"Alarmed for themselves", said Francis Place, "they have established soup-kettles to dole out broth in scanty portions to the industrious people who, but for their conduct, would have been living as became men—independent men—on their own earnings." By 1830 the agricultural labourer was becoming desperate, and was less easily doped into quiescence with soup.

E. WAGES

"When the tillage of the land afforded a fair remuneration to the farmer, the labourers reaped the due reward of their toil, and with their earnings maintained their families and trained them in habits of industry and sobriety. But now, no longer able to maintain themselves by the sweat of their brows, they are driven to the scanty pittance derived from parish funds"—so ran the petition for the abolition of duties on malt and beer, presented to Parliament by the farmers of Ely in December 1829. The

---

[1] Cooper, op. cit. IV, p. 464.

[2] At Wisbech the initiative was taken by the vestry, in December 1799. Subscriptions were to be raised to provide "good and wholesome meat-soup" to necessitous inhabitants at a penny per quart. A committee was appointed and the aid of the corporation to the extent of 50 guineas successfully solicited. A similar proceeding was again resorted to in 1816. (MSS. relating to the town of Wisbech, Peckover Collection, Wisbech.)

miserable condition both of independent worker and of pauper at this date few were likely to deny. Blinded, however, by their own present difficulties the farmers' memory of earlier days was dim! "If", said the sturdy Denson, "the petitioners allude to any period between 1792 and 1812, I deny it!—As corn rose, wages fell and the poor's rates increased in proportion." Statistics, he argued, gave a crushing answer to the plaintive farmers:[1]

Years	Average price of wheat per qtr	Average wages for husbandry	No. of loaves wages would buy	Price of qtrn. loaf	Poor rates in millions
1792	42s. 11d.	9s.	15	7d.	£2·6
1803	56s. 6d.	10s.	12	10d.	£4·1
1811	94s. 6d.	12s.	12	12d.	£5·9
1812	125s. 5d.	15s.	9	1s. 8d.	£6·5

The wages of the independent labourer in Cambridgeshire varied a good deal from district to district in 1833. The figures given to the Royal Commissioners[2] sometimes included and sometimes excluded beer, which was reckoned at a shilling weekly. Harvest wages were quoted by some parishes as summer wages. Taking the whole of the summer months wages ranged from 7s. to 15s., exclusive of beer, and for the winter months from 7s. to 12s. The average summer rate was 10s. or 11s., with no beer; the average winter rate 8s. or 9s.—"when employed", as some correspondents significantly added.

For a few weeks during harvest the labourer could usually count on getting 12s. a week; at Wimpole the exceptional sum of 25s. was said to be earned weekly at this season. The arbitrary

[1] J. Denson, op. cit., quoting Monthly Magazine for March 1815 and Companion to Almanack, 1829, p. 56. It should be noted that Denson selected peak years and quoted no years after 1812. In 1813 wheat sold at 109s. 9d. per qtr; in 1814 at 74s. 4d. For cost-of-living index cf. J. H. Clapham, Econ. Hist. of Mod. Brit. (1926), p. 127.

[2] P.L.C. Rept. 1834, App. B 1, Pt. 1, Query 8, pp. 49–72.

manner in which deductions were made from the stipulated wages is illustrated from the private account book of Farmer Blow of Whittlesford.[1] The farmer engaged about a dozen men at 12s. 6d. a week to help with the harvest of 1802. The weather was propitious and in less than four weeks the corn was completely garnered—"Three Weeks 4 Days, a Good Harvest. Not 4 Hours loss of time this year. Peace and plenty, thanck God. For the first time I paid my harvest men in one and two pound Bank of England Notes", ran the farmer's cheerful diary. Tom Cooper, one of the labourers, viewed the business less complacently and protested violently against the long, overtime hours, for which not even the novelty of bank-notes was adequate recompense. The only result of his remonstrance, and of the sympathy shown by a fellow-labourer, was noted by the farmer as follows:

Thos. Cooper, Set of 5s. for throwing the pint pot and Bracking 2 panes of sash, to larn him Good maners, £2. 1s. 6d.
Henry Neves, For mowing part of time. Set of 5s., £1. 11s. 6d.

John Gray, one of the farmer's regular hands, was docked of 10s. 6d. in payment of the rent owing to his master. Only seven of the men got their full wages from Blow. Part of the wages of two paupers was made up by the parish:

C. Munn, Jun[r], 15s. 6d. from the parish, £2. 6s. 0d.
J. Tomson 12s. „ „ „ £2. 6s. 0d.

There was little farm work done by women and children in Cambridgeshire during the winter, and spinning was no longer a profitable by-employment. During the other months of the year women and children did to some extent contribute to the family income. In the best-paid instances women earned 5s. and children 4s. a week—rising to 9s. and 6s. respectively for the few weeks of harvest. The average weekly wages were, however,

[1] MS. Maynard Collection, Saffron Walden Museum.

only about 3*s*. in summer or 2*s*. to 2*s*. 6*d*. for the whole year.[1] It is hardly surprising that marriage at any price, or even illegitimate relations, seemed to some women the only solution to life.

Piece-work rates were paid in some parishes, for certain occupations—threshing, chaff-cutting, turnip-hoeing and mowing in particular. On the whole the labourer gained little by this system: to quote Metcalfe, the able correspondent of Foulmire, "The mode defeats any benefit to the poor man, who is well aware that if he works hard and overtime, and consequently has to receive for a week or two a few shillings more than the regular weekly wages, the prices will immediately be lowered".[2]

"Could the family subsist on their earnings? If so, on what food?" enquired the Commissioners.[3] The following replies convey the more general opinions:

Bassingbourn: On very plain food.
Bottisham: Yes. On potatoes, bread and tea.
Histon: Certainly not, except on potatoes.
Great Shelford: They could not subsist in this parish on what they would earn, exclusive of parish relief.
Wisbech: We believe they may, but much depends on the economy of the man and woman.

Here and there, as at Chatteris, where the summer average of wages rose to 14 or 15*s*., it was considered that labourers "could live well on common food".

With only two exceptions, every parish interrogated replied that it would be totally impossible for the labourer in 1834 to lay by any savings in the course of the year.[4]

"It is obvious", said Denson in 1829, "that the labourer's earnings are no more than shall keep him merely in existence, and when deductions are made for house-rent, firing etc., his income is not

[1] *P.L.C. Rept.* 1834, App. B 1, Pt. 1, Query 12, pp. 49–72.
[2] *Ibid.* Query 9, pp. 49–72.
[3] *Ibid.* App. B 1, Pt. 2, Query 14, pp. 49–72.
[4] *Ibid.* App. B 1, Pt. 1, Query 15, pp. 49–72.

equal to what is allowed to a felon! Men are better paid for plunder than for habits of industry!...In their state of wretchedness men have indeed become more vicious, and are striving politically to learn the causes of their altered state."[1]

Such was the economic background of the agricultural risings of the 'thirties. "The disturbances of two years ago", said Alfred Power,[2] "show the sense of need for a vital change. The general opinion points rather to a total change than to partial and palliative treatment....Certainly affairs go on very ill in this county." It was through these Augean stables that the broom of the Reformed Parliament swept ruthlessly.

[1] Denson, *op. cit.* p. 47.
[2] *P.L.C. Rept.* 1834, App. A, Pt. 1, p. 240.

Chapter XVI

CONSTITUTIONAL STRUCTURE AND SOCIAL POLICY

The primary aim of this book has been to examine in detail the way in which the Poor Law actually worked in the hands of a variety of local authorities within the limits of Cambridgeshire. Frequently, as has been seen, the laws produced effects undreamed of by their framers. Probably no social service played so large a part as did the Poor Law in moulding the constitution of the authorities which administered it; and it was in turn moulded by them. It is therefore fitting that the more outstanding features of the constitutional machinery itself should be traced here.

A. THE COUNTY

The inclusion within the bounds of Cambridgeshire of the extensive franchise of the Bishop of Ely—among special jurisdictions second only to Durham in importance—makes it possible to institute certain comparisons regarding the development and social effects of gradual changes in county government. For most administrative purposes throughout the period 1597–1834, as for centuries before, the Isle of Ely was exempt from the jurisdiction of what may be called Cambridgeshire proper, the Bishop claiming prerogatives normally vested in the Crown.[1] The Isle had its own Chief Justice and its own justices of the peace and other county officers.[2] In the main, however, the legal

---

[1] The episcopal franchise dated back to the seventh century.

[2] There was no Sheriff for the Isle: his functions were fulfilled by the Chief Bailiff, a life official appointed by the Bishop and responsible only to him. The Bishop appears to have retained the right to appoint justices of the peace till 27 H. VIII, c. 24. The Chief Justice was appointed by the Bishop till 1837: the Act of 7 W. IV, c. 53, transferred this privilege to the Crown. The Isle was in 1888 made a separate administrative county. It retains to

framework of administration here was based on the constitution of an ordinary county. The only other authority claiming exclusion from the jurisdiction of the county was the borough of Cambridge. For most purposes, Poor Law and other, this exemption held, but in the important matter of settlement disputes appeal lay, after 1697, to the County Bench and not to the Quarter Sessions of the town.[1]

1. The Personnel of the Cambridgeshire Magistracy

(a) THE ASSEMBLED BENCH

The county, like the parish, existed to ensure that voluntary services should be rendered by the "consumers" in the interest of the whole community.[2] According to statute the justices were to be "of the most sufficient knights, esquires and gentlemen of the law" resident within the county, a certain quorum being required to have special knowledge of the law. By 1689 in most

the present time its own Commission of the Peace and supplies, by custom, the joint High Sheriff for Cambs. and Hunts. every third year.

[1] Disputes arose occasionally in the eighteenth century concerning the respective jurisdictions of county and Isle, especially in connection with settlement appeals. The Act of 1692 (3 W. & M. c. 19) apparently recognised in such cases the jurisdiction of liberties, as well as towns corporate having their own Quarter Sessions. The Act of 1697 (8 and 9 W. & M. c. 30), however, took away jurisdiction in settlement appeals from towns and liberties not "counties of themselves". The town of Cambridge never attempted after this date to hear such appeals, but the position with regard to the Courts of the Isle was very dubious. (Cf. MS. Q.S.R. Cambs. 1719, 1720, 1727.)

[2] The consolidating Act of 1590 was the basis of the justice's authority for the period 1597–1834. It laid down his qualifications and the sphere of his labours (a) individually, (b) in conjunction with one or more of his colleagues of the division, (c) in co-operation with his fellows, sitting collectively, at least four times a year, with the full equipment of a Court of Justice for the whole county. Certain expenses were statutorily allowed to eight magistrates of each county—4s. per day, during the sitting of the Court.

counties the legal quorum had become a mere formality.[1] Cambridgeshire, however,[2] was distinguished by a group of leaders consistently above the average in intellectual attainment. The number of justices normally attending Quarter Sessions varied from four or five to a dozen, rising to a score or more on occasions of special moment.[3] The General Sessions for the county proper were held only in the county town of Cambridge, and the majority of regular members of the assembled Bench consisted of those justices residing in and around the university centre. At least from the sixteenth century, the Vice-Chancellor and Heads of Colleges[4] were in the commission for the county as well as for the town, and a few other county justices had college or town residences. Hence in the group of county leaders the influence of the university was remarkably strong. Medical men, distinguished lawyers and jurists figured prominently beside Doctors of Divinity and baronets.[5] Some increase in clerical membership

---

[1] S. and B. Webb, *The Parish and the County* (1906), p. 302.

[2] *I.e.* the county outside of the Isle.   [3] In both county and Isle.

[4] As early as 1456, the Provost of King's College was in the commission for both county and town (Cooper, *op. cit.* I, p. 207). In 1587 the Vice-Chancellor and 5 Heads of Colleges petitioned to be similarly admitted and appear to have been so admitted soon after this date (*ibid.* II, p. 432). The Mayor was in the commission for the county in 1380 (*ibid.* I, p. 119). The Act of 1734 exempted the Mayor as well as Heads of Colleges from the property qualification, on the ground that it was customary for them to be justices of the county (*ibid.* IV, p. 216).

[5] In the early seventeenth century such writers of legal handbooks as Michael Dalton and John Layer sat on the Cambs. Bench. In the later part of the century the most familiar figures were Robt. Eade, M.D., Wm. Cook, LL.D., James Duport, Dean of Peterboro', Sir T. Wendy, K.B., Sir Chrisr. Hatton, Sir T. Willis and Sir Saml. Clark. In the early part of the eighteenth century Sir Marmaduke Darryll, Sir John Hind Cotton, Sir Geo. Downing and Sir Robt. Clarke were the leading figures. The families of Pern, Jenyns and Pepys contributed active members through many generations. The Millicents, Sclaters and Richers dominated the parochial life of Linton for over a century, backed by their credit on the Bench. Wm. Cole, the famous antiquary, Edward Bassett, M.D., Chrisr. Jeaffreson and Samuel Gatward, a legal light of the town of Cambridge, were repeatedly deputed to supervise county activities in the eighteenth

was the only significant change in personnel during later generations—an increase more marked in the county as a whole than in
the leading clique. Stable rather than enterprising, lacking perchance the stimulus of commerce, at times even reactionary, yet
animated by the best Conservative thought of the age and maintaining from generation to generation a fairly consistent level of
trained intelligence and honesty, the Cambridgeshire Bench on
the whole compares favourably with the magistracy of other
counties.

(b) THE JUSTICES OUT OF SESSIONS

Much of the work of the justice lay out of sessions and all
justices were not of the calibre of the governing clique, though
they were largely of the same political and religious colour: comparatively few of England's merchants or moneyed men were
domiciled either in Cambridgeshire proper or in the Isle, hence
Whig influence here was never strong. The county had literally
its "Squire Western", but he had little in common with his
namesake of fiction: neither "Justice of mean degree" nor
"Trading Justice"[1] was a type characteristic of rural Cambridgeshire. It is true the fee system prevalent in the eighteenth
and early nineteenth centuries easily lent itself to misuse, and
there was apparently a shortage of justices[2]—especially in the

century. Gregory Wale of Shelford, magistrate and Cam Conservator,
wielded considerable influence as County Treasurer from 1707 to 1739—
he received only a salary of 10 guineas per annum, but county balances,
sometimes amounting to as much as £66, remained in his hands. Among
the most outstanding of the clerical justices of the early nineteenth century
was Wm. Metcalfe of Foulmire, warmly commended by the Poor Law
Commissioners of 1834 for his zeal in reducing parish account-keeping to
order.

[1] S. and B. Webb, *op. cit.* pp. 322 *et seq.*

[2] An examination, for example, of the signatories to pauper removal
warrants of the eighteenth century reveals the wide areas for which particular justices acted—half a dozen names recur repeatedly. It reveals also
the loose interpretation of such statutes as required the concurrence of the
"nearest justice". Gregory Wale of Shelford, for example, signed warrants

isolated fens of the Isle—but in most districts such shortage does not seem to have resulted in a general raising to the commission of men to whom fees were a major consideration. It was stated in the early nineteenth century that paupers, after refusal of parochial aid, often tramped for miles to secure an order for relief from some compliant magistrate. In the neighbourhood of Cambridge and Royston this state of things certainly did prevail. Individual magistrates undoubtedly differed from one another on the desirability of over-riding parochial decisions—and they were never too prone to look to the County Bench for guidance—but for the most part conviction rather than negligence dictated their attitude.

2. The Evolution of County Organisation

The great increase in the scope and extent of the justice's work between 1597 and 1834 led in particular to three developments which had unforeseen effects on the real constitution of county government and through it upon the life of the community. These developments came slowly in Cambridgeshire: even by 1834 they were far less marked than in more industrialised counties.

(a) THE DELEGATION OF AUTHORITY TO LOCAL GROUPS

(i) Divisional Meetings—Monthly or Informal

By the general terms of his commission, as well as by specific statutes, the duties of the individual justice, or of the justice in

for Bourne, Gamlingay, Linton, Trumpington and Whittlesford. Parish officers from as far afield as Boxworth, Chesterton, Elsworth, Fen Ditton, Fulbourne, Ickleton, Milton, Waterbeach and Whittlesford sought warrants from Anthony Thompson of Cambridge. Many of the names of rural magistrates are above suspicion: of town magistrates one is far less assured. It may well be that overseers found it to their advantage, at the expense even of fees and journey, to seek warrants from such justices as could be relied on to oblige without too close a scrutiny. Some few magistrates were in the commission of both county and Isle, and settlement and other disputes occasionally resulted.

conjunction with one or more of his colleagues, had been increasing from the outset. Though expressed in judicial form his decisions in the main were on matters of social expediency, and of these Vagrancy and Poor Law formed a large share. By Statute, for example, the approval of two justices was necessary for the settling of the poor-rate, for the appointment of the parish overseers and surveyors, for the binding of parish apprentices, and from 1662 onwards for the granting of removal warrants.[1] Considerable power in the granting of relief was put into the hands of the individual justice by the Act of 1692;[2] and though this was checked to some extent in 1723[3], later eighteenth- and nineteenth-century legislation allowed to the justice a very effective voice.[4]

During the sixteenth and seventeenth centuries Poor Law and other orders were not infrequently issued by the Bench itself as a Court of First Instance.[5] By 1700 these were becoming rare in

[1] One justice was sufficient in the case of a vagrant. Up to 1729 two justices were the authority for granting alehouse licenses.

[2] 3 W. & M., t. 11. Cf. *supra*, p. 177.

[3] 9 G. I, c. 7. Cf. *supra*, p. 178.

[4] Among Cambs. vestry papers for the early eighteenth century one occasionally finds an order of some J.P. requiring the parish to provide relief. By the middle of the century such orders are sufficiently common in the town of Cambridge for printed forms to be in use. In the rural districts they are not common till the close of the century, and not in every area even then.

[5] Cambs. Quarter Sessions Records are not extant for the years before 1660, but references to such Orders occur in overseers' accounts and in the Records of the town of Wisbech. In 1661 the overseers of Thriplow were ordered by the Cambs. Bench to provide "fitt cloathes and apparrell for Roger Tayler, a poore childe". In the same year the Court, on the petition of Robert Carter, ordered the overseers of Chesterton to relieve him. In 1706 the Court gave detailed directions regarding a bastard child, "the two next justices not making any order, but the same coming originally to be heard before the last Quarter Sessions" (*ibid.* 1706). It would seem almost as though, during the seventeenth century, orders for the removal of persons were sometimes issued, in the first instance, by the Cambs. Bench (*ibid.* 1692, 1693), and in other instances by divisional meetings (*ibid.* 1702).

Cambridgeshire: the Court had its hands full with more complicated business. Even in the seventeenth century the interest of Quarter Sessions in Poor Law affairs was chiefly as a Court of Appeal: prior to 1662 the poor-rate was the main subject of contention; after that date pauper removals acquired a rapidly increasing prominence.

It was decreed by the County Bench, in 1660, that their order respecting the relief of a certain Jeremy Chambers of Soham should continue "until this Court or the two nearest Justices shall otherwise determine". The practice of thus referring questions to two or three justices of the division concerned— either for final determination or for detailed investigation—was a method of relieving the congestion of work at the centre very frequently employed in the seventeenth, and the early part of the next, century. Many matters demanding local knowledge were so relegated, but Poor Law affairs, especially pauper settlements, were among the most common in this county.

The more regular local gatherings of justices date back to Tudor and early Stuart days, when Privy Council pressure was constantly exerted to compel the holding of monthly divisional meetings for the control of local affairs.[1] It was sometimes to

[1] The area of the "division" may originally have coincided with the ancient "hundred", but by the Restoration period whilst this was the case in the larger or more populous hundreds of Cambs., two or even three of the smaller hundreds were grouped to form à division. There were two divisions in the Isle: the hundred of Wisbech and the north part of the hundred of Witchford formed one; the hundred of Ely and the south part of Witchford the other.

The Chief Constables' Sessions, or Petty Sessions, held in each hundred still survived in Cambs. after the Restoration, for the purpose of registering contracts of service under 5 Eliz., c. 3. By this date the meetings were clearly subordinate to Quarter Sessions, but they were not identical with the justices' divisional meetings (cf. *supra*, pp. 55, 56). In the case of the Isle of Ely it is difficult to distinguish between the Chief Constables' Sessions and the magistrates' divisional meetings. Both were evidently being held in the early seventeenth century. (MS. Corp. Minute and Order Book, Wisbech, and Records of Courts Halimote and Courts Leet, Eliz. & Jas. I.)

these divisional meetings that matters were referred during the succeeding half century: at other times to a less formal conclave, dictated by the needs of the moment.[1] By the beginning of the eighteenth century, however, instances in which the defeated party declined to accept the verdict of local bodies, sitting without the aid of jury or counsel, were becoming too numerous.[2] With respect to settlement questions especially, the complexity of the law rendered a separate tribunal of high authority and conducted with full publicity more and more necessary. After the first decade of the century appeal cases tended to come more exclusively before the central court of the county.[3] Simultaneously with the taking over of complicated issues, the Bench was gradually ceasing to function as a Court of First Instance.[4]

[1] For example a complaint made to Quarter Sessions in 1667, concerning the non-payment of a Sawston woman's wages, was first referred to the nearest justice. The result proving unsatisfactory, the Court then referred the dispute to the next monthly meeting for the combined hundreds of Whittlesford and Chilford.

[2] In 1702 the disputed settlement of Diana Davis was referred by Quarter Sessions to the justices of the combined hundreds of Wetherley and Thriplow at their next monthly meeting, with the proviso that should either party still feel aggrieved the case should be reconsidered by the Court. (MS. Q.S.R. 1702; cf. also *ibid.* 1670.)

[3] Poor-rate disputes were occasionally decided by divisional meetings as late as 1749, but settlement cases practically ceased to be so decided in Cambs. twenty years earlier.

[4] The Bench also began—quite extra-legally—to depute whole departments of administration to local groups, or "Special Sessions", meeting privately. This development was very slow in Cambs. Highway Sessions, under the Act of 1691, are first recorded here in 1727. Licensing Sessions were held from 1729 onwards.

"Special Sessions", in the original sense of meetings for the county as a whole for some particular branch of work, were held in the Isle of Ely to the end of our period. In Cambs. proper on two exceptional occasions meetings representative of the whole county were held in places other than Cambridge, probably for peculiar reasons of convenience—in Jan. 1742 at Little Abington, in Nov. 1747 at Kneesworth.

(ii) *Petty Sessions*

In the course of the later eighteenth century the monthly meetings seem to have lost something of their regularity, though in Cambridgeshire one area differed from another.[1] During the 'eighties, whether at monthly or longer intervals is not evident, the magistrates of the hundred of Whittlesford were assuming to themselves astonishing legislative functions. Quite independently of direction from the Bench they drew up a bread scale for their neighbours. From 1790 to 1821 in district after district of the county local justices, meeting quite privately, with only very general direction from the Bench, formulated extra-legal, and often illegal policies for the treatment of such vital matters as unemployment and poverty. Sometimes—though rarely before 1821—the central Bench directed activities.[2]

The name "Petty Sessions" does not seem to have come into common use in Cambridgeshire till about 1816, when it was applied to the Sessions thenceforward held regularly in the respective divisions for the testing of weights and measures. Permanent clerks were attached to each area.[3] One finds the Bench, in 1828, circularising the magistrates through the medium of these clerks on the subject of a uniform scale of pauper allowances. It was complained in the course of the discussion that assemblies for the consideration of poor-relief were rarely held every month and a strong appeal was made for more regular meetings of Petty Sessions. During the disturbed state of the agricultural population in 1830–1, the appeal became a mandate issued by a Central Committee, meeting under the unusual

[1] The Petty Constables of Bottisham, for example, presented accounts to the vestry, between 1738 and 1775, for "goen to ye gestesesmetens" at dates which suggest monthly assemblies. The Chief Constables also seem usually to have been present. (MS. Constables' Accounts, Bottisham.)

[2] In 1795, for example, the justices were required by the Court to communicate to the vestries within their respective divisions the general views of the Bench on the systematising of grants from the rates.

[3] At first paid by fees, but also receiving sums from county funds when duties had been peculiarly heavy.

auspices of the Lord Lieutenant himself. In January 1832, pursuant to an "Act for the better regulation of Divisions in Counties",[1] a redivision of the county for the purpose of Petty Sessions was effected.

(b) THE ORGANISATION OF A COUNTY EXECUTIVE

The accretion of a group of paid officials, completely subservient to Quarter Sessions, was a very slow process in this county. The County Treasurer was receiving but a paltry six guineas in the middle of the eighteenth century, whilst in some agricultural counties he received eight times this sum. Control over the most important of subordinate officials—the Chief Constables —had indeed been assumed early. Certainly as early as 1660 they were either appointed directly or their appointment confirmed by Quarter Sessions,[2] but no definite salaries were paid to them till as late as 1827.[3] Systems of fees and contracts still dominated most sides of administration down to 1834, and by these means no efficient staff for the slowly evolving county executive could be built up on the lines of more progressive counties.

(c) CENTRAL COMMITTEES FOR THE COUNTY AS A WHOLE

The practice of delegating certain branches of business not to local but to central committees, consisting of sundry members of the assembled Bench, was gradually established. It was in vogue

[1] 9 G. IV.

[2] At that date the nomination was often stated to have been made by the Court Leet, but was confirmed by Quarter Sessions. Before the end of the seventeenth century in Cambs. the appointment was a life-appointment or till old age. It was evidently a lucrative post, for, except in cases of friction, the successor was nearly always a son or relative. The status of Chief Constable had clearly degenerated by the middle of the eighteenth century: frequent reprimands were administered by the Bench on the subject of fee-taking, and scales of charges were drawn up at intervals.

[3] Salaries were customary in the Isle of Ely by 1805.

here at least as early as 1691 for the annual examination of the Treasurer's accounts, and in 1728 a Vagrancy Committee was nominated. Thenceforward similar temporary bodies, for these and other purposes, were appointed at intervals. One of the most important of the central groups was the committee which came into being with the building of the new Gaol and House of Correction in 1801. This Gaol Committee soon became a standing committee, and when other bodies developed similarly local government had assumed one of its most characteristic modern forms.

In the realm of Poor Law it was not till October 1828, "in consequence of the present high price of bread", that an important central committee was appointed, consisting of one magistrate from each division.[1] The committee reported to a special Adjourned Sessions, by which it was reappointed as a semipermanent body to supervise the carrying into effect of the remedies suggested. A standing committee of five magistrates was nominated the following year to report regularly to Quarter Sessions. From this time onwards standing committees were the rule. It is noteworthy that, influential as such private committees were, report to Quarter Sessions was always insisted upon in the county proper.

3. *The Development of Legislative Functions*

The original conception of the Court of Quarter Sessions as a strictly judicial authority still dominated most County Benches at the end of the seventeenth century, but in the course of the following century a gradual distinction was often made between business needing a jury, or the hearing of counsel or disputants, and that which justices could settle privately.[2] Outside the franchise of Ely this process had made strikingly little headway

[1] There is no record in Quarter Sessions' minutes of the meeting which drew up the general Bread Scale of 1821—of which we know from parish references and from the *P.L.C. Rept.* of 1834 (App. A, Cowell's report, p. 584). This may be due to clerical oversight.

[2] S. and B. Webb, *The Parish and the County*, pp. 437 *et seq.*

in Cambridgeshire. Committees did sometimes adjourn to the comfortable privacy of the Rose Inn or the Falcon, but Adjourned Sessions were usually held in open court. It is true that by the nineteenth century the discretionary powers accorded by Tudor and Stuart statutes had been interpreted as granting untrammelled power to the justices actually to make the law upon which they themselves would adjudicate. If the pronouncements of the Bench in 1828, for example, were in accordance with the statutory Poor Law of Elizabeth, then clearly the bread-scale policy of seven years earlier was in defiance of it. Such mandatory enactments did undeniably affect vitally the happiness and well-being of the community, yet they were at least made here in open court.

More remarkable in this county was the assumption of legislative authority by the local groups of magistrates. The assembled Bench held its hand almost to the point of futility. The scheme, for example, put forward in 1814, on behalf of well-organised district workhouses as an alternative to bread scales, was bold and generous, but it was withdrawn when local support was not forthcoming.

4. The Isle of Ely

General Quarter Sessions for the Isle were held alternately at Wisbech and Ely; in addition annual Special Sessions[1] met at March or Chatteris for the purpose of examining the general finances. Most promulgations of Quarter Sessions theoretically applied to the whole franchise, but in practice much of the business dealt with had reference only to the hundred and half-hundred in the vicinity of Wisbech or of Ely respectively. The distinction between the two divisions of the Isle[2] was in some respects a formal one: separate county rates were levied and separate Treasurers appointed apparently throughout our period. Each division maintained a separate House of Correction—the

[1] At any rate during the nineteenth century, for which period alone adequate records survive.

[2] Cf. *supra*, p. 226, note.

one at Ely, the other at Wisbech. The group of regular members of the Bench, moreover, naturally tended in either case to be those of the division concerned. In the northern area outstanding members were invariably Capital Burgesses or other inhabitants of the vigorous township of Wisbech—a fact which has much to do with the greater vitality of some branches of administration in this part of the Isle.

By the beginning of the nineteenth century, changes in organic structure had gone further here than in the county proper. The surviving nineteenth-century Minute and Order Books of Quarter Sessions suggest at least a clear discrimination between the two branches of magisterial work. The records have curiously little to say on subjects of local government, but relate with exceptional detail criminal and other matters requiring formal presentment. It is conceivable that separate books were kept for the two departments and that one series only has survived,[1] but it is much more likely that record was made only of matters coming before Court and jury, and that other affairs—practically the whole of "county business"—were indeed transacted here by "two parsons and five squires", adjourning behind the closed doors of a neighbouring inn, " amidst the smoking of pipes, the cluttering of pots and all the ordure of a narrow room".[2] In the privacy of so large a share of local government[3] may lie the ex-

[1] A possible explanation may be found in the lack of adequate provision for the salary of the Clerk of the Peace. In the county proper certain clerical expenses were reclaimable from the National Exchequer, through the "cravings of the Sheriff", but customary fees supplemented this source. It was therefore a temptation to the Clerk to enter such items only as it was legally compulsory to record, or those for which fees were obtainable. In the case of the Isle the Clerk was dependent entirely on fees, for there was no Sheriff and no Exchequer grant. The entries do nevertheless suggest a division of the Court.

[2] Timothy Nourse, *Compania Felix* (1700), p. 166. (Quoted by S. and B. Webb, *op. cit.* p. 244.)

[3] The Court itself felt some compunction concerning the abuse of adjournment and in 1824 ordered that only one adjournment should be permitted for each session, except in an emergency, after due notice. (MS. Q.S.R. Ely, 1824.)

planation of the inhuman negligence which characterised certain branches of central administration in the Isle.[1]

Local magistrates were left to their own devices even more strikingly than in the county proper. This did not necessarily entail local inertia: in the northern division, at any rate, it stimulated initiative. Nasmith, Chairman of Quarter Sessions for the Isle, writing in 1799, expressed full confidence in the vigorous exercise of the discretionary powers vested in the individual magistrates,[2] and local records justify his opinion.

5. Reaction and Reform

With the final accession to power of the Reform Party in 1832, county government, no less than municipal and parochial, called for scrutiny. The abuses patent in the metropolis and in the new industrial regions could not be laid to the charge of the magistracy of rural Cambridgeshire, but even here complaint was loud on the subject of rising expense. Some of the most significant changes which had been quietly evolving in county government for more than a century passed without comment: it was the irresponsible authority of an unrepresentative body which lay, said the critics, at the root of all evil. Yet constitutional revision stopped short at the county. Magistrates were still to the reformer of the 'thirties essentially judicial authorities and elective judges were unthinkable even to him.[3] To strip the justice of accreted powers and to subject him to control seemed therefore

[1] Especially the conduct of the Ely bridewell and gaol. The gaol here had not passed, as in most counties, into the hands of the magistrates, but the bridewell was under their immediate control and maintained by a rate on the south division of the Isle. The bridewell shared the inhuman, illegal regulations and the neglect which made the gaol a terrible commentary on the private ownership of prisons. The combined gaol and bridewell at Wisbech was, largely as a result of town influence, much better regulated; half of the keeper's salary was raised by a rate on the north division of the Isle and half by a town contribution.

[2] Jas. Nasmith, *Charge to Grand Jury* (1799).

[3] S. and B. Webb, *op. cit.* p. 606.

the correct policy. Perhaps the most vital change in county government came when the Poor Law Amendment Act of 1834 swept from the magistrate his supervision and control of the largest branch of parochial expenditure.

B. THE PARISH

Whether or not an independent entity in the eyes of the law, the parish did in fact develop as the unit of local government.

Outside the Isle of Ely the small rural community of several hundred inhabitants formed the typical parish. In perhaps a dozen cases by the beginning of the nineteenth century the population was double or treble this figure.[1]

Conditions within the franchise were somewhat different. Geographical circumstances had led to the clustering of the population on the one-time islets of higher, gravel-tipped ground rising above the surrounding peaty marshes.[2] As a result the typical parish was a decidedly larger unit than in the county proper. Grouped around the parent villages there were often dependent hamlets—again the direct outcome of fen conditions.[3]

[1] Out of some 200 parishes in county and Isle, in 1801, only 28 had a population of over 600. Of these 28 parishes only 10 had a population of over 1000. No less than 6 of the 10 were within the Isle. Four parishes, 3 of which were in the Isle, had above 1500 inhabitants.

Excluding Cambridge, Linton was the sole market town in the county proper in 1801, though markets had been held at a few other places at earlier periods. In the Isle markets were still held at Wisbech, Ely, March and Thorney, and had only recently been discontinued at Whittlesey. Soham had a market throughout the seventeenth century. (D. and S. Lysons, *Magna Britannia*, ii.)

[2] The higher grounds of gravel or boulder clay still bear names having the termination "ea" or "ey", signifying island—*e.g.* Whittlesey, Thorney, Manea, Stonea, Eastrea, Stuntney.

[3] The hamlet of Parson Drove with its chapelry grew up because the mother-church of Leverington was too distant and "the way and passage from the same troublesome and dangerous in the time of winter" (W. Watson, *An Historical Account of the Ancient Town and Port of Wisbech*, 1827, p. 474). Similarly the chapelry of Murrow was licensed by the Bishop

The custom of intercommoning on the wastes, moreover, fostered communal interests between adjacent parishes.

whilst in 1388, owing to the danger of leaving the banks and dykes untended the difficult journey to Wisbech was undertaken. Guyhirne, Tholomas Drove and Wisbech St Mary were also dependent on Wisbech. Emneth was an offshoot of Elm. The parish of Doddington was the largest in Isle or county, and indeed one of the most extensive in the kingdom, comprising no less than 38,000 acres of good land. The rectory—held in the middle of the seventeenth century by the Lord of the Manor—was one of the richest in England. Courts Leet and Baron were still held there in 1827. There were three dependent hamlets—Benwick, Wimblingdon and March. In 1821 the combined population of the parish was 5899. By this date March (3850) far outstripped the mother-parish (676) in population.

Many of these chapelries were originally associated with wealthy gilds, in control of numerous charities. An examination of the official Returns of Charitable Donations (1798, pp. 104 *et seq.*) shows a quite disproportionate share of large benefactions, often in the form of land, enjoyed by parishes of the Isle as compared with the rest of the county. Some of these endowments were transferred from the gilds to a body of Feofees at the Reformation. Lands left in this way at Parson Drove were misapplied by the body of Feofees. Under order of the Court of Chancery a new board of ten trustees was appointed in 1698, and lands enclosed from the waste added to the charity for the upkeep of the chapel and the maintenance of the poor. Though certain precautions were taken, the system of co-option was still retained. Since the funds were to be used for the alleviation of the rates and taxes very naturally the parish officers were the leading trustees, and the personnel of board and vestry soon became indistinguishable. At Leverington St Leonards charity lands—worth over £290 annually in 1827—were similarly vested in Feofees, under the direction of a "Town Bailiff" nominated annually from among their own number. The gildhall was for long used as a workhouse. So, too, at March the gildhall was used as an asylum or workhouse from 1575 till the new workhouse was erected in 1823—"replete with every convenience, an ornament to the town" (Watson, *op. cit.* p. 594). Valuable charities here amounted to £460 annually in the early nineteenth century, though much mismanagement had necessitated a Chancery decree at that date. It was probably the exceptionally spacious old gildhalls which set the standard of workhouse buildings in the Isle—a gentleman's residence, with fine decorated ceilings, was purchased at Elm in 1801 as "the house of reception for the poor" (*ibid.* p. 595). The Poor Law Commissioners of 1834 were impressed by the airiness and comparative comfort of the workhouses of the Isle—as well as by the more methodical systems of account keeping.

Though the population was fairly evenly distributed over the county proper, means of communication were notoriously bad and village life was in consequence remarkably isolated. Now and again unsuccessful attempts were made by one of the more fortunately situated parishes to introduce some element of co-operation between the villages of the neighbourhood. From the end of the eighteenth century local magisterial activity did sometimes secure a measure of agreement as to some particular social policy. Nevertheless every effort in Cambridgeshire to group parishes for the purpose of achieving the better administration attained in other counties by means of District Unions ended in failure.

Incorporation on the lines of the famous East Anglian Hundreds was equally difficult in the Isle, though many desired it. The spirit of parochial particularism was less marked here: the whole of the parishes within the ambit of Wisbech influence looked to that enterprising township for inspiration. Dependent hamlets, and even adjacent villages, did indeed co-operate to some extent in the administrative measures adopted by certain of the larger parishes. Nevertheless intervening swamps prevented more formal and effective union of wider areas. In the larger villages of the Isle much greater willingness to make administrative experiments is discernible than in the small, unprogressive parishes of the county proper. The reasons are to be found partly in the distinguishing features noted above and partly in the fact that valuable charities were, to an unusual extent, at the disposal of parish authorities. Ecclesiastical influence in the Isle may, in pre-Reformation days, have fostered the widespread support of

A board of ten trustees managed the joint lands of Sutton and Mepal. Some 1200 acres were controlled by the "Governors of the Lands and Possessions of the Poor" at Ely.

A few similar instances of wealthy parishes are to be found in the county proper. The Feofees of the Soham charity lands are elsewhere described (*supra*, pp. 207 *et seq.*). The body of Feofees at Burwell almost certainly developed from the manorial court, of which some records are still extant: the Feofees were not identical with the vestry, but by the eighteenth century the distinction was a fine one.

PLATE X

I. LEVERINGTON WORKHOUSE, ISLE OF ELY

II. LINTON TASK HOUSE, BUILT IN 1737

village gilds which are traceable as the origin of many of these charities. Extensive lands, as well as gildhalls and almshouses, were thus to be found during our period in the hands either of parish officers or of bodies of Feofees. It was within one or other of such ancient buildings that the more modern workhouse was often first established: it was the control of valuable estates that largely determined parochial policy.[1] The most striking example of gild influence is afforded by the Brotherhood of the Holy Trinity of Wisbech, from which grew the incorporated township and which gave the decisive bent to the town's administration through succeeding centuries.

The fourteen small urban parishes of the much-divided town of Cambridge, suspicious of each other and above all suspicious of corporate regulation, present in many respects a striking contrast on the one hand to the most populous parish of the Isle[2]—that of St Peter's, Wisbech, coterminous with the township and dominated to an extraordinary degree by corporate policy—and on the other to the united parishes of Royston, with their unique,[3] extra-legal, representative constitution.

1. Parish Government

Certain undefined rights appertained, by custom and Common Law, to the inhabitants at large, meeting in the parish vestry, especially at Easter. It was in their control over the churchwardens—the most ancient parish officers—that the main possibilities of democratic government lay. The churchwardens were held[4] to be representative of and responsible to the parishioners in the execution of wide, if somewhat vague, services for the common good, whilst the overseers by law owed allegiance to none save the justices.[5] The statutory association, however, of the

---

[1] Cf. *supra*, p. 234, note 3.

[2] The population in 1821 was 7877 (including the dependent village and hamlets).

[3] Unique so far as this county is concerned. Cf. *supra*, p. 106; *infra*, p. 244.

[4] By custom and Common Law.   [5] Under 43 Eliz., c. 5.

churchwardens with the overseers[1] did in practice necessitate some measure of popular consent to the activities of the overseer —for certain of which, indeed, after 1691 sundry statutes definitely required the approval of a vestry. By assimilation to one or other of the various methods commonly employed in the selection of churchwardens, the parish frequently took over the real choice of the overseers to be presented for magisterial confirmation. In other cases the onerous obligation of the parish officers to remain in harness till formally relieved led to the practice of nominating their own successors and paved the way for the rule of the close vestry.

In the early part of the seventeenth century Privy Council supervision probably achieved a measure of regularity in the monthly meetings of churchwardens and overseers enjoined by statute. In many Cambridgeshire parishes till the middle of the eighteenth century the officers do seem to have worked simultaneously throughout the whole year, whether continuing to meet formally or not. The serious increase in the complexity of their duties and in the financial outlay involved—particularly in connection with settlement disputes and the erection of workhouses—tended, however, to prevent the monthly official gatherings from developing into an exclusive governing clique: overseers were not anxious to risk meeting the charges of litigation out of their own purses. By the end of the eighteenth century, moreover, it was a common practice in both county and Isle for the overseers to divide the year between them, each officer accepting responsibility only for some months.[2] The churchwardens at this date frequently withdrew entirely from routine duty in connection with Poor Relief. In such circumstances the parish officers could hardly assume the sole government of the parish. The intimate economic and personal relationships existing between the members of small rural communities nevertheless almost inevitably entailed the concentration of power in

---

[1] And with the constables for certain purposes.

[2] This was true of some few rural parishes even in the early seventeenth century.

the hands of a little knot of leading inhabitants, among whom churchwardens and overseers, and sometimes constables and surveyors, figured prominently.[1] An oligarchy of this nature, governing by the tacit consent of the rate-payers at large, worked harmoniously right down to 1834 in many of the small parishes of the county. In other parishes the approval of a larger body—rarely of the whole community of rate-payers[2]—was definitely sought on occasions of importance. Government of these informal types might, however, develop in one of two directions: in certain parishes one traces the gradual evolution of something approximating to an open vestry; in others the oligarchy becomes a completely close body.

It is only in the more populous or wealthy communities that the evolution is at all clear. In several of the parishes of the Isle of Ely, for example, where large trust funds existed, the personnel of the close body which administered them was, by the later eighteenth century, more or less identical with that of the vestry, which seems to have become equally exclusive: in other parishes such developments were frustrated by the vigour of the

---

[1] Certain Tudor Statutes indeed implied the existence of such authorities. (Cf. S. and B. Webb, *op. cit.* p. 175.)

[2] "It was customary to omit from the rate-book all premises of low rental", say the Webbs (*op. cit.* p. 105). This was not universally true of Cambs. parishes at all periods. Rate-books are extant for many parishes: sometimes separate lists were made for church-rate and poor-rate, though the tendency to use a common assessment spread. The former lists generally included rather more names than the latter. There were 172 inhabitants of Great St Mary's parish assessed to the church-rate in 1629, of whom 42 were defaulters. There could hardly have been more than about 150 householders at that date. The list included even parish servants and almsfolk. By far the majority of the parishioners were rated at Bassingbourn in the sixteenth century. Undoubtedly the settlement policy gave the overseers a strong incentive for cutting down the lists. Nevertheless, even in the eighteenth and nineteenth centuries many of labouring rank were often assessed. In reply to a direct question of the Poor Law Commission, in 1833, a very considerable number of Cambs. parishes replied that small cottages were usually rated, even though the rates remained as bad debts.

inhabitants at large. Protests—originating usually in connection with the malversation of charities and sometimes involving expensive law-suits—terminated in the establishment of an open vestry, simultaneously with the reconstitution of the bodies of trustees.[1]

Interesting developments can also be traced in the larger rural villages, or small market towns, of the county proper. Among these Linton was perhaps the most active and may serve as an illustration.

2. *Rural Developments*

Linton

The seat of regular magisterial gatherings from the sixteenth to the nineteenth century and geographically well situated, Linton[2] made successive attempts to organise the parish as a centre of local government for the district. Three of the landed families of the neighbourhood actively contributed to the work of Quarter Sessions, led the local meetings of justices and dominated the vestry of Linton for many generations. It is difficult indeed at times to distinguish between their activities as vestrymen and as magistrates. It was they, together with the incumbent—aided at times by some of the past or present officers—who not only controlled the routine work of the parish but also made decisions involving new and important departures.[3] A standing committee of five parishioners—of which the three justices were the most important members—was practically self-appointed in 1710, for the purpose of controlling the administration of both regular and

---

[1] For examples see Ely MSS., under heading "Schools". (Registry, Ely.)

[2] With a population of 1519 in 1821 and 1678 in 1831. (Census Returns.)

[3] *E.g.* in 1710 it was decreed by a vestry consisting of justices and minister that relief should be distributed only upon Sundays, after Evening Prayer, and that no additions should be made to the list of regular pensioners or casual money distributed but by written order of one of the justices, or of certain "substantial inhabitants". (MS. Vestry Minutes.) Cf. *supra*, p. 180.

casual relief. Committees—some temporary, some more permanent—continued to be appointed for Poor Law and for other purposes, but in the course of the eighteenth century it became increasingly usual to summon what was styled "a general town meeting", sometimes numbering over twenty "substantial inhabitants", to give consent to whatever project was in debate and to nominate the committee which should carry it into execution.[1] In 1754 the services of a solicitor were engaged. At the close of the eighteenth century the authority of the governing group came more openly into question: public opinion made its voice effective in 1801, when the vestry agreed that "the inequality of the assessment for the maintenance and relief of the poor" demanded a general revaluation. Thenceforward an open vestry sought to steer the parochial ship through the troubled waters of the early nineteenth century. Good intention rather than efficiency marked its efforts.

3. The Urban Parishes of Cambridge

In certain parishes of the university town changes were more formal than in the average rural parish. Metropolitan movements influenced a public interested in pamphlet and journalistic literature and even in law cases. It was naturally within the walls of the university church of Great St Mary that the most heated controversies raged. Apparently the parish was under the governance of a close body, recruiting itself by co-option, as

---

[1] *E.g.* twenty-two parishioners assembled in 1700 to consider the conversion of the old almshouse into a real workhouse; twenty-three in 1737 to give consent to the raising of £100 loan for a workhouse—a committee consisting of two justices, two overseers and two churchwardens was appointed; thirteen in 1756 to agree that the parish should bear the expense of prosecuting parishioners guilty of hedge-breaking—half a century earlier the vestry had threatened to refuse relief to any such offenders.

The committee took a more permanent form in the case of surveyors: from 1753 onwards from four to seven vestrymen were elected yearly to attend to highway regulations. (MS. Vestry Minutes.)

early as 1504,[1] and there is no record of any change before 1738. This body elected the churchwardens, who then elected four overseers, from whom two were finally chosen by the town justices.[2] The vestry meetings were usually attended by six to a dozen members, but even at this period double that number were occasionally present at "a public meeting of ye parishioners".[3] Dissentient elements were already in evidence in 1697, when the vestry attempted to alter the basis of assessment and to levy both church- and poor-rate according to a more equitable pound-rate. The Mayor, as magistrate, refused consent, and a vestry of seventeen members thereupon decided to return to the "old and usuall custom". It was not uncommon at this period, as at a later date, for the vestry to appoint several of its members as a temporary committee to negotiate some project, the general lines of which had been agreed upon.

During the half-century between 1693 and 1743 a wave of opposition to Select Vestry government—set in motion partly by Whig, partly by anti-clerical sentiment—swept the Metropolis, where the evil results of the system were peculiarly obvious, and spread to some extent to the provinces.[4] Though the practical results were small, the interest aroused was considerable. The wave reached Great St Mary's in 1738. "A majority of the parishioners" in that year elected two churchwardens in opposition to those elected by the Select Vestry. The minutes of the proceedings state the case fully. The parish, it was declared, had in time past "consented to Select Vestrys with a view to prevent clamours", the inhabitants being "pretty numerous". Latterly this custom had proved to be "ill-grounded". The present parishioners had surely "as good a right to set aside such Select Vestrys as their Ancestors could ever have had to consent

[1] At which date the extant vestry records begin.

[2] *I.e.* after the statutory institution of overseers. Cambridge was accustomed to complicated modes of election for corporation offices.

[3] For such purposes as defying the magistrates' order to assist other parishes (1635); apprenticing children (1656, 1682, and many subsequent dates); owning persons as settled parishioners (1675, 1685); agreeing to badge the poor (1682).   [4] Webb, *op. cit.* chaps. v, vi, vii.

thereto ". It was unfitting that parochial expenditure should be determined by "six or eight people, who take the Liberty of unstringing their Neighbours purses by Artifice and Contrivance, contrary to their inclinations and goodwill ". The determination of the majority carried the day and the two churchwardens then proceeded to elect the overseers according to ancient custom. The following year a pound-rate was successfully substituted as the basis of assessment. Nominally the vestry remained open, but as enthusiasm died down the ordinary business gradually fell as heretofore—without definite election—into the hands of a small group. At moments of special interest[1] the more alert rate-payers put in an appearance, but there is little to distinguish the parish government of the later eighteenth century from the earlier Select Vestry.

It was stated in the course of the attack upon the close vestry of Great St Mary's that the town parishes of Holy Trinity, Great St Andrew, and St Botolph had at one time been ruled by like select bodies, but that these had been "abolished for many years ".[2] The sixteenth- and seventeenth-century account books of churchwardens, overseers and surveyors of St Botolph's do indeed reveal an organisation under a Select Vestry, whose members in the later sixteenth century were termed "headboroughs" and were at that date twelve in number.[3] The transition to a nominally open vestry here, however, and also in the

[1] *E.g.* in 1742 to dispute the vagrancy rate imposed by the Bench; in 1750 to contest the General Workhouse scheme for the town. (MS. Vestry Book.)

[2] MS. Vestry Book, 1738. Definite reference was made to the London revolt.

[3] Extracts from Church Book of Accompts, 1583 (preserved in Bowtell MSS, 6, 2511, Downing College Library). Two sidesmen, one nominated by the incumbent and one by the vestry, were included among the parochial officers of St Botolph's from the sixteenth century. The churchwardens were elected in like manner: the overseers and surveyors of the next century were selected by the vestry; the constables by the Court Leet. At a vestry meeting of 1663, the members still styled themselves "headburrowes", though only seven were present; they met to co-opt two further headboroughs.

parishes of Great St Andrew and Holy Trinity, was a very unobtrusive one and seems to have made little difference to the ordinary conduct of parish affairs.

4. *Royston*

More revolutionary than any of the experiments so far discussed were the changes inaugurated, in 1781, by the two combined parishes of Royston. A rapidly increasing poor-rate and a swelling tide of vagrancy drove the town to drastic reorganisation. A representative body was set up, consisting of one churchwarden, two overseers and eight elected members from the Hertfordshire parish, the same number of officers together with three elected members from the Cambridgeshire parish. The new body proceeded forthwith to engage a salaried vestry clerk, to draw up standing orders and to arrange that printed notices should be circulated to announce the time and object of all meetings.[1] It was indeed the Poor Law which had provoked the change, but the new body took over all the functions of local government—including the control of public morals. Administrative efficiency, combined with public control, might perchance have been achieved but for the constant friction resulting from two county jurisdictions. Other sources of weakness existed, though these might have been remedied. Certain executive functions, for example, were still carried out by the parish officers, full control over whom could hardly be secured whilst they sat on the legislative council and were not its direct, salaried nominees. It is not clear, moreover, how frequent were the appeals to the general body of rate-payers. The constitution, however, was maintained till the general legislation of 1818–19. It was hoped that under the aegis of statutory authority—at least in the sphere of Poor Law—freedom from friction might be attained. The Sturges-Bourne legislation was consequently adopted. The verdict in 1834 was still favourable: "We think it impossible to do without a Select Vestry".

This leads to a consideration of the general influence in Cambridgeshire of the legislation of 1818–19.

---

[1] Cf. *supra*, p. 106.

5. Sturges-Bourne's Acts

It was the very rapid rise of the poor-rate in the second decade of the nineteenth century—more obvious to the average rate-payer than the equivalent growth of national wealth—together with the disorderly character of the meetings of the crowded Metropolitan vestries, that concentrated attention upon Poor Law administration and resulted in the Acts of 1818 and 1819. The main effect of these Acts was to legalise the formation of a parish committee, annually elected by and subject to the control of an open vestry, the officers being completely subordinated to the committee. Certain clauses fixing the suffrage were compulsory in all parishes, but the main administrative changes were merely optional. The section permitting the appointment of a salaried assistant overseer, moreover, might be adopted independently of the rest of the Act.

The choice of the obnoxious term "Select Vestry" for what was in reality a representative committee was an unfortunate one, but more serious objections were disclosed when the Act was put into operation. The functions of the parish were manifold, yet the new organisation was legally concerned only with the Poor Law: dislocation was therefore likely to ensue. The system of plural voting which the Act introduced, moreover, led in practice to riotous meetings and sometimes involved resort to a referendum, where the number of votes to be counted was large.

6. Select Vestries in Cambridgeshire and the Isle

The majority of the small rural parishes of Cambridgeshire ignored or disapproved of the suggested vestry reorganisation, but about half of those interrogated in 1833 had appointed a salaried assistant overseer. In the Isle of Ely a considerable proportion of the larger parishes adopted a Select Vestry as well as a paid overseer: in these cases the parish did not scruple to extend the new organisation to matters unconnected with Poor Law. Nevertheless the difficulty of obtaining a quorum commonly arose. The full number of Select Vestrymen was usually twenty, but the experience reported by Whittlesey was very generally repeated: "One set attend one meeting, another the next".[1] Hence continuity of policy was lacking.

The urban parishes of Cambridge proved a finer touchstone. Little interest seems to have been taken here before 1825. The labouring population of the parish of Little St Andrew, however, had been increasing with startling rapidity. A small community of 251 souls in 1801, the parish numbered no less than 2211 in 1821 and trebled again during the next decade. In 1825 a Select Vestry was instituted and much-needed reforms began. Weekly meetings were held and the list of applicants for relief was cut down by a rather ruthless "offering of the house". Expenses fell markedly but a loud outcry arose from the poorer classes. At the general parish meeting, in 1828, for the annual election of the Select Vestry, the small rate-payers rolled up in numbers and a scene of confusion followed. "A low mechanic was called to the chair by general acclamation and the elections fell upon a class of persons whose appointment the magistrates refused to sign."[2] Henceforth no Select Vestry was appointed. Holy Trinity and Great St Andrew's also made the experiment. The former parish abandoned the Select Vestry but retained an assistant overseer. The experience of Great St Andrew's was more fortunate: the parish was much less populous than Little St Andrew's and the proportion of substantial householders much larger. The Select Vestry was adopted here about 1829; well-attended meetings were held every fortnight and the new constitution was maintained down to 1834.

Since parish and township of Wisbech were coextensive, vestry government in this case is most conveniently considered in connection with corporate constitution.

---

[1] *P.L.C. Rept.* 1834, App. A, Query 17. (Everett's Report.)
[2] *Ibid.* 1834, App. A, p. 239. (Power's Report.)

C. THE TOWNS

(1) *Cambridge*

Whether in respect of constitutional structure or of resulting social activity, it would be difficult to find a more striking contrast than that existing between the democratic township of Wisbech and the close corporation of Cambridge. The latter town alone was a full municipality by prescription,[1] possessing an independent magistracy.[2]

The corporate rulers of Cambridge were vigorous enough in medieval days, and indeed in Tudor and Stuart times exerted very considerable authority over poor relief, as over other social affairs. As joint-trustee for Hobson's Workhouse in the early part of the seventeenth century, the town in fact took over from the parish authorities the essential control of the able-bodied poor. Rivalry between Town and Gown, however, tended to distract attention from mere parochial affairs and when, in the succeeding century, inertia and corruption to a large extent replaced rivalry, what few efforts were made to co-ordinate parish policy met with more suspicion than support.[3] From the end of the seventeenth century onwards the body of freemen, or burgesses, became increasingly futile in social administration as they became increasingly exclusive in character.

The exercise of considerable care to secure impartiality—within the prescribed limits of the electorate—is suggested by the complicated, indirect method by which the choice of Mayor was settled, according to ancient by-law. So far, however, had practice diverged from early intention that the half-century following 1784 found the office completely within the control of a single family, enjoying boundless influence. The elections of the twelve aldermen and the twenty-four common-councilmen

---

[1] Subject to the regulations of numerous charters.

[2] From 1380 onwards. (Cooper, *op. cit.* I, p. 119.)

[3] "The corporation has no concern in the management of the poor", it was reported in 1835. (*First Reports from Commissioners on Municipal Corporations* (1835), VI, Pt. iv, p. 2195—hereafter referred to as *R.C.M.C.*)

were theoretically conducted similarly to that of the Mayor: by the end of the eighteenth century members of both bodies held office for life. Most of the civic posts at this date were temptingly lucrative.[1]

To the freedom of the town, with its treasured privileges, there were four avenues of approach—birth, apprenticeship, purchase and gift. From the beginning of the eighteenth century, however, these routes were guarded with ever-growing jealousy.[2] In 1736 the number of freemen polling was 246: by 1835 it had fallen to 118, though in the interim the whole population had trebled.[3] To the freeman alone was the management of corporate affairs open or the parliamentary franchise granted, yet in 1834 no less than eleven-twelfths of the rates of the borough[4] were paid by those who were unconnected with the corporation and who had no control over its officers.[5]

Political influence was "perfectly notorious" at Cambridge— exercised for a long series of years prior to 1834 by the Duke of Rutland, the High Steward of the town.[6]

Acting magistrates of the eighteenth and early nineteenth centuries were also inevitably party in character and usually subservient in mentality. The earlier disputes between Town and Gown had led to repeated, though ineffectual, efforts on the part

[1] The four Bailiffs were likewise elected annually, but were commonly re-elected for four years. The annual election of the two Treasurers was, by 1787, a farce.

[2] By the nineteenth century only one or two per annum entered by birth or apprenticeship. Entry by purchase or gift was dependent on the approach of a parliamentary election and on the party colour of the applicant.

[3] The population was about 20,000 at this date.

[4] The borough-rate was levied by the Town Bench.

[5] No standing committees were at any time appointed. Temporary committees were always the immediate nominees of the Mayor and their reports were rarely discussed. The eight auditors were appointed by the Mayor and passed the Treasurers' accounts without examination, for the items were often their own bills.

[6] Convivial meetings of the Rutland Club were never "disturbed by anything so disgusting as a bill". (*R.C.M.C.* (1835), p. 2205.)

of the university to obtain an independent magistracy. From the seventeenth century onwards academic representatives tended to withdraw disdainfully, except when their own interests were at stake, from the ordinary meetings of the Town Bench. Though the Bench definitely strove in Stuart times to exert a beneficial control over the growing particularism of the petty parochial authorities, magisterial influence was weakened by the absence of those most skilled in the law.[1] After the Revolution vested interests were secure and the slumbers of the university as a body were scarcely lighter than those of the town. But the eighteenth century gave scope to the individual, and the university rarely lacked a small group of active and intelligent representatives upon the County Bench. Unfortunately for the town, however, though the quondam rivals now sacrificed peacefully before the same altar, the ineptitude of town magistrates did nothing to revive the support of their academic colleagues. The Cambridge Bench became a by-word for inefficiency and individual magistrates were notoriously prone to make fees their primary consideration. One town justice, an alderman, it was reported in 1835, issued from his own office half at least of all the town pauper removal warrants. The overseer of St Bene't's stated that he himself had often occasion to go three or four times a week to this magistrate and that he usually paid six to eight shillings per visit in fees. When a colleague was necessary the magistrate called in the aid of his son and had latterly dispensed with the services of a clerk, to whom alone fees were legally due[2]—the suspicion was strong that the clerk had been merely a cat's-paw before.[3] "Town magistrates", said an Esquire Bedell of the same period, "are in great disesteem with respectable people of all political parties, and other magistrates named in the commission decline to act with the aldermen."[4]

Had the corporation managed its large benefactions with integrity the town might well have been one of the most pro-

[1] Cf. *supra*, p. 222.
[2] Regulated at intervals by Quarter Sessions.
[3] *R.C.M.C.* (1835), p. 2191.   [4] *Ibid.* p. 2194.

sperous in the country, but malversations, it was gravely reported in 1835, had occurred "to a very great extent". Of twelve out of eighteen charities nothing whatever was known; of others the only beneficiaries were the members of the governing body. Property derived from Crown grants, as well as from bequests, was let out on long leases, at very low rentals, to members of the corporation. From 1791 onwards there was a "general scramble among the corporators" for the purchase of valuable town lands at merely nominal prices. The theory of corporate property was brazenly expressed by one of the common-councilmen in 1835: "The corporation has a right to expend their income on themselves and their friends, without being bound to apply any part of it to the good of the town".[1]

"Neglect of municipal duty and abuse of municipal power in a great variety of forms"[2] had proved the result at Cambridge of government by a close corporation. It was in face of just such conditions that Reformers "saw red".

(2) Wisbech

Whilst at Cambridge parish authorities, for over a century and a half, pursued their several ways untrammelled by corporate policy, at Wisbech the position was reversed: the town rulers here dominated parochial administration till well into the eighteenth century to an extent hardly envisaged by the laws of the land. The geographical coincidence of parish and manorial borough, or township, of necessity made the link between the two authorities a close one. Moreover gild traditions were exceptionally persistent and greatly strengthened the hold of the town over the parish.

---

[1] E.g. in 1791 the corporation sold land estimated to be worth £400 to Stephen Robinson for £21. Leases were commonly from 60 to 999 years. A limit of 40 years was fixed in 1823. (R.C.M.C. (1835), p. 2199.)

[2] Ibid. p. 2206.

(a) THE GILD

The early history of the borough is practically the history of its religious gild, founded in 1379.[1] It was to the usages established in these days that the distinguishing features of later development were largely due. Membership increased rapidly and the wealth of the gild was augmented by benefactions to such an extent that the appointment of a Bailiff was necessary in 1463. His management of the landed estates was from the outset subjected to the strict control of committees nominated by the governing body of the gild.[2] As early as 1512 the device of a standing committee had been adopted for the supervision of the gild almshouse. Efficiency and integrity became the hall-marks of gild activities, the scope of which steadily extended. Many of the functions later performed by the corporation were already exercised by the Brethren: the distribution of relief, the care of orphan children and the granting of loans to tradesmen, for example, were important duties. Association between gild and church was naturally close: apart from paying for special religious observances, the Brethren often contributed to the general expenses of the churchwardens.[3] Even in these early days a quasi-judicial authority—such as was exercised more extensively during the first generation or so after incorporation—was occasionally assumed by the Inquest or governing body of the gild.[4] The exceptional vigour of the communal spirit manifested

[1] Founded "for a free scoll, yer to admatt and bryng up yoyoth, and to celebratt yer divine servis and to relyffe steyne poore pepull". The gild also maintained certain piers and banks. (Answer to Ed. VI's Commissioners. MS. Gild Records, 1547.) The number of Brethren seems in 1379 to have been sixty-seven, whose payments then amounted to £13. 14s.

[2] No long leases were to be arranged without special consent. (MS. Gild Records, 1514.)

[3] It was the Alderman (who was also the vicar) and the churchwardens who were summoned before Ed. VI's Commissioners when the gild was dissolved. They contributed, for example, to "ye buyldyng of ye stepull".

[4] E.g. two individuals were presented and fined 3s. 4d. each for abusing the Alderman. (Watson, History of Wisbech (1827), p. 159.)

by the Brethren begat trust and this in its turn called for increased watchfulness, for the temptations of office were many. The last ordinance issued by the gild, in 1547, may well have served as the motto for its successors: "We will and ordeyn y^t ye aldmā and bayley shall do nothing w^t out ye consent of xii". There is hardly yet that direct control of the people of which later Wisbech inhabitants were so proud, but there is already the tradition of purity of administration and public zeal. It was on the ground of the efficiency of the social services rendered and of the management of the landed estate that the possessions of the gild were restored and the town raised, in 1547, to a corporation.

(*b*) THE CHARTERED TOWNSHIP

The first Royal Charter was unusually democratic in form: ten of the "better, more honest and more discreet inhabitants"— the "Ten Men", or "Capital Burgesses" as later charters styled them—were to be elected annually by the inhabitant householders of Wisbech. Beyond an implied grant of authority to maintain the customs of the community the charter had nothing to say about government, yet it was through the gradual extension or modification of the simple functions of gild days that the town developed into a body differing only from a full municipality in the absence of a corporate magistracy.

In the course of the following half-century some limitation of the franchise was introduced by general consent in the interest of efficiency.[1] No head of the corporation was recognised by charter, but in actual fact a Town Bailiff was elected by the Ten as their executive head, with the allowance of so small a stipend

---

[1] In 1564 the Ten were required to be 40s. freeholders. In 1611 the general electorate was similarly confined, after a contest with those who would have converted the body into an autocracy by limiting the franchise to £10 freeholders. In 1688 not only did an attempt to obtain the election of "Capitall Burges for ther lives" fail, but the public inspection of all accounts and their submission to the Common Hall were secured. From 1818 the accounts were printed and published.

as barely to cover out-of-pocket expenses. Monthly meetings of the Ten were held regularly and sometimes interim gatherings also. An annual meeting[1] of the freeholders was required by charter, but from the outset the Ten Men frequently consulted the electorate, or even the whole body of inhabitants, and continued to do so during succeeding centuries.

The powers assumed in the early days of the corporation clearly owed much to gild precedent. The direct administration of certain branches of poor relief—the giving of money, clothing and medical aid from corporate funds—was in the old tradition. It was indeed as a result of the substantial monetary assistance granted to the parochial authorities that these officials were reduced to a state of subjection warranted by neither statute nor charter.[2]

[1] Following the custom of gild days a feast was held on these occasions.

[2] To the churchwardens assistance was given, for example, in 1597 and 1625 for building repairs; in 1604 for communion wine; in 1607 for the salary of the preacher; in 1671 "for the general ease of the inhabitants of their church rate". In 1690 the salary paid to the parish clerk was stopped, but two years later a reduced salary was again voted.

The control over other parish offices is seen repeatedly. In 1591 the Ten assembled to "view the Book for the Collections of the Poor". In 1592 they excused two men payment to the poor-rate because the men had assisted a widow to find employment, and the widow herself was ordered to be taken off the "collection" for twelve weeks; in 1586 Robt. Chandler was ordered by the Ten to be "discharged of his Menworks and Watchinge" and to be given a coat in consideration of his taking an orphan child. The Ten passed the accounts of the "Collectors for the Poore" and of the churchwardens, constables and surveyors. During the seventeenth century it was the Capital Burgesses who decided whether the overseers should collect a single or a double rate (e.g. in 1674); who ordered a new assessment, and even appointed and paid an assistant overseer to aid in reassessing and to keep a regular watch for undesired settlers (1675 et seq.); who insisted upon the attendance of members of their own body at the weekly distribution of relief by the overseers (1677). From 1576 onwards the Ten frequently apprenticed children, but probably in these cases obtained the legal sanction of the justices among their own members.

(c) THE VESTRY

In the absence of churchwardens' or overseers' accounts there is little evidence respecting the early constitution of the vestry. Though in a subordinate position till the eighteenth century, the vestry seems to have worked in harmony with the Capital Burgesses; the two bodies were not, however, identical in personnel. The strongly-marked devotion of the town to democratic principles would lead one to presume the existence of an open vestry.

The problems of poor-relief increased simultaneously with the extension of corporate obligations in many directions and the Capital Burgesses gradually withdrew from the more routine duties of Poor Law administration. At the end of the eighteenth century the vestry was a vigorous organisation, so numerously attended indeed as to embarrass discussion. The corporation still contributed to the financing of parochial projects, but either left organisation entirely to the vestry or delegated members to a joint committee of town and parish. By this date, in fact, the old custom of reference by the Capital Burgesses to the inhabitants at large usually meant appeal to an open vestry meeting.[1]

The practical difficulties attending open vestry organisation in a populous area led the parish to adopt the Select Vestry system of Sturges-Bourne. The wide influence of Wisbech was mani-

[1] In 1786, for example, the establishment of Sunday Schools was discussed before large gatherings of the vestry. A joint committee of Capital Burgesses, clergy and others was appointed. (Ely MSS. "Schools", Registry, Ely.) During the dearth of 1799 the parish assembled, "after regular notice read in church", to discuss the setting-up of a Soup Kitchen. A parish committee was appointed. The Capital Burgesses contributed £50 but left organisation entirely to the vestry. In 1810 the corporation decided to legalise its position by applying for a Local Improvement Act. The measure was submitted to a vestry meeting and being disapproved of was temporarily dropped. A similar proposal was carried a little later. In 1826 the Select Vestry and the Capital Burgesses combined to finance an enlightened public utility scheme. (MS. Corp. Minute and Order Book, 1799, 1810, 1826. For establishment of Select Vestry see also P.L.C. Rept. 1834, App. A, Query 17. (Everett's Report.))

fested in the unique extra-legal arrangement whereby the salaried assistant overseer served jointly for the parish of Wisbech St Peter (with the dependent village of Wisbech St Mary and the hamlets of Guyhirne, Tholomas Drove and Murrow) and for the parish of Emneth and the hamlet of Elm. His duties were confined to distributing relief, the ordinary overseers attending to rate-collection. Apparently the Select Vestry worked fairly well, though but a small proportion of the twenty members attended regularly. The reorganisation of Poor Law administration here caused little dislocation of other services, since much of the responsibility for these latter had for long devolved in practice upon the Capital Burgesses.

(d) THE MAGISTRACY

What was the relation of the corporate body to the magistracy of the Isle? During the sixteenth and seventeenth centuries the town assumed, as a result of earlier customs, not only the powers of control legally belonging to the parish officers but in some cases powers vested by law in the justices. In the instances of corporate action adduced above[1] there is no reason to suppose that the justices as such played any part. For the first few decades of corporate life, moreover, the Ten Men, meeting together with "others ye inhabitants of ye most best, wysest and substantialest of ye said Towne", acted as a voluntary semi-judicial tribunal.[2] Nevertheless one is often aware of the justices in the background. The organisation of the town and outlying hamlets during the

[1] Cf. *supra*, p. 253, note 2.
[2] "For the appeasyng of such controversyes as doe aryse...betwene any of o^r neyghbours." Some of the disputes were such as would normally have fallen within the summary jurisdiction of a magistrate; others might well have been matters for presentment before the Court Leet. Yet the Court Leet was functioning actively till a much later period. (The MS. Records of "Court Leet and Courts Halimote held at Wisbech", extant for the late years of Elizabeth and the beginning of James I's reign, show the two courts working separately.)

plague of 1584–7 was carried out by the Capital Burgesses hand-in-glove with the magistrates for that part of the Isle.[1]

It was, however, the Court Leet which, in 1587, drew up orders to prevent the influx of strangers[2], and presumably it was the same body which issued further orders on the subject in 1591 —"in the Court at Wisebech".[3] In the latter part of the seventeenth century the extrusion of would-be settlers and the demolition of cottages on the Lord's waste were effected by means of presentment at the Court of Quarter Sessions, through the medium of the Grand Jury for the hundred.[4]

A memorandum was made in 1593 of a "metynge of the Ten Men and others of the Bynche". Thirteen years earlier it was the "Tenne Men and others of the cheif Hedborrows of the said Towne, with the Consent of the Justices of the Peace", who settled certain matters with the Queen's Purveyor[5].

The activities of Capital Burgesses, Courts Leet, Quarter Sessions and justices' divisional meetings are indeed often inextricably confused in the records.[6] In actual practice, moreover, the same individuals acted in more than one capacity. The Chief Constable of the Hundred of Wisbech was, at least at some periods, also a Capital Burgess, and on the Grand Jury for the Hundred Court sat many prominent townsmen. Several of the Capital Burgesses were magistrates for the Isle and, as already pointed out,[7] the magistrates in or near Wisbech dominated the

---

[1] The assessments levied were "with the consent of the justices". The printed regulations and penalties were also "by order of the justices", though carried out with a fairly free hand by the Ten Men and their assistants, in their capacity as Governors of the ten wards into which the town was divided in 1587—as it was again later to meet the dearth of 1595.

[2] MS. Corp. Records, 1587.

[3] Ibid. 1591. The Court Leet was still fining offenders of this type in 1620. (MS. Corp. Minute and Order Book, Records of Courts Leet, etc.)

[4] MS. Corp. Minute and Order Book, 1674, 1682, 1693.

[5] It was the Chief Constable and seven others who were deputed by the Ten to settle an apprenticeship dispute in 1577.

[6] In assessments for drainage purposes there is the additional confusion of orders of Commissioners for Sewers.

[7] Supra, p. 232.

counsels of the Bench of Quarter Sessions. The inclusion within the parish of an outlying village and hamlets increased the hold of the town over the rural neighbourhood, whilst the communal use of extensive wastes brought the whole of the hundred into still closer unity and fostered the vitality of the Hundred Court and the influence of its leading members. Hence resulted the harmony between magistrates and Capital Burgesses and the informal assumption of magisterial authority on occasion.

(e) CONSTITUTIONAL DEVELOPMENTS OF THE CORPORATION

The delegation of authority to committees dates back, in rudimentary form, to the days of the gild. After the incorporation of the town the practice continued, though it was not till the middle of the eighteenth century that it grew to importance. From this period onwards the Town Bailiff constantly sought the support of two or three colleagues for his rapidly extending duties. By the end of the century committees were at work drafting full reports on this problem and on that.

The gradual organisation of a salaried staff began in the seventeenth century, if not earlier. Various minor offices were created, some to be retained permanently, others to be abolished after a period of trial.[1] The salaries, however, were never high and the posts were never sinecures. As the executive officer of the Capital Burgesses for all purposes, the Town Bailiff found his duties increasingly onerous, yet even in 1834 only a small annual gratuity of £5 was voted to him, whilst strict control was maintained by "the Hall" over his most trivial expenditure. A salaried Town Clerk was appointed in 1679.

---

[1] In 1626 a beadle and scavenger was appointed. His salary was 40s. in 1647 and 60s. in 1677. In 1673 a warner-off of poor strangers was engaged "so long as the Burgesses do aprove of his diligence and no longare". The beadle undertook this duty a little later, being rewarded according to the town's favourite device of "payment-by-results". A separate bellman was engaged intermittently from 1676.

It is perhaps rather misleading to say that "at no time and for no purpose did the corporation levy a rate",[1] where the relation between parish and borough was so intimate and where the Capital Burgesses were in very real control of the parish purse. A Parish Clerk was regularly appointed at some period before 1579 and by that date the collections for the payment of his wages were for practical purposes a compulsory rate—a rate which was used at the dictate of the Ten Men as the basis for other occasional levies.[2] In 1685 the Capital Burgesses abolished the rate and paid the Parish Clerk a salary of £10, but reverted to the old practice in 1690. The actual outlay of the constables was sometimes repaid from corporate funds and at other times by a semi-voluntary collection—a form of levy which persisted to the nineteenth century. The insufficiency of corporate funds and voluntary or semi-voluntary collections to secure adequate service in a rapidly growing urban community was becoming obvious by the end of the eighteenth century, especially in matters of police organisation. The Capital Burgesses were deeply concerned to improve matters, but the reluctance to impose a definite borough-rate was hardly a virtue by this date. Certain public services were provided out of the magistrates' rates for the northern part of the Isle: in the case of a fully-fledged municipality like Cambridge these of course had to be met by a borough-rate. The most striking feature in the government of Wisbech is, nevertheless, the skill and integrity with which public funds had been managed, with but few failures, for nearly five centuries. The rents of gild property and later benefactions, together with the ancient tolls and dues arising from the trade of the port, were the essential means by which the services of the town had been maintained,

---

[1] S. and B. Webb, *English Local Government. The Manor and the Borough* (1908), p. 144.

[2] In 1579 to assist a poor scholar at St John's College, Cambridge; in 1584, and at later dates, for the relief of the poor; in 1583 for the repair of the Great Bridge, and later in the same year to meet the fine imposed by the Court for the non-repair of a certain causeway. (MS. Corp. Minute and Order Book.)

yet few towns could boast a more continuously active and enlightened policy. The lead which Wisbech gave to the whole of the north part of the Isle in Poor Law matters was paralleled by the town's enterprise in many other directions.[1] "The affairs of the town", said the Commissioners of 1835, "are managed by a representative body", whose activities are checked by "annual elections and publicity of accounts.... Corporate officers are few and their salaries moderate". Public meetings are held before any serious debt is incurred. Charity funds—in startling contrast to those at Cambridge—are "appropriated to their legitimate objects, without party distinctions. The corporation exists, in fact as well as in words, for the common benefit of the inhabitants".[2] Whilst the municipal reforms of 1835 were met at Cambridge by a storm of protests, at Wisbech they were hailed with approval, as ushering in an era of complete democratic rule and full municipal status.

[1] The Capital Burgesses maintained a Grammar School continuously; from 1710 onwards they spent much on river improvements; in 1714 opened a public library; in 1758 completed a new stone bridge; and in 1811–13 reorganised, on the lines of Lancaster and Bell, their Charity Schools established a century earlier. The workhouse schemes are described fully in other chapters.

[2] *R.C.M.C.* (1835), p. 2564.

Chapter XVII

CONCLUSIONS

Any attempt to define within accurate chronological limits the trends of thought or practice which developed in the long period during which the Elizabethan statute formed the basis of Poor Law administration is fraught with serious difficulty, for even within the confines of a single county contradictory policies repeatedly characterise places but a few miles apart. This is less true of the first forty years of the seventeenth century, during which time the administrative hierarchy, with the Privy Council at its head, made unflagging efforts to establish a centralised and uniform system, but in the course of the two succeeding centuries complete local autonomy resulted in the most varied administration—legal, extra-legal and illegal.

The explanation lies essentially in the isolated character of the very small communities with which we are essentially concerned. Communications were notoriously bad through the fenland county of Cambridge, yet it is in the marshy Isle of Ely rather than in the county proper that the influence of common impulses at various periods can more easily be traced. The more significant villages of the Isle were, in the main, situated on the drier ridges, and population tended to concentrate here, or in hamlets looking to the larger communities as centres. The successive series of experiments initiated by the enterprising little industrial town of Wisbech, bordering upon the East Anglian textile district, definitely gave the lead to the larger parishes of the Isle. This is particularly true with respect to workhouse activities. Valuable benefactions, moreover, often made experiment possible. In the county exterior to the Isle, on the other hand, villages were more evenly scattered: geographical considerations defeated all attempts to combine for purposes of local government till the dictators of 1834 swept every difficulty aside.

The university town itself—the one full municipality within the county—was divided into fourteen small parishes, and already in the early years of the seventeenth century there were manifestations of the spirit of jealous particularism evoked by the stress laid upon parochial responsibility for the poor. Constant conflict between Town and Gown, however, kept alive some sense of corporate unity, especially whilst the university still posed as the pampered child of the Privy Council. As the headquarters of the Eastern Association during the Civil War, however, Cambridge experienced something of the welding power of enthusiasm for a common cause, and from the Restoration era onwards the rivalry between Town and Gown was less marked. During the course of the eighteenth century there grew up that deification and monopolisation of vested interests, which characterised academic and municipal bodies alike, and which brought in its train the notorious corruption in high places. Whilst Mayor and Vice-Chancellor were now prepared to join hands, parochial jealousy and natural suspicion of authority thwarted the repeated efforts to unite the town under a common system of Poor Law administration.

If an attempt be made to group the activities of Cambridge with those of the other urban communities, generalisations must be made warily, for the towns of Cambridge, Wisbech and Royston differed widely from one another in many respects.

Nevertheless certain distinctive features do emerge from the detailed study embodied in the foregoing chapters.

PRIVY COUNCIL CONTROL

"Instruction for youth, employment for the healthy, comfort for the aged and infirm, reformation for the profligate", these it was held by the Cambridgeshire Bench in 1814 had been the guiding principles of the Elizabethan Poor Law. How far had they dictated the policy of succeeding centuries?

Privy Council control was more comprehensive and continuous in rural Cambridgeshire during the first four decades of the seventeenth century than at any other period, and matters concerned with poor relief were more often the occasion of Privy Council interference in the university town than they had been even in the sixteenth century: in the case of Wisbech central influence made itself felt less directly by way of the neighbouring East Anglian towns. Nevertheless difficulties in the working of the law early disclosed themselves—in the town of Cambridge obstacles arose particularly when attempts were made to levy upon the wealthier parishes rates in aid of the poorer, or alternatively to equalise the rate over the whole town. In the rural districts the Act was put into force where distress was marked, but there was no sudden or widespread change from earlier semi-voluntary systems. It was only during the second decade of the century that most of the larger villages began to conform more precisely to the technique of administration laid down by law. For more than a century Wisbech continued its earlier gild tradition of direct corporate control, so far as the sick and the casual poor were concerned, and kept a close supervision over the parochial officers' activities on behalf of the children. The urban authorities interfered occasionally at Cambridge in the early seventeenth century, and in both towns the control of unemployment was regarded at this date as a matter for corporate arrangement—in Wisbech it continued to be so to the end of the eighteenth century and to some extent even later. The provision of work was naturally the most difficult of the duties imposed upon unsalaried, unspecialised parish officers. Whilst the Privy Council was supreme, a stock of materials was sometimes provided in the larger parishes; most often it was worked up in the homes of the poor, but occasionally in a semi-institutional Task House. The smaller villages preferred to encourage unemployed men to wander into the better-equipped parishes, but after the outbreak of the Civil War work was rarely available even in these. At no time was the County House of Correction at Cambridge used as an ordinary workhouse: it stood in the background, representing the coercive attitude to be adopted towards the deliberately idle and turbulent. In the towns for more than a century a marked reluctance to devote the rates to the relief of unemployment was manifest—any alternative source of municipal income seemed preferable. Benefactions for this purpose came to the relief of the authorities of both Cambridge and Wisbech. No stigma, however, was as yet attached to the honest applicant for public employment: the deterrent policy was reserved for the idle and vicious.

THE DOCTRINE OF PROFITABLE EMPLOYMENT

The change of heart on the subject of profit-making which followed the Protestant Reformation, the Calvinistic identification of virtue with success, the breakdown of the older industrial régime as a mere result of war, and the pressure which fear of Dutch rivalry exerted upon the industrial world, combined to bring into prominence the doctrine of profitable public employment as the solution of poverty. This was a conception not envisaged by the Statute of 1597, and it was not till nearly a century later that it aroused widespread interest. Together with the growing recognition of the unsuitability of the parish as an administrative unit, this interest in public employment of the poor continued to express itself in waves of practical experiment during the eighteenth century—at first tending to stress the element of profit; when this failed seeking support in the disciplinary aspect of work.

As early as 1600, however, the Ten Men of Wisbech had evolved, with the aid of private venture, a scheme of employment basing itself upon the profit-making creed. The failure of the employers to secure a remunerative turn-over, when the scale of wages was fixed and the number of employees was entirely outside their control, did nothing to destroy the faith of the town rulers in the essentials of the doctrine: they merely concentrated upon discovering more effective ways of putting it into practice. Before the Restoration era Schools of Industry for children had been started, and for adults workhouses and other schemes in which the contract system was applied—nearly seventy years before contracting was statutorily allowed. Experiment followed experiment to the end of the century. Seeking at first to dispose of the pauper manufactures in the open market, the authorities were gradually compelled to use the products more and more exclusively for consumption by the employees themselves—an experience repeated everywhere in the course of the following century.

Unemployment, however, was not at this date a serious menace in rural Cambridgeshire, and the university town was opposed to municipal action. It was, in consequence, the Charity School movement which gained most ground here during the first two or three decades of the eighteenth century. Recognising the repeated failure of its industrial plans, even Wisbech threw in its lot with the educational cause, though favouring the inclusion of manual labour in the curriculum.

THE WORKHOUSES

The history of Cambridgeshire shows that poorhouse and workhouse were not always so distinct in origin as some authorities have asserted, but the rural institutions of the seventeenth century perpetually tended, like their eighteenth- and nineteenth-century successors, to lapse into abodes for the impotent, the children, or the casual pauper only. The application, in 1700, for permission to erect a House of Correction at Linton sounds the note of deterrence which characterised this period in the country generally and gave rise to the various private Workhouse Acts which preceded the general permissive legislation of 1723.

Alert and independent as usual, Wisbech proceeded in 1720 to erect a new institution without consulting the legislature, and with the foresight gained by a century of experience avoided certain of the pitfalls inherent in the Act of 1723—a vigilant board of management replaced the statutory contractor, and paupers entirely incapable of work were excluded from the house. The Wisbech establishment, conducted successfully for some years, served as a model for the rest of the Isle, where throughout the succeeding century the workhouse policy was much more widely adopted than in the county proper.

In the town of Cambridge the failure of a corporate workhouse scheme, in 1727, resulted in the small parochial buildings assuming the character only of poorhouses, with but little regulation of any kind—the character which, in the main, they retained till 1834.

At Royston a disciplinary building was opened in 1735, but the town clearly accepted the legislation of 1723 as giving authority for the use of the rates for the purpose of establishing a workhouse, without entailing obligation to adopt the Act in its entirety. The deterrent principle soon resulted in driving the able-bodied to risk the life of the roads, and consequently in limiting the inmates to those who, through infirmity or extreme youth, were compelled to accept the "test".

In rural Cambridgeshire outside the Isle only gradually, from the later 'thirties onwards, did about one-tenth of the villages found some kind of institution—far more often a poorhouse than a disciplinary, industrial establishment.

At no period and in no part of the county—urban or rural—was it customary for any length of time to "offer the house" to every applicant. In no case, moreover, were the recipients of out-relief farmed to a contractor. These features would seem to distinguish the county from many parts of England.[1] The system of farming the workhouse alone was, however, common in Cambridgeshire, but it was very rarely adopted before 1750 and not widely till the 'sixties and 'seventies. In the years between 1785 and 1834 there was marked hesitation about the wisdom of contracting: many parishes swung backwards and forwards between this system and direct parochial management. Apparently they recognised the evils, but finally considerations of expense rather generally in the Isle of Ely—to a less extent in

[1] Cf. Webb, *English Local Government. English Poor Law History*, Pt. I, p. 283: "Contracts of this description indemnifying the parish against all its obligations under the Poor Law, with such exceptions only as were expressly provided for, may be traced in all parts of England".

the county proper—weighed in favour of the contract. Since the contractor was not responsible for out-relief, he at least was under no pecuniary inducement in this county to refuse to maintain any applicant otherwise than in the house.

It appears to have been the recognition that the contractor was subjected to strong temptation to wield oppressive power that led to the frequent substitution of a *per capita* system of payment for the earlier lump sum in most parts of England. In Cambridgeshire, however, one sometimes finds the *per capita* basis tried and then deliberately discarded in favour of the more rigorous system—though usually with special precautions. This was probably one aspect of the curious tendency, noticeable in certain areas of the county, to revert, during the 'eighties and 'nineties, to the harsher spirit of half a century earlier. It is the more striking in view of the general swing towards humanitarianism, which is quite obvious in Cambridgeshire as elsewhere. It is noteworthy in this connection that, whilst sympathy with the improved mode of administration suggested by Gilbert's Act of 1782 was evident, the town of Cambridge rejected the idea of the workhouse as a mere asylum for the helpless. When, moreover, the two parishes of Royston were united in the 'eighties, it was the "Test Act" of 1723 which was definitely adopted, in spirit as well as in technique. In the final unsuccessful effort made by the County Bench, in 1814, to meet the fully-recognised need for larger administrative units and better management, Gilbert's Act was cited as the basis for the suggested unions, but the workhouses proposed were to be mixed establishments—asylums and industrial institutions—though, be it noted, of a genuinely kindly nature, "places of refuge or desirable resort".

With certain exceptions, however, during the régime of outdoor allowances between 1790 and 1834, it is generally true that the workhouses of Cambridgeshire proper, as of most counties, degenerated into the ill-kept lodging-houses—if they had ever been anything else—where no pretence was made either of discipline or of profitable labour. In the Isle, on the contrary, although the profits from work amounted to little, the workhouses were usually clean and well-conducted.

SETTLEMENT AND REMOVAL

Perhaps the most constant reflection forced upon the delver among obscure annals mouldering in the parish chests of county and Isle, or among the more orderly records of Quarter Sessions, is the large part played by the Settlement Laws, directly or indirectly, in the life of the poorer section of the community. During the greater part of the period considered quite two-thirds of the time of the County Bench must, on an average, have been occupied with appeals touching this matter; quite two-thirds of the extant parochial papers are concerned with the movement of pauper pawns across the chess-board of Cambridgeshire.

It is possible of course to overstress the mere financial side of this question, and also the extent to which labour was rendered immobile, but the repressive element which the policy necessarily fostered in the attitude to poverty cannot easily be exaggerated. The Act of 1662 and its successors became the fly-wheel around which, in Cambridgeshire, the Poor Law administration revolved.

There are in the sixteenth and early seventeenth centuries examples of harsh—even illegal—removals in this county, but the new enactment did mean a much more comprehensive and ruthless use of the power of ejectment, and it did mean the concentration of attention upon this to the detriment of interest in improved modes of relief, especially in the more remote parishes. Needless expense was entailed, fraud and casual employment were encouraged, the ties of family life were loosened at every point, and, up to 1795, callous brutality, frequently resulting in actual death, marked the attitude towards sick (and especially pregnant) persons. Brutality of course was not confined to the Poor Law in eighteenth-century England and, moreover, a close investigation of details does show that in practice the Settlement Laws did not invariably work with the harsh and wasteful rigidity often assumed.

Certificates were sometimes used in this county before the

Act of 1697, and after that date they were commonly employed. On occasion the system hampered movement, but on the whole it did mitigate the severity of settlement restrictions, especially between the years 1740 and 1780. After 1795 certificates were granted mainly to pregnant single women, exempted from the Act of 1795 which prohibited removal before application for relief had been made.

The custom of maintaining paupers in distant parishes, without insisting upon removal—common in Cambridgeshire after about 1780—in a similar way lessened the hardships involved by the Settlement Laws.

Prior to 1795 it is clear that many overseers did not await actual chargeability to the rates before removal was secured, and in not a few cases honest, industrious labourers, in definite employment, were removed. In spite of the laws, however, there was much circulation of labour. Statistics for the county show that the laws fell far more heavily upon decrepit people, women enceintes and married labourers with one child or more, than upon healthy single men.

From the late eighteenth century onwards there is evidence of a more sympathetic desire to consider the effect of removal from the pauper's standpoint.

PAUPER APPRENTICESHIP

Much stimulation of local authorities by the Privy Council had been necessary before masters could be prevailed upon in this county to take pauper apprentices. The whole organisation of industry was breaking down during the Restoration period, but the Settlement Laws gave a new lease of life to the apprenticeship system. The Act of 1692 emphasised the right of settlement which apprenticeship gave, and an increased use of apprenticeship for the purpose of securing the child's claims upon another parish is noticeable in Cambridgeshire after 1692. Nevertheless children were rarely bound in distant parishes, though they were usually bound to petty tradesmen who cared only for the small premium offered, or for the cheap service of the child. Cases of ill-treatment undoubtedly occurred, but most parishes paid the premium in instalments, so that some opportunity was offered for supervising the master's conduct. Probably the worst consequence of pauper apprenticeship in this county was the overstocking of the market in low-grade occupations. On the whole the Cambridgeshire child fared better than many of his contemporaries.

BASTARDY

A marked increase in immorality was in part the result of the handicap which the married man endured by reason of the Settlement Laws, but by far the most rapid growth of bastardy offences occurred in the period between 1796 and 1834. It had become obvious to Cambridgeshire authorities by about 1770 that the prosecution of poor men was as inefficacious a way of combating the evil as was the imprisonment of women offenders, which had long been discontinued, and after 1770—with the exception of one interlude—parishes ceased to prosecute poor men, unless they belonged to a different parish which could be made financially responsible. There was consequently far more immorality among labouring men in the period of economic depression after 1796 than a mere examination of Court cases reveals.

Parochial pressure, accompanied by bribery and corruption, was frequently exerted to compel the marriage of unwilling parties: many instances of desertion resulted, and in any case the atmosphere of such homes could not possibly have been a moral one.

The saving of the parochial purse, moreover, was not secured, though every consideration, in this sphere as in so many others, had been sacrificed to it.

RELIEF OUTSIDE THE WORKHOUSE
1601–1782

Long before the Elizabethan statute it had been customary for parishes to board-out or to place in almshouses the aged, the impotent and those children too young to be apprenticed or put to work; occasionally to pay rents on behalf of the distressed; to give temporary monetary assistance in case of sickness and to grant weekly pensions to others in their own homes. The statute introduced no vital change of method. In many cases the pensions paid were clearly supplementary to the insufficient wages earned by decrepit people, by children or by widows. By the beginning of the eighteenth century grants were sometimes made in Cambridgeshire even to able-bodied men who were "overcharged with children". It was true the Elizabethan Poor Law had not authorised the supplementing of wages out of the poor-rate, but the Statute of Artificers had provided for the assessing of wages. When this latter practice ceased it was not unnatural that parish officers should come to regard the man burdened with a large family in much the same light as they always regarded the widow. The assumption underlying the overseer's attitude towards married labourers, under the Settlement Law, was that customary wages could not be expected to meet the needs of a large family. When this theory was generalised the emergency measures of the French War period were born.

The steady growth of the "collection list" is noticeable even in the later seventeenth century. From about 1760 or 1770 the "by-expenses", or casual payments, increased disproportionately—a feature to be expected in a county where the workhouse was never the sole method of dealing with poverty. By the middle of the eighteenth century the surveyor's rate had begun to be drawn upon as a poor-rate, in lieu of paying full wages for honest labour on the roads.

1782–1832

Gilbert's Act showed the changed attitude of the legislature itself to the principle of supplementing wages. A year later, in 1783, the Whittlesford justices drew up a scale of relief for the hundred —the earliest scale as yet discovered.[1] During the 'eighties and

[1] Cf. F. G. Emmison, *Relief of the Poor at Eaton Socon*, 1706–1834 (Pubs. of Beds. Hist. Rec. Soc. vol. xv, 1933), p. 51. This interesting publication has appeared while the present book was in the Press.

'nineties the number of men at work on the roads, sent on the rounds, or relieved without work, increased in the county generally.

In the famine year of 1795 the Cambridgeshire Bench, after much discussion, turned down the minimum wage policy, suggesting that allowances from the rates would prove a less permanent derangement of economic life. A general scientific bread scale for the whole county was not issued till 1821, though different scales for particular parts of the county were common by 1800. The scale of 1821 was distinctly less generous than that of Speenhamland: there could have been little encouragement of large families, unless it were encouragement born of despair. It is nevertheless curious to find a general scale first sanctioned at the very moment when the country resounded with criticisms of a policy adopted merely as a war measure. Though officially dropped in 1829, the county scale, or a modified form of it, was still adhered to by many parishes.

The evil effects of the allowance system upon the wages and opportunities of the independent labourer, upon the small independent cultivator employing little or no labour, and upon the morale of the pauper himself, were as evident in Cambridgeshire as they were in other agricultural areas in which the system prevailed. In this county, to an exceptional degree, town work offered no alternative to agricultural labour: hence absence of competition prevented a rise in wages in response to the alarming rise in prices engendered by war and harvest failure. The settlement policy had taught folk that it was criminal to seek work beyond the confines of their own parish: it was natural that, as real wages sank lower and lower, men should desire to anchor in their one secure haven. The man with just a little property found himself driven from employment to make room for those whom the parish must support, yet unless he parted with his property there was no public assistance for him—the parish was rigidly applying the "means test" of the present day.

Certainly the poor-rates grew seriously, though the rise in population, as well as the general rise in national wealth, must be borne in mind. The period of most rapid poor-rate increase in Cambridgeshire occurred earlier than the decade of most rapid growth of population, but the inflation of prices during the war must be allowed for in estimating the real increase per head of the burden. If such adjustments be made, the added burden is less than is usually assumed. Nevertheless Cambridgeshire stands out none too favourably in comparison with the country at large. The fact that the county figures among those where enclosures accompanied a disproportionately extensive granting of allowances is not without significance, though it calls for more detailed investigation.

One lingers regretfully over the discarded policy of fixing minimum wages; it may well be that even the kindly disposed magistracy would have experienced insuperable difficulty in adjusting wages to prices without even the modern aid of index numbers, yet the magistrates were forced to make adjustments through the medium of the poor-rate, with the bread scale as a crude guide. The temporary character of the emergency measure was of course the genuine excuse for its adoption.

It has been argued by many writers that, with all its deficiencies, the Elizabethan system of public relief repeatedly saved England from the revolutions which occurred elsewhere; the greatest strain thus far in its history was put upon the Poor Law during the Napoleonic Wars. Scotland, it is true, never supplemented wages, but distressed Scots, like twentieth-century Americans, were driven literally to beg their bread or to steal it —"il y a deux côtés de la médaille".

In spite of a repressive background, the outstanding aim of Elizabethan legislation was the prevention of poverty: the comprehensive Labour Statute was framed largely with this end in view. The Tudors, moreover, had finally recognised the problem to be a national one, and for half a century the Privy Council made premature efforts to act for the country as a whole. Unfortunately, the technique adopted in 1597 was inadequate, and the evils accompanying workhouse schemes, settlement policies, apprenticeship and allowances were the miserable outcome of throwing upon petty localities the whole expense of a malady which was essentially national. The purpose of the 1834 reformers was to prohibit rather than to prevent, and the remedies were drastic: they did enlarge the areas and provide for more efficient administration; they did result in the reabsorption of the able-bodied into industry in those regions where genuine work was to be found. In Cambridgeshire reabsorption was not easy of achievement. The spinning-wheel and reel had figured a generation earlier in nearly every humble home; the loss of textile by-employment was not accompanied here by the growth of new industries in neighbouring towns, and the poor, like other mortals, had "often an unaccountable affection for some particular habitation": they were not easily attracted by the cotton mills of the north. "They have an amazing prejudice against the Poor Law Bill", said a Cambridgeshire farmer in 1836.[1] "Last year they were in a very deplorable state indeed....Several of the best and most honest labourers have said to me that...before they will go to the Union Workhouse, they will rob on the highway."

What the Poor Law of 1834 had above all failed to do was obvious when England passed through the vale of industrial depression half a century later. Repression could not drive the workless into occupations which did not exist, yet no local Poor Law authority was a fitting body to deal with a widespread disease occasioned by the fluctuations of modern commerce. The passing-bell of the system was tolled in 1929. Supersession of the Boards of Guardians by local authorities empowered to deal with destitution, if they so please, through channels unsullied by the taint of pauperism, and withdrawal of a large proportion of wageless workmen from the sphere of Poor Relief and from local control, have cleared the ground for the final contest waged over the remains of the old system to-day.

[1] Commons' Committee on the State of Agriculture (1835), quoted by Fay, *op. cit.* p. 103.

APPENDIX

I

Testimonial under 5 Eliz., c. 3

Form of Testimonial required under 5 Eliz., c. 4.

[Quoted MS. Q.S.R. Cambs. 1670]

Memo: y^t A. B. servant to C. D., of E., husbandman or taylor etc., in ye said County, is licensed to depart from his sd. Master, and is att libty to serve elsewhere according to the statute in y^t case made and pvided. In wittness whereof etc—
Dated ye day, month, yeare and place etc of making hereof.

II

(1) Suspension of a Removal Order during Sickness.
(2) Cancellation two months later.
(Printed form on back of ordinary Removal Order)

(1) It appearing to us the within-named Justices, that it would be attended with danger to remove the within-named Elizabeth Cooke, by reason of her being dangerously ill at this time; We do authorise and direct that the execution of the within order be suspended until we shall be satisfied that it may be safely done. Witness our hands this 13th day of September, 1802.

Roger Kerrison (*Mayor*)
John Browne.

(2) It being certified to us Sr Roger Kerrison Knt., Mayor, and John Browne Esq., that the above-named Eliz. Cooke may now be removed without danger, We do hereby direct that this our order be carried into immediate execution; and it being this day proved upon oath before us, that the charges incurred in consequence of the above suspension, amount to the sum of £6. 9s., viz the sum of £4. 3s., the charges of James Robinson, Surgeon, for medicines, attendances, etc. and the sum of £2. 6s. the charges of Christmas Church for

Relief for the said Eliz. Cooke, We do hereby direct and require the Churchwardens and Overseers of the Parish of Royston in the County of Harts, on sight hereof to pay the above-mentioned sum of £6. 9s. to the Officer removing the said Eliz. Cooke.

Given under our Hands this 13th day of November, 1802

Roger Kerrison, *Mayor*
John Browne.

III

Certificate of Legal Settlement granted by Parish of Wilbraham to Parish of Bottisham, 1707

(In manuscript)

1707 Cantabr: Wee the Churchwardens and Overseers of the Poor of the Parish of Wilbraham parva in the County of Cambr. Do hereby owne and acknowledge That William Hatly his Wife and Children are Inhabitants Legally settled in our said parish of Wilbraham parva, and we doe hereby oblige our said parish to Receive the said William Hatly his Wife and Children at any Time hereafter when Chargeable, And to provide for them according to Law. Witness our hands and Seales this 6th day of May Anno dom. 1707.

Witness hereunto   Rich: Brand ◯
the marke of Robt.   *Churchwardens*
Miller ✕   Joseph: Crabb ◯
the marke of Mary
Wheatston ✕

William Challis
  his mark ✕ ◯
✕ Batts
  Mark ◯

Allowed by us her Maties Justices of the Peace for the County of Cambridge.

P. Whitcote
Max Hill.

IV

Advertisement of a Firm of Contractors

(Royston Vestry Papers)

WANTED

POOR TO FARM

To the Churchwardens, Overseers and Inhabitants of the different Parishes, who are inclined to Contract for their Poor in the House and out of the House, or in the House only, for one Year or more, where a Manufactory will be established if required,—Also Lunaticks and Refractory Poor taken in at per Head per Week—A Reference may be made for a Character and Security if required.

Letters Addressed (Post Paid) to Messrs Butler and Rockett, Contractors for Biggleswade, Beds., or at Waltham-upon-Thames, Surry, will be duly attended to.

Biggleswade, Sep. 25th 1803.

V

Inventory of Pauper's Goods taken by the Parish

An Invatory of the Houshold ferniture of John Piper of Bottisham Load, Dec. 7th, 1782.

	£	s.	d.
A Fether Bed Bolster and one pillow one Sheet two Blankets and a quilt a Bed Stead	1	10	6
One hutch		2	0
One Obel Table		2	6
One Deal Table			9
A pliss Cubbard		5	0
Seven Chairs		1	6
A pucket and pail			9

	£	s.	d.
Seven Earthen plates			6
Six Earthen Dishes			6
Two Earthen Pots			2
A pare of pothocks		1	3
A glass beker two Tea pots a pint Bason		2	3
A pair of Bellows			6
A pair of Tongs			6
Three Candle Sticks			6
One Trunk		2	0
One Buffet Stool			6
One Wash Ciller		2	0
One Weel		1	0
One Reel		1	0
One Iron Pot		1	0
A Flock Bed one pillow and 2 Blankets		5	0
A Tea kettle		3	6
A large Iron Pot		3	0
	£3	8	2

VI

Agreement concerning the Putting out of a Pauper Boy not by Indenture

An Agreement made between Edward Sharp and Jekyl Wilson, Overseers of the Parish of Royston, Herts, and Segrave Faircloth or Royston, afsd., yeoman, 30th Aug. 1765, as follows (to witt)
Consideration money: £3. 10s. 6d.

To live after the nature of a Servant, for the term of 4 years.
Segrave to find and provide sufficient meat, drink, washing, lodging, wearing aparell, and all other necessaries, and endemnifie the sd. psh. from all expenses etc.

S. F.

Witness,
M. F.

VII

Bastardy Proceedings

(1) The Examination of the Woman before the Justice

(In this case two justices were present)

Examination of Sarah Hornsey of Royston, in this County, Singlewoman, taken Oct. 5th, 1738.

This examinant says, upon Oath, that she comes freely and voluntarily, to declare that she is with Child; that she was born in the psh. of Royston, is one and twenty years old, and that Henry Watson, of the same parish, Barber, is the father of the Child she goes with, and no man else has had carnal knowledge of her. That about a fortnight before Shrovetide last past, the sd. Henry got his ends of her, having follow'd her for near a twelvemonth; has at several times promised her Marriage. And farther says not.

Sarah ⨯ Hornsey
her mark

J. Savage
Ed. Forester.

(2) Warrant for the Apprehension of a Putative Father 1770

Cambs.} To all Constables and other his Ma[ties] Officers of the Peace for the s[d] County of Cambs.

Whereas Martha Swain of the parish of Royston, in the sd. County of Cambs., single Woman, in her Exam[n]. taken this Day in Writing, and upon Oath, before us (one of H.Ma[ties] Justices of the Peace etc.) hath voluntarily declared that she is with child, and that the sd. Child is likely to be born a Bastard, and to be Chargeable to the sd. Parish of Royston, and the sd. M. S. hath in the sd. Exam[n]. charged Richard Farr of Royston afsd. with having begotten the sd Child on her Body, with which she is now pregnant. And whereas Sam Coxall and Henry Coe, Overseers of the Poor of the sd. Parish of Royston, have made application unto me, for the immediate apprehending the sd. R. F., to answer these Premises: These are, therefore, in His Maties Name to Authorize and Require you, and every of you, to apprehend the sd. R. F., and to bring him before me, or some other of His Maties Justices of the Peace, that he may be proceeded against as the Law directs. Given under my Hand and Seal this 6th Day of Dec. in the Year of our Lord, 1770.

Chas. Weston

(3) The Prosecution of Thomas Fagg for Bastardy, Royston 1790

(a) *Notice of Warrant*

23rd June, 1790

Sir,

As Vestry Clerk of Royston I am desir'd by the Overseers to acquaint you that a Warrant was issued against you on a Charge of Bastardy by Sarah Gear on Saturday last, and that the Magistrates will on that day fortnight, the 5th of July, about 12 o'clock at Noon, be ready at the Rose Inn in Cambridge to make the Order of Filiation, if you shall think proper to attend at that time, and let me know in a few days whether you mean to do so, and the Parish Officers with the woman will also attend.

I am Sir,
Yr hble Servant,
Henry Watson.

Mr. Thos. Fagg,
Bell and Crown Inn, Holborn, London.

(b) *Reply*

Bell and Crown, Holborn.
July 2nd, 1790.

Sir,

Yours of ye 23 June. I have rece^d. I believe I shall be at Cambridge on Saturday ye 5th inst.

I am etc.
Yours etc.,
Thomas Fagg.

(c) *Expenses incurred*

Mr Thos. Fagg Dr to the Parish of Royston, Cambs.:

		£	s.	d.
June 7th:	Horsehire and Expenses to Cambridge to obtain a Warrant against Mr Thos. Fagg, for a Bastard Child sworn to him by Sarah Gear, which I cd not obtain then		6	10
„ 21st:	Horsehire and Expenses to Cambr. on same business		6	7½
	Pd. Carriage and Expense of Sarah Gear		4	8
	Pd. for Oath and Warrant		2	0
July 5th:	Horsehire and Expenses to Cambr. to meet Mr Fagg who did not attend		7	0
	Pd. Carriage and Expenses of Sarah Gear		3	10
Aug. 16th:	Pd. Lord Mayor of London for backing the Warrant		1	0
„ 19th:	Pd. Mr Reeves the Const. for Executing the War^t.		10	6
	Horse and Chaise 3 days		18	0
	My own Expenses—horse included—3 days	1	16	0
Sep. 13th:	Horse and Expenses to Cambr. to obtain a Summons for Mr Fagg		6	10½
	Pd. for Oath and Summons		4	0
	Pd. Carriage and Expenses of Sarah Gear to Cambr.		4	6
„ 14th:	Expenses to London to serve summons on Mr Fagg	1	8	8
„ 17th:	Horse-Chaise and Expenses to Landbeach to obtain an Order against Mr Fagg		13	3
	Pd. for Orders		4	0
„ 20th:	Expenses to London to serve Order on Mr Fagg	1	8	8
		£9	6	5

The Parishioners of Royston to R. Flack,
Dr Jany, 1790

	£	s.	d.
Expenses at Foulmire when Sarah Gear swore her bastard child to Thos. Fagg		3	6
Two Journeys to Soham to get security of Thos. Fagg for the Maintenance of Sarah Gears Child— Horsehire and Expenses	2	1	6
Horsehire and Expenses to Cambge. on acc. of Mr Faggs entering into recognisance for his appearce at the Q. S.		6	0
A Journey to Cambridge at the Q. S., if required, respecting the above business. Horsehire and expenses		10	6
Thos. Watsons Bill	1	2	7
	£4	4	1

Mr Thos. Fagg Dr to the Parish of Royston, Cambs.

		£	s.	d.
Oct. 17th:	Pd. Master of Workhouse for the Month of Lying-in of Sarah Gear	2	0	0
	Pd. for maint. of child of S. G. for 44 weeks at 2s.	4	8	0
	Expense of Mr Geo. Phillips, Overseer of Royston		3	4
	Carriage and Expense of S. G.		4	9
	Journey and Exps. of Thos. Watson, Const., with S. G. to Cambridge		9	2
	Journey and Expenses of Thos. Watson to Landbeach with S. G.		16	10
		8	2	1
	Mr Lowes Bill	9	6	5
		17	8	6

	£	s.	d.
[Brought forward	17	8	6]
Pd. Master of Workhouse for keeping child 11 weeks	1	2	0
Mr Watson as by Bill	4	4	0
	22	14	6
Journey to Cambr.		2	6
Horsehire etc.		4	0
My expenses		2	6
	£23	3	6

Result of Trial

	£	s.	d.
Charges reduced from £23. 3s. 6d. to	12	2	11½
and 40s. costs allowed the Respondents	2	0	0
6 weeks maintenance Dec. to Jan.	12	0	
	£14	14	11½

Final Statement of the Whole Expense of Mr Fagg's Business

		£	s.	d.
Mr Flack as by Bill		4	4	1
Mr Lowe	do.	9	6	5
Mr Watson, Constable Bill		1	18	7½
Mr Geo. Phillips	do.		8	1
Mr Watson	do.	3	0	1½
Mr Sealy	do.	1	13	4
Mr Ward	do.		9	0
Mr Day, Solicitor	do.	118	6	4
		139	6	0

	£	s.	d.		£	s.	d.
Recd of Mr Flack what remd. of the £40 recog. after deducting Mr Flacks Bill	35	15	11				
Recd of Mr Fagg by Mr Flack the Cost settled by the Justices at the Sessions	14	15	0		50	10	11
Adverse Balance					£88	15	1

VIII

Total Disbursements on the Poor in the Hundreds of Cambs. and the Isle of Ely, and in the Town of Cambridge

(Parl. Repts. 1776, 1785, 1804)

Hundreds of	1776	1785	1804
Armingford	£1104	£1274	£2776
Chesterton	511	813	1958
Cheveley	553	944	1587
Chilford	839	1276	2729
Flendish	464	739	1496
Longstow	842	1231	2276
Northstow	360	769	1856
Papworth	672	1156	3168
Radfield	817	1129	2431
Staine	618	1089	1948
Staploe	1380	1832	4383
Thriplow	758	1120	2345
Wetherley	595	793	2400
Whittlesford	368	718	1567
Town of Cambridge	1761	2643	3900
Total in Isle of Ely	6452	8543	19254
Total in County and Isle	18094	26069	56074

MS. SOURCES AND BIBLIOGRAPHY

A. MANUSCRIPT SOURCES

Quarter Sessions Minute and Order Books of Cambridgeshire: 1660–70; 1689–94; 1699–1834.

Sessions Bundles—loose papers for a few inconsecutive years during the eighteenth century.

Cambridge Corporation Common Day Book, 1562–1835.

Bowtell Collection of MSS. relating to county and town of Cambridge (including Accounts of the Treasurer of the Town). (Downing College Library, Cambridge.)

Baker Collection of MSS. relating to county and town of Cambridge. (Cambridge University Library.)

Cole Collection of MSS. relating to county and town of Cambridge. (British Museum.)

Wisbech Gild and Corporation Records: vol. I, 1379–80, 1423–1540, 1547, 1551, 1560, 1564–6; vol. II, 1562–4, 1566–80, 1584–99; vols. III–XI, 1600–1835.

Records of Courts General, Courts Leet and Courts Halimote held at Wisbech, 1582–1619.

Vestry Books and Papers of fifty-four Cambridgeshire parishes.

Manuscript Collections relating to Parishes of Cambridgeshire at Wisbech Museum and at Saffron Walden Museum.

Wills and Inventories.

B. OFFICIAL STATE PAPERS

Statutes of the Realm.

Chantry Certificates, 1388. (Record Office.)

Acts of the Privy Council, 1540–97. (Printed J. R. Dasent.)

Acts of the Privy Council, 1601–4. (Printed J. R. Dasent.)

Acts of the Privy Council, 1615–16. (Printed H. C. Maxwell-Lyte.)

Privy Council Register and Proclamation Books. (1621–3.)

Privy Council Abstracts, 1547–1611. (B.M. Add. MSS. 11402.)

Privy Council Orders and Justices' Replies. (British Museum.)

Book of Orders (1630). (Cambridge University Library.)

State Papers Domestic, Eliz., Jas. I, and Chas. I.

Subsidy Rolls, Hy. VIII.

Ministers' Accounts and Patent Rolls, Ed. VI and Eliz.

Royal Commission on Historical MSS. Reports.

House of Commons' Journals.

Reports of the Committee on the Laws which concern the Relief and Settlement of the Poor, and the Laws relating to Vagrants, and also the State of the Several Houses of Correction. (1775–6.)

Returns relative to the State of the Poor. (1786.)

Returns relative to the Expense and Maintenance of the Poor in England. (1804.)

Report of Select Committee of the House of Commons on the State of Mendicity in the Metropolis. (1815.)

Report of Select Committee on Parish Apprentices. (1815.)

Report of Select Committee on the Poor Laws. (1817.)

Report of the House of Commons' Committee on the Police of the Metropolis. (1819.)

Reports of Commissioners appointed to Enquire concerning Charities and the Education of the Poor. (1815–39.)

Digest of Charity Reports. (1831–2.)

Reports of the Charity Commissioners. (1819–42.)

Report of Select Committee of the House of Commons on Vagrancy. (1821.)

Report of Select Committee of the House of Commons on Scotch and Irish Vagrants. (1828.)

Report of the House of Lords on the Poor Laws. (1831.)

Report of Select Committee on State of Agriculture and of Persons employed therein. (1833.)

Returns Relative to the Poor. (1833.)

First Report of the Royal Commission on the Poor Laws. (1834.)

C. PAMPHLET LITERATURE, JOURNALS, ETC., ANONYMOUS AUTHORS

Cambridge Chronicle and Huntingdonshire Gazette, eighteenth and nineteenth centuries.

Gentleman's Magazine, eighteenth and nineteenth centuries.

Reports of the Society for Bettering the Conditions and Increasing the Comforts of the Poor. (1798–1814.)

Second Report of the Association for the Relief of the Manufacturing and Labouring Poor. (The Pamphleteer, vol. vi, 1816.)

On the Means of Benefiting the Poor. (The Pamphleteer, vol. xvi.)

English Historical Review, vol. xiii. (Norfolk Assessment of Wages.)

Account of the Benevolent Society for the Relief of the Sick and Aged Poor. (1801.)

An Ease for Overseers of the Poore. (1601.)

Greevous Grones for the Poor. By M. S., London. (1622.)

A Clear and Evident Way for Enriching the Nation of England and Ireland. By I. D. (1650.)

An Account of Several Workhouses. (1725 and 1732.)

An Examination of the Alterations in the Poor's Laws proposed by Dr Burn, And a Refutation of his Objections. (1766.)

The Poor Laws England's Ruin. By a Country Overseer. (1817.)

The Vagrant Act in relation to the Liberty of the Subject. By a Barrister. (1824.)

A Letter to the Magistrates of the South and West of England on the expediency of correcting certain abuses of the Poor Laws. By one of their Number. (1828.)

The Settlement and Removal of the Poor considered. (1847.)

Sketch of the State of the Children of the Poor in 1756 and of the Present State and Management of all Poor in the Parish of St James, Westminster. (1797.)

Collections relative to the systematic relief of the Poor at different periods and in different countries. (1815.)

Historical Review of the Poor and Vagrant Laws, from the earliest periods upon record to the present time. (1838.)

Articles to be Enquired into by the Churchwardens, Exeter. (1636.)

Inquisition on Charitable Uses, 1729. (Cambridge, 1729.)

D. WORKS MAINLY EARLIER THAN 1834

ADOLPHUS, J. Observations on the Vagrant Act. (1824.)

APLETRE, J. Proposals for the Better Maintenance of the Poor of the County of Worcester. (c. 1696.)

AWDELEY, J. Fraternitye of Vacabondes. (1561.)

BAILEY, W. Better Employment...of the Poor. (1758.)

BANKS, S. Catalogue of Subscriptions for the Relief of Sufferers from Cattle Plague at Cottenham, 1747. (Camb. Antiq. Soc. Publ. 1865.)

BARRINGTON, DAINES. Observations on the More Ancient Statutes. (1795.)

BELLERS, J. Proposals for Employing the Poor in a College of Industry. (1714.)

BLOMEFIELD, F. Collectanea Cantabrigiensia. (Norwich, 1750.)

BOTT, E. A Collection of Decisions of the Court of King's Bench on the Poor Laws. (1773.)

BOTT, E. and C. F. On the Laws relating to the Poor. (1815.)

BURN, R. Justice of the Peace. (1754 and 1869 ed.)

—— History of the Poor Laws. (1764.)

BURROWS, Sir J. Decisions of the Court of King's Bench. (1754 and later.)

CARTER, E. History of Cambridgeshire. (1749.)

CARY, T. Proposals offered to the Committee of the Hon. House of Commons. (1699.)

—— Essay towards regulating the Trade and employing the Poor in this Kingdom. (c. 1700.)

—— Proceedings of the Corporation of Bristol. (1700.)

CELLIER, ELIZ. Scheme for the Foundation of a Royal Hospital. (1687.)

CHILD, Sir J. New Discourse of Trade. (c. 1669.)

CHRISTIAN, E. Charges delivered to the Grand Juries in the Isle of Ely. (1819.)

CLAPHAM, S. A Collection of Several Points of Sessions Law. (1818.)

COBBETT, W. Rural Rides. (1909 ed.)

—— Works. (1839–40.)

—— Cottage Economy. (1927 ed.)

COLQUHOUN, P. The State of Indigence and the Situation of the Casual Poor in the Metropolis. (1799.)

—— Treatise on the Police of the Metropolis. (1800.)

COOPER, T. Observations upon the Vagrant Laws. (1742.)

COPLAND, R. Hye way to the Spyttel Hous. (c. 1535.) (Reprinted E. V. Utterson, Select Pieces, 1817.)

Cox, E. W. The Practice of Poor Removals. (1848.)
Crabbe, G. The Village. (1783.)
—— The Borough. (1810.)
—— Collected Poems. (1823.)
Dalton, M. The Country Justice. (1630 ed.)
Davenant, W. Essay upon Ways and Means. (1695.)
—— Essay upon Probable Means of making a People Gainers in the Balance of Trade. (1697.)
Davis, D. Case of Labourers in Husbandry. (1795.)
Davison, J. Considerations on the Poor Law. (1817.)
Defoe, D. Tours. (1724–7.)
—— Giving Alms no Charity. (1704.)
Dekker, T. The Belman of London. (1608.)
—— Guls Horne-booke. (1609; reprinted 1905.)
Denison, W. Tracts on Poor Laws. (1837.)
Dennis, J. Vice and Luxury. (1724.)
Denson, J. A Peasant's Voice to Landowners. (Camb. 1830.)
D'Ewes, Sir Simonds. Journals. (1682.)
Dugdale, W. History of Imbanking and Draining the Fens and Marshes. (1662 and 1772 ed.)
—— Monasticon Anglicanum. (1846 ed.)
Dunning, R. Plain and Easy Method showing how the Office of Overseer may be managed. (1685.)
Dyer, G. History of the University of Cambridge. (1814.)
Eden, F. M. State of the Poor. (1797.)
Farish, W. M. Plan for immediately ameliorating the present conditions of the Agricultural Poor. (1830.)
Fielding, H. A Charge to the Grand Jury of Westminster. (1741.)
—— Inquiry into the Cause of the late Increase of Robbers. (1751.)
—— Proposal for making an Effectual Provision for the Poor. (1753.)
Firmin, T. Proposals for Employing of the Poor. (1678.)
Foley, R. Laws relating to the Poor, with Cases adjudged in the King's Bench. (1751 ed.)
Francis, C. Decisions of Court of King's Bench upon Laws relating to the Poor. (1793.)
Fuller, T. Church History. (1655.)
—— History of the University of Cambridge. (1655.)

GEE, J. Treatise on Trade and Navigation. (c. 1728.)

GILBERT, T. Considerations on the Bills for the Better Relief of the Poor. (1785.)

GOFFE, W. How to advance the trade of the Nation and employ the Poor. (Harl. Miscell. vol. IV.)

GOOCH, W. Agriculture of Cambs. (1813.)

GOSLING, R. Laws concerning the Poor. (1720.)

GREENE, R. Ghost-haunting Coney-catchers. (1626.)

HALE, Sir M. Discourse touching Provision for the Poor. (c. 1659.)

HANWAY, J. An Earnest Appeal for the Children of the Poor. (1766.)
—— Letters on the Importance of the Labouring Part of our Fellow Subjects. (1767.)
—— A New Year's Gift. (1784.)

HARMAN, T. A Caveat or Warning for Common Cursetors vulgarly called Vagabones. (1566.)

HARRADEN, R. Cantabrigia Depicta. (1809.)
—— New Cambridge Guide. (1809.)

HARRISON, W. Description of England. (1577.)

HAY, W. Remarks on the Poor Laws. (1735.)

HAYNES, J. Great Britain's Glory, or an Account of the Great Numbers of Poor employed in the Woollen and Silk Manufactures. (1715.)

HOARE, Sir R. COLT, and others. The History of Modern Wiltshire. (1822–44.)

HOWARD, J. State of the Prisons. (1786.)

HOWLETT, J. The Insufficiency of the Causes to which the Increase of our Poor and of the Poor's Rates have been ascribed. (1788.)

KEMBLE, J. M. A Few Remarks upon the Supposed Antiquity of Church Rates. (1837.)

KENNETT, WHITE. Parochial Antiquities. (1818.)

KING, GREGORY. Natural and Political Observations and Conclusions. (1680.)

LAMBARD, W. Duties of a Constable (incl. Overseers and Collectors). (1588.)
—— Eirenarcha. (1610 ed.)

LAYER, J. The Reformed Justice. (MS. Corpus Christi College, Cambridge.) (1633.)

LEGAT, J. An Ease for Overseers. (Cambridge, 1601.)

LOCKE, J. On Education. (1693.)

—— Report to Board of Trade. (1698.)

LOGGAN, D. Cantabrigia Illustrata. (1690.)

LYSONS, D. and S. Magna Britannia. (1808.)

MANDEVILLE, G. Essay on Charity and Charity Schools. (1733.)

MARRIOTT, Sir J. Argument in the Case of the Poor's Rate charged on the Colleges of Christ and Emmanuel, in the University of Cambridge, 1768. (Cambridge, 1768.)

MARTINEAU, HARRIET. Poor Laws and Paupers illustrated. (1833.)

—— Forest and Game Law Tales. (1845.)

MASSIE, J. A Plan for the Establishment of Charity Homes. (1758.)

MASTERS, R. Catalogue of Baker MSS. (Cambridge, 1784.)

MERE, J. Diary and other Documents, 1500–72. (Ed. J. Lamb, 1838.)

MICKLEBOURGH, J. The Great Duty of Labour and Work, etc. (Cambridge, 1751.)

MORANT, P. History and Antiquities of Essex. (1768.)

MORE, T. Utopia. (1516.)

NASMITH, J. A Charge to the Grand Jury at the General Quarter Sessions of the Isle of Ely. (Wisbech, 1799.)

NICHOLS, J. History of Barnwell Abbey. (1826.)

NIELD, J. State of the Prisons. (1812.)

NORTH, Hon. ROGER. Discourse on the Pernicious Tendency of the Laws for the Maintenance and Settlement of the Poor. (1753. Written before 1689.)

ONELEY, R. An Account of the Care taken in the Most Civilised Nations for the Relief of the Poor. (1758.)

PRATT, J. T. The Laws relating to the Poor. (1827.)

RIDLEY, Bp. N. Works. (1841 ed.)

RUGGLES, H. History of the Poor. (1793 and 1794.)

SAUNDERS, R. Abstract of Observations on the Poor Laws, with Reply to Rev. J. Nasmith. (Cambridge, 1802.)

SCOTT, J. Observations on the Present State of the Parochial and Vagrant Poor. (1773.)

SELDEN, J. History of Tithes. (1618.)

SMITH, J. T. Vagabondia. (1817.)

SMITH, SYDNEY. Edinburgh Review. (1820.)

SMITH, SYDNEY. Works. (1839–40.)

STRYPE, J. John Stow. A Survey of the Cities of London and Westminster. (1720.)

—— Ecclesiastical Memorials. (1721 and 1822 ed.)

TOWNSEND, J. The Injustice of the Poor Laws. (1787.)

TUCKER, Dean J. Defects of the Poor System. (1760.)

VANCOUVER, C. Agriculture of Cambridgeshire. (1794.)

WALKER, T. Observations on the Nature, Extent and Effects of Pauperism. (1826.)

WATSON, W. An Historical Account of the Ancient Town and Port of Wisbech. (1827.)

WHISTON, W. A Sermon Preach'd at Trinity-Church in Cambridge. (1705.)

WOOD, I. Some Account of Shrewsbury House of Industry. (1791.)

YARRANTON, A. England's Improvement. (1677.)

YOUNG, A. Considerations on the Subject of Poorhouses. (1796.)

E. MODERN WORKS

ANDREWS, W. Old-time Punishments. (1890.)

ASCHROTT, P. F. and PRESTON-THOMAS, H. The English Poor Law System. (1902.)

ASHBY, A. W. One Hundred Years of Poor Law. (Vinogradoff, Oxford Studies, vol. III, 1912.)

ASHLEY, Sir W. Introduction to English Economic History. (1894.)

ATKINSON, J. C. N.R. Yorks Quarter Sessions. (1884.)

ATKINSON, T. D. Gilds of Cambridge. (Camb. Antiq. Soc. Proc. 1897.)

ATKINSON, T. D. and CLARK, J. W. Cambridge Described. (1897.)

ATTENBOROUGH, F. L. The Laws of the Earliest English Kings. (Cambridge, 1922.)

BABINGTON, C. C. History of the Infirmary and Chapel of the Hospital and College of St John the Evangelist at Cambridge. (1874.)

—— Ancient Cambridgeshire. (1883.)

BAKER, T. H. Records of Seasons, Prices, etc. (1885.)

BATESON, M. Cambridge Gild Records. (1903.)

—— Borough Customs. (1904.)

BEARD, C. The Office of Justice of the Peace in England. (1904.)

BEEVES, W. A. Church Briefs. (1896.)

BOOTH, C. Poor Law Reform. (1911.)

BROWN, A. E., BLAND, P. A. and TAWNEY, R. H. English Economic History. Select Documents. (1925 ed.)

BURDETT, H. C. Addenbrooke's Hospital. (1898.)

CANNAN, E. History of Local Rates. (1927 ed.)

CHADWICK, W. E. The Church, the State and the Poor. (1914.)

CHANDLER, F. W. Romance of Roguery. (New York, 1899.)

—— The Literature of Roguery. (1907.)

CHEYNEY, E. P. History of England with an Account of English Institutions during the Later Sixteenth and Early Seventeenth Centuries. (1914.)

CLAPHAM, J. H. An Economic History of Modern Britain. (1926.)

CLARK, A. Working Life of Women in the Seventeenth Century. (1919.)

CLARK, H. W. A History of Tithes. (1891.)

CLARK, J. W. Annals of St Mary the Less. (1857.)

—— Cambridge and its Neighbourhood. (1881.)

—— Letters Patent of Eliz. and Jas. I addressed to the University of Cambridge. (1892.)

—— The Observances in use at the Augustinian Priory of St Giles and St Andrew, Barnwell. (1897.)

CLAY, Sir A., and others. The Principles of Poor Law Reform. (1910.)

CLAY, J. W. Visitations of Cambridgeshire, 1575 and 1619. (Harl. Soc. Proc. 1897.)

CLAY, ROTHA M. Medieval Hospitals of England. (1909.)

CLAY, W. K. History of Parish of Waterbeach. (Camb. Antiq. Soc. Proc. 1859.)

—— History of Parish of Landbeach. (Camb. Antiq. Soc. Proc. 1861.)

—— History of Parish of Horningsea. (Camb. Antiq. Soc. Proc. 1865.)

—— History of Parish of Milton. (Camb. Antiq. Soc. Proc. 1869.)

CLEMENTS, J. H. Brief History of Ely and Neighbouring Villages. (1868.)

COODE, Sir G. Report on Laws of Settlement and Removal. (1851.)
COOPER, C. H. Annals of Cambridge. (1845.)
—— Memorials of Cambridge. (1866.)
COULTON, G. G. Medieval Studies. (1910.)
—— Monastic Schools in the Middle Ages. (1913.)
—— Five Centuries of Religion. (1923.)
—— The Medieval Village. (1925.)
COX, J. C. Three Centuries of Derbyshire Annals. (1890.)
—— The Parish Registers of England. (1910.)
—— Churchwardens' Accounts. (1913.)
—— Cambridgeshire. (1914.)
CREIGHTON, C. History of Epidemics in Great Britain. (1891.)
CUNNINGHAM, W. Growth of English Industry and Commerce. (1910 ed.)
—— The Economic History of Cambridgeshire. (1903.)
—— The Story of Cambridgeshire. (1920.)
—— Common Rights at Cottenham and Stretham in Cambridgeshire. (Camden Miscell. vol. XII, 1910.)
DUNLOP, J. O. Apprenticeship and Child Labour. (1912.)
FARRER, W. Feudal Cambridgeshire. (1920.)
FAY, C. R. Life and Labour in the Nineteenth Century. (1920.)
FENNER BROCKWAY, A. A new Way with Crime. (1928.)
FOSTER, J. E. Churchwardens' Accounts of St Mary the Great, Cambridge, 1504–1635. (1905.)
—— Diary of Alderman S. Newton, 1662–1717. (1890.)
FRERE, W. H. and KENNEDY, W. P. M. Visitation Articles and Injunctions of the Period of the Reformation. (1924.)
GARDINER, F. J. History of Wisbech. (1898.)
GASQUET, Card. F. A. Henry VIII and the English Monasteries. (1888.)
—— The Eve of the Reformation. (1900.)
—— English Monastic Life. (1904.)
—— The Greater Abbeys of England. (1908.)
—— Parish Life in Medieval England. (1906.)
GIBBS, A. E. Corporation Records of St Albans. (1890.)
GONNER, E. C. K. Common Land and Enclosure. (1912.)
GOODMAN, A. W. Notes on the Church of St Botolph. (1913.)

GOODMAN, A. W. A Little History of St Botolph's. (1922.)

GRAY, B. KIRKMAN. History of English Philanthropy. (1905.)

GRAY, J. M. History of the Perse School, Cambridge. (1921.)

GREEN, Mrs A. S. Town Life in the Fifteenth Century. (1894.)

GREGORY, T. E. The Economics of Employment, 1660–1713. (Economica, 1921.)

GROSS, C. Bibliography of Municipal History. (1890.)

HAILSTONE, E. History and Antiquities of the Parish of Bottisham. (1863.)

—— Supplement to above. (1878.)

HALE, W. H. Antiquity of the Church Rate Considered. (1837.)

HAMILTON, A. H. A. Quarter Sessions from Elizabeth to Anne. (1878.)

HAMMOND, J. and B. Village Labourer. (1924 ed.)

—— Town Labourer. (1925 ed.)

HAMPSON, E. M. Settlement and Removal in Cambridgeshire. 1662–1834. (Cambridge Historical Journal, vol. II, No. 3, 1928.)

—— Cambridge County Records. (Camb. Antiq. Soc., Communications, vol. XXXI, 1931.)

HARDY, W. J. Hertfordshire County Records, 1581–1698. (1905.)

HARDY, W. J. and PAGE, W. Bedfordshire County Records, vol. I, 1714–1832. (Bedford, 1907.)

HARRIS, M. D. Life in an Old English Town. (1898.)

HEATON, H. The Yorkshire Woollen and Worsted Industry. (Oxford, 1920.)

HOBHOUSE, Bp. E. Churchwardens' Accounts. (Somerset Record Soc. 1890.)

HOLDSWORTH, W. A. The Handy Book of Parish Law. (1886.)

—— History of English Law. (1922 ed.)

HOTTEN, J. C. The Book of Vagabonds and Beggars. (Translation, 1892.)

JAMES, M. R. Suffolk and Norfolk. (1930.)

JUSSERAND, J. A. A. J. English Wayfaring Life. (Translation, 1889.)

KENNEDY, W. H. Elizabethan Episcopal Administration. (1924.)

KINGSTON, A. East Anglia and the Great Civil War. (1894.)

—— History of Royston. (1906.)

KNOWLES, M. History of Wicken. (1902.)

LEACH, A. F. Schools of Medieval England. (1915.)

LEADAM, I. S. Domesday of Enclosures. (1904 ed.)

LECKY, W. E. History of England in the Eighteenth Century. (1892.)

LEONARD, E. M. Early History of English Poor Relief. (1900.)

LILJEGREN, S. B. The Fall of the Monasteries and Social Changes in England. (1924.)

LOCH, C. S. Charity and Social Life. (1910.)

MAITLAND, F. W. The Court Baron. (1891.)

—— Township and Borough. (1898.)

MAITLAND, F. W. and BATESON, M. The Charters of the Borough of Cambridge. (1901.)

MARSHALL, D. M. The English Poor in the Eighteenth Century. (1926.)

MOSELEY, J. Evils of Apprenticing the Children of Paupers. (1830.)

NICHOLLS, Sir G. History of the English Poor Law. (1898 ed.)

PALMER, P. G. The Statutes of the Hospital of the Blessed Trinity, Guildford, 1629. (1927.)

PALMER, W. M. Meldreth Parish Records. (1896.)

—— The Village Gilds of Cambridgeshire. (Cambs. and Hunts. Archaeol. Soc. Trans. 1903.)

—— The Reformation of the Cambridge Corporation, 1662. (Camb. Antiq. Soc. Proc. 1913.)

—— History of Melbourne and Meldreth. (1923.)

—— Cambridge Castle. (1930.)

PASHLEY, R. Pauperism and Poor Laws. (1852.)

POWELL, E. The Rising in East Anglia. (1896.)

PROTHERO, G. W. Constitutional Documents. (1913.)

REICHEL, O. The Rise of the Parochial System in England. (1905.)

RIBTON-TURNER, C. J. History of Vagrants and Vagrancy. (1887.)

ROBERTSON, J. G. W. The Laws of the Kings of England from Edmund to Henry I. (1925.)

ROGERS, THOROLD. Six Centuries of Work and Wages. (1908 ed.)

—— History of Agriculture and Prices. (1866.)

ROSE, Rt. Hon. G. Observations on the Poor Laws. (1805.)

SALTER, F. R. Early Tracts on Poor Relief. (1926.)

SAVINE, A. English Monasteries on the Eve of the Dissolution. (Vinogradoff, Oxford Studies, vol. I, 1909.)

SELLERS, M. York in the Sixteenth and Seventeenth Centuries. (Hist. Review, 1897.)

SNAPE, R. H. English Monastic Finances in the Later Middle Ages. (1926.)

STOKES, H. P. Cambridge Parish Workhouses. (Camb. Antiq. Soc. Publ. 1911.)

—— Outside the Barnwell Gate. (Camb. Antiq. Soc. Publ. 1915.)

—— A History of the Wilbraham Parishes in the County of Cambridge. (1926.)

TANNER, J. R. Tudor Constitutional Documents. (Cambridge, 1922.)

TARRETT, BEDE. Social Theories of the Middle Ages. (1926.)

TAWNEY, R. H. Agrarian Problem in the Sixteenth Century. (1912.)

TAWNEY, R. H. and POWER, E. Tudor Econ. Documents. (1924.)

TOULMIN SMITH, J. The Parish. (1857.)

—— English Gilds. (1870.)

TROTTER, E. Seventeenth-Century Life in the Country Parish. (1919.)

TURBERVILLE, A. S. English Men and Manners in the Eighteenth Century. (Oxford, 1926.)

UHLHORN, J. G. W. Christian Charity in the Ancient Church. (Translation, 1883.)

WALKER, C. E. Records of a Fen Parish. (1909.)

WALKER, N. and CRADDOCK, T. History of Wisbech and the Fens. (1849.)

WARE, SEDLEY L. The Elizabethan Parish in its Ecclesiastical and Financial Aspects. (Baltimore, 1908.)

WEBB, S. and B. English Local Government. The Manor and the Borough. (1908.)

—— The Parish and the County. (1906.)

—— English Poor Law Policy. (1910.)

—— Statutory Authorities for Special Purposes. (1922.)

—— English Prisons under Local Government. (1922.)

—— English Poor Law History. Part I. (1926.)

WESTLAKE, H. F. The Parish Gilds of Medieval England. (1919.)

WILLIS-BUND, J. W. Social Life in Worcester. (Assoc. Archit. Socs. vol. XXIII, 1897.)

WITHERS, J. REYNOLDS. Poems. (1856.)

WOOLMER, T. A Beggar Poet. (The Nineteenth Century, vol. XXI, 1887.)

INDEX OF NAMES

INDEX OF PLACES

INDEX OF SPECIAL SUBJECTS

STATUTES, PRIVY COUNCIL ORDERS, PARLIAMENTARY REPORTS

Statutes

Parliamentary Returns and Reports

CAMBRIDGE: PRINTED BY WALTER LEWIS, M.A., AT THE UNIVERSITY PRESS

Printed in Great Britain
by Amazon.co.uk, Ltd.,
Marston Gate.